MONSTROUS NATURE

MONSTROUS
NATURE

ENVIRONMENT
AND HORROR ON
THE BIG SCREEN

Robin L. Murray and Joseph K. Heumann

UNIVERSITY OF NEBRASKA PRESS | LINCOLN AND LONDON

Acknowledgments for the use of copyrighted material appear on pages ix–x, which constitute an extension of the copyright page.

♾

Library of Congress Cataloging-in-Publication Data
Names: Murray, Robin L., author. | Heumann, Joseph K., author.
Title: Monstrous nature: environment and horror on the big
screen / Robin L. Murray and Joseph K. Heumann.
Description: Lincoln: University of Nebraska Press, [2016] |
Includes bibliographical references and index.
Identifiers: LCCN 2015044552 (print)
LCCN 2015046477 (ebook)
ISBN 9780803285699 (cloth: alk. paper)
ISBN 9780803294905 (epub)
ISBN 9780803294912 (mobi)
ISBN 9780803294929 (pdf)
Subjects: LCSH: Horror films—History and criticism. | Environmental
protection and motion pictures. | Nature in motion pictures.
Classification: LCC PN1995.9.H6 M875 2016 (print) |
LCC PN1995.9.H6 (ebook) | DDC 791.43/6164—dc23
LC record available at http://lccn.loc.gov/2015044552

Set in Sabon Next by John Klopping.
Designed by N. Putens.

CONTENTS

ILLUSTRATIONS

ACKNOWLEDGMENTS

We would first like to thank Bridget Barry and the University of Nebraska Press staff for supporting this project. We appreciate the professional climate that the University of Nebraska Press provided us. Our experience with the University of Nebraska Press continues to be pleasant because of history editor Bridget Barry's support for this project. We also thank Eastern Illinois University for supporting our work through a President's Fund grant. The grant assisted grant writing and research for the project. Thanks go to Professors Scott Slovic and Charles Stivale for contributing reference letters for three grant proposals encouraged by this grant: the American Council of Learned Societies, the Enhancing Life Project, and the National Endowment for the Humanities. We are also thankful for the assistance that office managers Sarah Miller and Jean Toothman and research assistants Katelyn Hartke, Seth Mowrer, and Shayna Hamm provided with support from the President's Fund. Thanks also to department chair Dana Ringuette for supporting our work.

Most importantly, we would like to thank our family and friends for their encouragement and understanding during this project. We also thank *Jump Cut* editors John Hess, Chuck Kleinhans, and Julia Lesage and *Studies in Documentary Film* editorial assistant Sally Wilson for their continuing support for our work.

Chapter 1, "*The Hellstrom Chronicle* and *Beetle Queen Conquers Tokyo*: Anthropomorphizing Nature for Humans" is derived in part from an article published in *Studies in Documentary* 7, no. 2 (June 2013) copyright Taylor & Francis, available online at http://www.tandfonline.com/ with DOI. 10.1306/odf.72.179_1 Parts of chapters 2, "As Beautiful as a Butterfly"? Monstrous Cockroach Nature and the Horror Film" (Fall 2014) and 3, "The Earth Bites Back: Vampires and the Ecological Roots of Home" (Fall 2014) were published in *Jump Cut* (http://www.ejumpcut.org/home.html) and are used with permission.

INTRODUCTION

Film, Environment, Horror

Perhaps the most iconic movie monster from the 1950s forward is Godzilla, a giant reptile that stars in dozens of movies from Toho Studios in Japan. As a creature of its age, beginning with its 1954 debut, Godzilla springs to life from the radiation left by nuclear testing and functions as a condemnation of the U.S. atomic attack on Hiroshima and Nagasaki in 1945. As Kyohei Yamane-hakase (Takashi Shimura) warns in the original film, "if we continue conducting nuclear tests, it's possible that another Godzilla might appear somewhere in the world again." As a monstrous result of humanity's destruction of the environment, Godzilla serves as a mixture of Maurice Yacowar's disaster categories, embodying a traditional natural monster but also illustrating Yacowar's natural attack subgenre. Godzilla also presents a cautionary symbol of the dangerous consequences of mistreating the natural world—monstrous nature on the attack.

Gareth Edwards's remake of *Godzilla* (2014) initially reinforces this view of nature run amok when Sandra Brody (Juliette Binoche), the wife of scientist Joe Brody (Bryan Cranston), is killed by a Japanese nuclear reactor breach. As Brody exclaims, "You're not fooling anybody when you say that what happened was a 'natural disaster.' You're lying! It was not an earthquake; it wasn't a typhoon! Because what's really happening is that you're hiding something out there! And it is going to send us back to the Stone Age! God help us all." For Brody the disaster was caused by a monster, not a natural catastrophe.

But later the attacks become something more: natural monsters seeking survival for themselves and their offspring as "MUTOs," Massive Unidentified Terrestrial Organisms that thrive on radiation. Godzilla enters the narrative

Godzilla (1956): Monstrous nature attacks Tokyo.

to save the Earth from these monsters. Unlike the original natural monster, Godzilla returns from the ocean bottom to destroy the MUTOs and restore the balance of nature, according to Dr. Ichiro Serizawa (Ken Watanabe). As Serizawa declares, instead of attempting to destroy both Godzilla and the MUTOs, the navy should "let them fight." For Serizawa "the arrogance of men is thinking nature is in their control and not the other way around." Horror films such as *Godzilla* provide a space in which to explore the complexities of a monstrous nature that humanity both creates and embodies.

Explorations of the monster and its representation in literature and media typically highlight ways to define the literary fiend. In *Monster Theory* Jeffrey J. Cohen argues, for example, "that the monster is best understood as an embodiment of difference, a breaker of category, and a resistant Other known only through process and movement, never through dissection-table analysis" (1996, x). In this same volume Ruth Waterhouse suggests that the monster can be most easily understood by reading its constructions "backward from the present" (x), so—for example—Grendel is filtered through later texts such as *Dracula*. By highlighting literary history, Waterhouse also points to some of the mythic roots of the monster, from Greek and Roman mythology to Christianity. Modern monsters also stem from the Gothic, according to Maria Beville's 2013 book, *The Unnamable Monster in Literature and Film*. According to Beville, studies of the monster should highlight this unnamability, emphasizing the fiend as "thing" instead of a classification that "serve [s] a social function by embodying all that is horrible in human imagination" (2).

More focused readings of the horror film, however, showcase other roots of the monster: human and nonhuman nature. Since both class struggles and evolution are addressed in the horror film, the genre is ripe for explicitly environmental readings. Film critics Paul Wells and Noel Carroll address these environmental underpinnings in differing ways. Wells takes an interdisciplinary approach to horror, asserting that, more than any other genre, horror film "has interrogated the deep-seated effects of change and responded to the newly determined grand narratives of social, scientific, and philosophical thought" (2000, 1). Specifically, Wells suggests the horror genre film responds to the philosophy of Karl Marx as articulated in *The Communist Manifesto* (1848) and the theories of evolution espoused by Charles Darwin in *On the Origin of the Species* (1859). For Wells horror films draw on the class struggles of Marxist theory by "explor[ing] modes of social 'revolution' in which naturalized ideas about bourgeois orthodoxy are transgressed" (4), as in *Frankenstein* (1931) and *Night of the Living Dead* (1968), while also examining the repercussions of humanity's desire to challenge natural selection and "'artificially' impose itself upon the conditions of material existence, while nature slowly but surely, organically and often invisibly, changes the world" (5). Horror thus responds to and addresses elements of both human and nonhuman nature—class struggles and evolution.

In his seminal *Philosophy of Horror*, Noel Carroll also highlights the genre's connection with a disrupted natural world when he declares, "In works of horror, the humans regard the monsters they meet as abnormal, as disturbances of the natural order" (1990, 16). For Carroll "horror involves essential reference to an entity, a monster, which then serves as a particular object of the emotion of art-horror" (41). Methods of creating these monsters integrate the natural world in multiple ways from creatures born out of fission between a nonhuman animal and a human to various forms of evolutionary change induced by a "mad scientist" figure or exposure to toxins of some sort. Yet even though both Wells and Carroll emphasize horror's roots in the natural world, readings highlighting the consequences of this connection are scarce.

We assert that the horror film and its offshoots often can be defined in relation to a monstrous nature that evolved either deliberately or by accident and incites fear in humanity as both character and audience. This interconnection between fear and the natural world opens up possibilities for ecocritical readings often missing from research on monstrous nature, the environment, and the horror film. As William M. Tsutsui explains in "Looking Straight at THEM! Understanding the Bug Movies of the 1950s," "Conceptions of nature in science fiction and monster films, and the broader cultural influence of these mass-culture depictions, are topics that environmental historians should explore in more depth" (2007, 252). Stacy Alaimo reinforces this point, asserting, "Ecocriticism, for the most part, has ignored monstrous nature, directing its attention toward texts that portray nature more favorably" (2001, 279). This project offers an opportunity to fill that gap in the research on the monstrous nature film.

Illustrating Monstrous Nature

Explorations of how trees transform into "monsters" seeking revenge against the human world that exploits them highlight the power of monstrous nature. In films as diverse as *The Wizard of Oz* (1939) and *The Lord of the Rings: The Two Towers* (2002), trees have fought back against humans, becoming "monstrous nature." In *The Wizard of Oz*, trees become animated when their apples are stolen (and a wicked witch intervenes). And in *The Two Towers*, trees called Ents seek vengeance against Saruman (Christopher Lee) and his army when their leader, Treebeard (John Rhys-Davies), sees a section of Fangorn Forest that Saruman has decimated to feed his iron forges.

Like the original *Godzilla*, monstrous nature films such as *Severed* (2005), *The Ruins* (2008), *Splinter* (2008), and *The Happening* (2008) highlight how trees might fight back against their human oppressors in the fantastic context of horror and science fiction. But the messages they convey also connect explicitly with current environmental issues. In *Severed* genetic testing in a logging camp meant to accelerate tree growth and increase timber output also proves deadly to humans when splinters from GMO logs transform humans into zombies who feed on other loggers. Although the "outbreak" seems isolated, its presence in the film serves as a warning against both genetic modification and overlogging of forests, environmental disasters condemned in recent news articles. The third annual International March against Monsanto on May 23, 2015, showcases a growing anti-GMO movement. And the Greenpeace website highlights protests against illegal logging in the Amazon rainforest ("Logging: The Amazon's Silent Crisis"). *The Ruins* also cautions against infiltrating rainforests when forest vines trap and kill American tourists trespassing on sacred Mayan land. In *Splinter* "splinters" like those in *Severed* parasitically invade human carriers and turn them into monsters, a cataclysmic result that underpins the possible consequences of climate change—the emergence and evolution of deadly parasites.

M. Night Shyamalan's *The Happening* takes this cautionary tale even further, explicitly connecting the behavior of trees to humanity's contribution to the disappearance of bees. Philadelphia high school science teacher Elliot Moore (Mark Wahlberg) underlines this connection during a class discussion prompted by a quote from Einstein scrawled on the blackboard: "If the bee disappeared off the surface of the globe then man would only have four years of life left." Moore's class focuses on the disappearance of bees, drawing on current theories addressing Colony Collapse Disorder explored in documentaries such as *Vanishing of the Bees* (2009). The film expands on this premise, asking what if a monstrous nature fought back? In *The Happening* the answer comes almost immediately after Moore's lecture on bees: as if reacting to our annihilation of the natural world, something from the trees in Central Park causes men and women to kill themselves.

These juxtaposed scenes suggest that humans have become a threat and must be defeated. As Moore's high school principal (Alan Ruck) explains, "All right, there appears to be an event happening. Central Park was just hit by what seems to be a terrorist attack. They're not clear on the scale yet. It's some kind of airborne chemical toxin that's been released in and around the park. They said to watch for warning signs. The first stage is confused speech. The second stage is physical disorientation, loss of direction. The third stage . . . is fatal."

According to an unnamed nursery owner (Frank Collison), "Plants have the ability to target specific threats. Tobacco plants when attacked by helio-this caterpillars will send out a chemical attracting wasps to kill just those caterpillars. We don't know how plants obtain these abilities, they just evolve very rapidly." When Alma Moore (Zooey Deschanel) asks, "Which species is doing it, if you think it's true," the nursery owner designates trees as the source of the human purge, explaining, "Plants have the ability to communicate with other species of plants. Trees can communicate with bushes, and bushes with grass, and everything in between." In *The Happening* trees and the plants with which they communicate transform into monstrous nature to attack the human species seemingly bent on their destruction.

Ecology and Horror Studies

By exploring monstrous nature, this work fills a gap in both film studies and ecocriticism, adding an ecocritical lens often missing from works exploring the horror film. Scholarship on the horror film examines horror in relation to myth, as does Richard D. Hand and Jay McRoy's edited volume, *Monstrous Adaptations: Generic and Thematic Mutations in Horror Film* (2007). Works such as George Ochoa's *Deformed and Destructive Beings* (2011) explore the purpose of horror films. Other works take feminist approaches to the horror film, such as Carol J. Clover's *Men, Women, and Chain Saws: Gender in the Modern Horror Film* (1992) and Linda Bradley's *Film, Horror, and the Body Fantastic* (1995). Noel Carroll's *The Philosophy of Horror: or Paradoxes of the Heart* (1990) combines his philosophical approach with theories of horror as a genre. Other works explore the horror film through cultural lenses. See, for example, Ian Conrich's edited volume *Horror Zone: The Cultural Experience of Contemporary Horror Cinema* (2010) and Robert G. Weiner and John Cline's edited work *Cinema Inferno: Celluloid Explosions from the Cultural Margins* (2010).

Other recent work in eco-horror informs our focus on monstrous nature. Although the volume concentrates primarily on print media, Bernice M. Murphy's *The Rural Gothic in American Popular Culture* (2013) explores some horror films. She asserts, for example, that the cabin has become an American replacement for the Gothic haunted castle in horror film and literature. Chapter 1, "The Cabin in the Woods: Order versus Chaos in the New World," suggests that this American Gothic cabin "has never lost its potency" (16).

Jeffery J. Cohen's "Grey" from his collection *Prismatic Ecology* (2014) explores the "gray" of the zombie in literature, television, and films. Organized according to the color spectrum, Cohen's collection seeks to expand definitions of environmentalism beyond the hallmark green ecology to include the brown, gray, and black found in literature, media, and the world.

Although Paul Wells describes revenge-of-nature horror films as "based on the idea that the everyday things that humankind take for granted in nature ... will one day cease to operate in the anticipated manner, and inexplicably rise to take its revenge on the exploitation and insensitivity of human beings" (2000, 115), few scholars examine horror films through an ecocritical lens. Our work seeks to begin addressing this by exploring nature horror in relation to multiple perspectives on monstrous nature.

Our work aligns most clearly with Stacy Alaimo's "Discomforting Creature: Monstrous Natures in Recent Films" and parts of Stephen Rust and his colleagues' edited volume, *Ecocinema Theory and Practice* (Rust, Monani, and Cubitt 2013), especially Stephen Rust's "Hollywood and Climate Change," Carter Soles's "Sympathy for the Devil: The Cannibalistic Hillbilly in 1970s Rural Slasher Films," and Sean Cubitt's "Everybody Knows This is Nowhere: Data Visualization and Ecocriticism." Sean Cubitt's *EcoMedia* (2005) also explores the depictions of nature in mainstream action films such as *The Lord of the Rings* and *The Perfect Storm* (2000). In their introduction to a special issue of *ISLE: Interdisciplinary Studies in Literature and the Environment* focused on horror literature and media, Rust and Carter Soles argue for "a more expansive definition of ecohorror" (2014, 509), which includes "analyses of texts in which humans do horrific things to the natural world" (509). Although most of the articles in this issue examine literary works, Rust analyzes *The Wall* (1982) as postmodern horror film, and Soles examines environmental apocalypse in *The Birds* (1963) and *Night of the Living Dead* (2002).

With its focus on monstrous nature, our work extends definitions of eco-horror and the monster beyond those found in recent studies. It also narrows such readings exclusively to monstrous nature movies. This book primarily explores the roots and ramifications of what Lee Gambin calls natural or ecological horror. Like Gambin our focus on nature run amok includes films outside Noel Carroll's "art horror" category. Gambin, for example, highlights natural attack films such as *Cujo* (1983), in which a St.

Bernard viciously attacks people not because he's possessed by a supernatural demon but because he's rabid. We extend genre definitions further by analyzing nature that is transformed into a monster in documentary and drama films outside traditional horror film parameters.

Monstrous Nature is organized in relation to four recurring environmental themes in films that construct nature as a monster: anthropomorphism, human ecology, evolution, and gendered landscapes. By applying ecocritical approaches that emphasize the multiple ways nature is constructed as monstrous or the natural world constructs monsters, we seek to build on the work of horror scholars who view genre film through a variety of theoretical approaches: theological, sociological, psychoanalytic, feminist, cultural, and genre studies.

Monstrous Nature primarily grows out of the groundbreaking work of Noel Carroll and Paul Wells, who at least begin to broach the monster's connection with the natural world. Our focus on anthropomorphism, human ecology, evolution, and gendered landscapes not only highlights the multiple ways in which nature is constructed as monster in traditional horror films and beyond; it also demonstrates what connects these seemingly divergent approaches: a human cause and a biotic solution. Humanity may contribute to the malevolent elements of nature on the big screen. But these films also suggest that embracing interdependent relationships with nonhuman nature may save us all. The structure of our text highlights the increasingly more complex ways in which nature becomes monstrous, first in relation to its connection with humans ("monstrous anthropomorphism"), next as human in a monstrous environment (a "human ecology"), then as a hybrid monster responding to either a comic or evolutionary narrative, and last as a gendered monster.

Monstrous Anthropomorphism

Our first two chapters apply multiple perspectives on anthropomorphism to documentary and feature films constructing insects as monsters or benefactors because they so closely resemble humanity. Whether the comparison between insects and humans is positive or negative, these films suggest that the real monsters are the humans who change the cockroaches rather than the bugs themselves.

Chapter 1, "*The Hellstrom Chronicle* and *Beetle Queen Conquers Tokyo*: Anthropomorphizing Nature for Humans," explores the approaches to anthropomorphism applied in *The Hellstrom Chronicle* (1971) and *Beetle Queen Conquers Tokyo* (2009), two insect documentaries that vilify and/ or glorify the insects on display by underlining similarities between the behaviors, cultures, emotions, and even appearances of humans and insects. The films construct insects as either monsters (as in *The Hellstrom Chronicle*) or model "persons" (as in *Beetle Queen Conquers Tokyo*) to promote an environmental message that either warns humans about their mistreatment of the natural world or encourages insect preservation through the protection of the natural world.

Chapter 2, "As Beautiful as a Butterfly"? Monstrous Cockroach Nature and the Horror Film," examines how altered and enhanced roaches on the big screen are anthropomorphized as either fiends or potential friends. They are presented as horrific monsters that must be destroyed, perhaps because they too closely resemble the malevolent side of humanity in *Damnation Alley* (1977) and *The Nest* (1988). *Mimic* (1997) and *Bug* (1975), on the other hand, examine the destructive repercussions of genetic engineering meant to alter cockroaches for human benefit, a more positive result that corresponds with the level of anthropomorphizing on the screen. *Cronos* (1993) more explicitly highlights the symbolic value of the cockroach as a seemingly immortal survivor. All these films, however, demonstrate a similar perspective on the cockroach, suggesting that manipulating nature, even for beneficial results, ultimately leads to destructive ends.

Human Ecology and Nature as Monster

Chapters 3 and 4 highlight readings of horror in film in relation to human ecology. The drive to reconnect with the Earth as home highlights the interdependent relationship between human and nonhuman nature illustrated by the films in this section. In the horror setting, this relationship may produce monsters instead of monstrous eco-trauma. This connection originated with the work of Ellen Swallow Richards, who viewed humans as part of nature and considered urban problems such as air and water pollution as products of human activity imposed on the environment and, subsequently, best resolved by humans.

Chapter 3, "The Earth Bites Back. Vampires and the Ecological Roots of Home," explores how two recent European comic vampire films, *Strigoi* (2009) and *The Pack* (2010), illuminate the interconnected relationship between blood, soil, and vampirism, highlighting the environmental underpinnings of the vampire myth in relation to a shattered ecology or home. Destroying that human ecology may lead to what clinical psychologist Tina Amorok calls an "eco-trauma of Being" (2007, 29). But in both *Strigoi* and *The Pack*, vampires rather than eco-trauma are the product of this devastated home, a soil desecrated by the blood of war or exploitation of human and nonhuman nature. In *Strigoi* and *The Pack*, a mistreated Earth bites back.

Chapter 4, "Through an Eco-lens of Childhood: Roberto Rossellini's *Germany Year Zero* and Guillermo del Toro's *The Devil's Backbone*," examines how these two films powerfully demonstrate the monstrous metamorphosis an environment destroyed by war causes children. The eco-horrors illustrated in the films shatter both human and nonhuman nature and fracture childhood landscapes, reinforcing the lasting environmental effects of warfare and the relevance of human approaches to ecology. In *Germany Year Zero* (1948) Rossellini amplifies the effects an eco-horror caused by total war and occupation has on innocence, especially the innocence of children whose external and internal landscapes have become broken. *The Devil's Backbone* (2001) explores these eco-horrors in an orphanage during the Spanish Civil War. *Germany Year Zero* and *The Devil's Backbone* translate a destructive human ecology into a fractured and horrific landscape of childhood.

Evolution and Monstrous Nature

Although most of the films explored in the three chapters in this section tell stories that present a pessimistic picture of humanity's future, they all provide a site in which we can try out new, sometimes destructive, evolutionary narratives. These stories seem to ask, what might happen if we continued down a dangerous path that includes nuclear warfare, ineffective toxic waste disposal, or unchecked chemical and biological experimentation? They also ask evolutionary questions about who we are, where we're going, and which story of ourselves we choose to construct: a tragic or comic evolutionary narrative. Chapters 5, 6, and 7 attempt to answer these questions.

Chapter 5, "Zombie Evolution: A New World with or without Humans," explores how *Land of the Dead* (2005) and *Warm Bodies* (2013) explicitly address evolutionary narratives of survival and reproduction and ultimately endorse interdependent relationships between humans and the zombies they may become. Even though June Pulliam's "Our Zombies, Ourselves: Exiting the Foucauldian Universe in George A. Romero's *Land of the Dead*" (2009) argues that zombies, not humans, form class-consciousness and can reorganize society in their own interests, we assert that *Land of the Dead* and *Warm Bodies* teach us that the most successful evolutionary narratives stress cooperation between species instead of war.

Chapter 6, "Laughter and the Eco-horror Film: The Troma Solution," asserts that two Troma Studios series, *The Toxic Avenger* (1984–2000) and *The Class of Nuke 'Em High* (1986–2013), demonstrate how laughing about the environment and its degradation may not only stimulate awareness; that laughter might also point out a path toward change. In spite of their sometimes overpowering campy humor and horrifying violence, these Troma films show the consequences of disturbing a pristine ecosystem and offer a viable solution to greedy humans' exploitation of the natural world.

Chapter 7, "Parasite Evolution in the Eco-horror Film: When the Host Becomes the Monster," highlights the evolution of parasites in films such as the *Frontline* documentary *Poisoned Waters* (2009), Barry Levinson's "found footage" horror movie response in *The Bay* (2012), and Shane Carruth's *Upstream Color* (2013). With some emphasis on a history of parasite films and their culmination in the vision and philosophy of David Cronenberg, this chapter examines the repercussions that humanity and the nonhuman environment face when we choose tragic evolutionary narratives rather than interdependence. In order to preserve the Chesapeake Bay as a source of recreation and sustenance, both *The Bay* and *Poisoned Waters* argue that we must address the environmental disasters and infectious monsters that our own destructive behaviors have created.

Gendered Landscapes and Monstrous Bodies

Our last two chapters apply an ecofeminist lens to horror films that bring gendered bodies to the fore. The films in this section seek to demonstrate the need for "a partnership ethic" like that historian Carolyn Merchant describes, in which "the needs of both humans and nonhumans would be dynamically balanced" (2013, 206). Chapters 8 and 9 highlight films that explore gendered bodies in relation to nonhuman nature.

Chapter 8, "Gendering the Cannibal: Bodies and Landscapes in Feminist Cannibal Movies," explores cannibal horror films in relation to both frontiers and gendered bodies. Although *Texas Chainsaw Massacre* (1974), *The Hills Have Eyes* (1977), *Motel Hell* (1980), and *The Lone Ranger* (2013) make similar statements about our desecration of the natural world, *Blood Diner* (1987), *Ravenous* (1999), *American Psycho* (2000), *Trouble Every Day* (2001), and *Jennifer's Body* (2009) explore multiple manifestations of cannibalism within a gendered framework that complicates colonial fantasies of land, women, and wendigo. At their best these films turn cannibal horror on its head, exploring bodies and landscapes from an explicitly ecofeminist or a feminist ecocritical perspective that condemns exploitation of women's bodies as frontiers.

Chapter 9, "*American Mary* and Body Modification: Nature and the Art of Change," examines Jen Soska and Sylvia Soska's feminist body horror film *American Mary* (2012) and masculine human-weapon films such as *RoboCop* (2013) and *Elysium* (2013) as body-modification films replicating the natural world they seem to transcend. When characters in *American Mary*, *RoboCop*, or *Elysium* modify their bodies to express their individuality and survive, they don't separate themselves from nature; instead they align themselves with the animal world. When either animals or humans change their appearance, they gain an evolutionary advantage that assures their reproductive and biological persistence.

Our conclusion synthesizes these four approaches by applying our four monstrous representations of nature on the big screen addressed in this work to climate-change films, part of the so-called cli-fi movement. Films such as *The Last Winter* (2006), *Half-Life* (2008), *The Thaw* (2009), *Snowpiercer* (2013), *Noah* (2014), and *Interstellar* (2014) draw on elements of a variety of genres (science fiction, animation, ecoterrorism, action-adventure, to name a few). But all these films center on themes that are connected explicitly with

The Happening: Trees' first attack immobilizes victims.

warnings against the negative consequences of rapid climate change. For us, exploring film in relation to a monstrous nature expands and refigures definitions of horror in productive ways. Such an exploration also demonstrates that the only viable solution to such "natural attacks" is to seek a middle ground that sustains both human and nonhuman nature.

1

Anthropomorphism and the "Big Bug" Movie

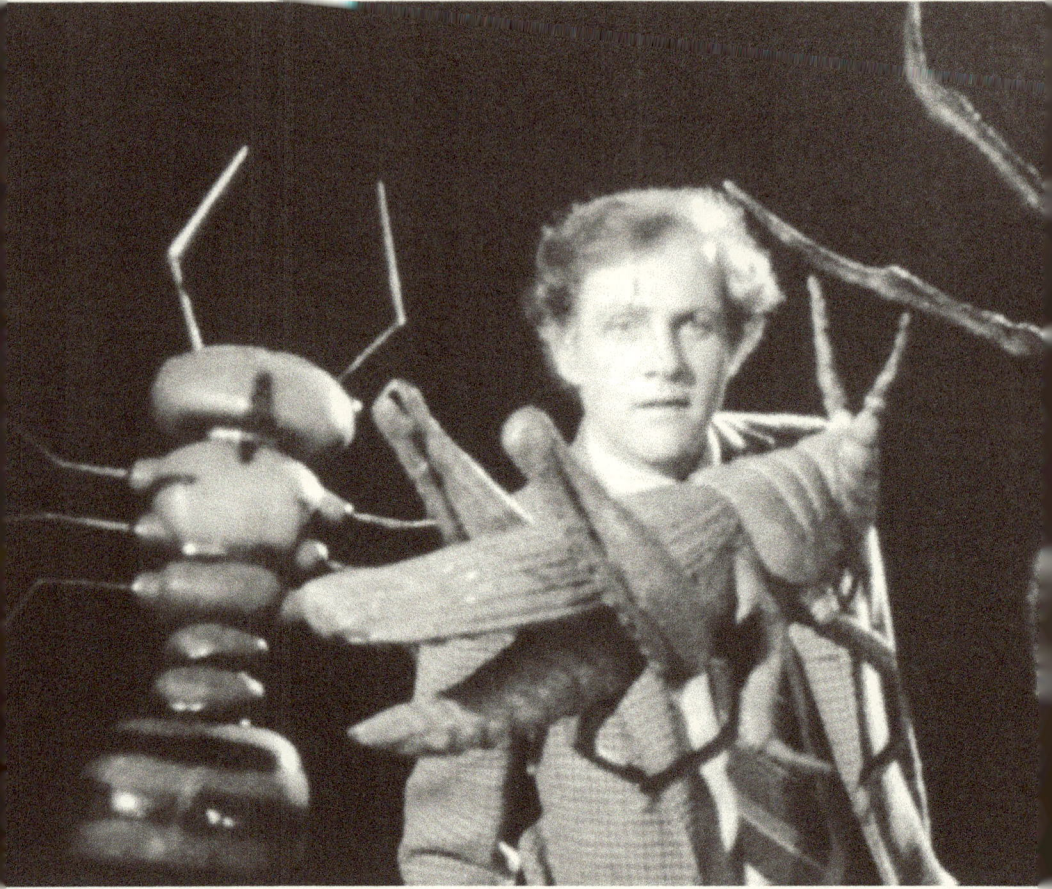

The Hellstrom Chronicle: Hellstrom illustrates insects as monsters.

1

The Hellstrom Chronicle and *Beetle Queen Conquers Tokyo*

Anthropomorphizing Nature for Humans

Near the center of the odd hybrid documentary–horror film, *The Hellstrom Chronicle* (1971), the film's narrator and actor, Dr. Hellstrom (Lawrence Pressman), emphasizes differences between insects and humans, contrasting them to separate humans from the natural insect world and justify the apparent conflict between them. Hellstrom explains, "Assuming for the moment that [an insect] is our opponent, let's see in a physical sense what he has going for him. Face is functional and without expression; only eyes and a mouth, just enough to keep the rest of the body alive. No muscles to smile with, or frown with, or in any way betray what's lurking beneath the surface." A more recent and traditional insect documentary, *Beetle Queen Conquers Tokyo* (2009), on the other hand, literally separates insects from humans by observing people capturing and caging beetles, crickets, and other species as revered pets.

Initially, both of these documentaries seem to distinguish humans from insects and the natural world they represent by highlighting differences between their worlds. But both films also vilify and/or glorify the insects on display by underlining similarities between the behaviors, cultures, emotions, and even appearances of humans and insects. These films build on a history of insect films from Percy Smith's short film, *The Strength and Agility of Insects* (1911), and the hand-drawn animated *How a Mosquito Operates* (1912) by Winsor McCay to narrative stop-action animated films such as Wladyslaw Starewicz's *Mest kinematograficheskogo operatora/The Cameraman's Revenge* (1912) and Loyshki's *The Beetle's Deception* (1913). Other films include the hyperrealistic Fleischer Brothers animated feature, *Mr. Bug (Hoppity) Goes to Town* (1941), and Disney's television documentaries *Nature's Half Acre* (1951) and the True Life Adventure *Secrets of Life* (1956).

Like these earlier films, *The Hellstrom Chronicle* and *Beetle Queen* compare the characteristics and behaviors of insects to those of human beings, connecting them with the human world. These films move beyond those before them by anthropomorphizing insects with a purpose in mind other than entertainment or science education. They construct them as either monsters (as in *The Hellstrom Chronicle*) or model persons (as in *Beetle Queen Conquers Tokyo*) to promote an environmental message that either warns humans about their mistreatment of the natural world or encourages insect preservation. Although the films begin by contrasting the human world with that of insects and approach their subject for varied purposes, they ultimately contend through their narrative and visual rhetoric, as Hellstrom asks at the end of *The Hellstrom Chronicle*, "Is it possible that these creatures are us?"

Problems and Benefits of Anthropomorphism

According to psychologist Alexandra C. Horowitz and evolutionary biologist Marc Bekoff, "in studies of animal behavior, there is near official consensus about anthropomorphism; it is to be avoided" (2007, 23). As they assert, "while the term anthropomorphism literally refers to the characterization of nonhuman behavior or inanimate objects in human terms, it has been further appropriated to refer to such characterization specifically when it is *erroneous*" (23), even though "it is the nearly exclusive method for describing, explaining, and predicting animal behavior—whether the animals are kept as pets, visited in the zoo, or observed in nature" (24). In their introduction to *Thinking with Animals* (2005), science historians Lorraine Daston and Gregg Mitman illuminate the origin of this aversion to anthropomorphism, explaining, "Originally the word referred to the attribution of human form to gods, forbidden by several religions as blasphemous" (2). Contemporary versions of anthropomorphism maintain this "religious taboo," they assert, "even if it is animals rather than divinities being humanized" (2). According to Daston and Mitman, anthropomorphism is critiqued on both scientific and moral or ethical grounds, becoming "almost synonymous with anecdote and sloth and opposed to scientific rigor and care" (3) or "a form of self-centered narcissism" (4).

Recent work in psychology, biology, and science history, however, demonstrates that despite the negative implications associated with anthropomorphism, it may serve practical, psychological, and evolutionary purposes. As Bekoff asserts in *Animal Passions and Beastly Virtues*, "Hard data do not tell the only story, and in my view it is perfectly okay to be carefully anthropomorphic" (2006, 16). In fact, Bekoff explains, "by being anthropomorphic, we can more readily understand and explain the emotions or feelings of other animals" (25). Bekoff and bioethicist Jessica Pierce declare, "There's nothing unscientific about using the same terms to refer to animals and humans, particularly when we're arguing that the same phenomenon is present across species" (2009, 41). And Horowitz and Bekoff suggest, it may illustrate "features of responsiveness that make early infant-caretaker relationships develop" (2007, 28). It may also "help . . . predict animal behavior" (30). It may advance animal rights arguments and, as Daston and Mitman declare, elucidate "the performance of being human by animals and being animal by humans, and the transformative processes that make thinking with animals possible" (2005, 6).

From an organismic-ecology perspective, anthropomorphism that highlights humans as animals may also provide a way to preserve a biotic community, a land ethic in which all parts of the "land" are of equal value. Organismic ecologist Aldo Leopold applied human ethics to the natural world, constructing a manifesto he called "The Land Ethic." This manifesto outlined in Leopold's *A Sand County Almanac* encourages an ecologically centered view of the land as a biotic pyramid in which humans are a part, a principle that rests on the belief that humans are simply members of a community of living things who interact cooperatively and with equal ethical value. One species—humans or other "sentient" beings—is not constructed as a conqueror but as a group of "biotic citizens" (Leopold 1949, 223).

In her study of the image of scientific authority in *March of the Penguins*, "Onward, Christian Penguins: Wildlife Film and the Image of Scientific Authority," Rebecca Wexler also acknowledges that anthropomorphism may have its benefits. Even though underwater shots from a penguin's point of view require "physical contact of the camera with the penguin's body," so "it is even more anthropomorphizing" than other sequences, "this shot also indicates the presence of science; it represents a scientific procedure" (2008, 277). For Wexler anthropomorphic techniques may advance science, helping biologists and ecologists, for example, better observe animal behaviors. In a study of interspecies love between ants, "Interspecies Love in an Age of Excess: Being and Becoming with a Common Ant, *Ectatomma ruidum* (Roger)" (2014), S. Eben Kirksey suggests that the little fire ant "might be accorded a dignity analogous to the human" connecting anthropomorphism with a biotic community.

Computer scientists Per Persson, Jarmo Laaksolahti, and Peter Lonnquist expand on these arguments about the benefits of anthropomorphism in their "Anthropomorphism: A Multi-layered Phenomenon." They begin by defining it as "a way of simplifying and thereby making sense of the environment by projecting a host of expectations about human life onto aspects of that environment." But they also expand that definition beyond one process. The authors explain that "anthropomorphism means different things on different levels" and in relation to different phenomena and schools of thought: primitive psychology, folk psychology, traits, social roles, and emotional anthropomorphism. Primitive psychology includes lower-level "expectations about needs, drives, life preservation, sensations, and pain" (Persson, Laaksolahti, and Lonnquist 2000), including the human need for food, water, and shelter and the ability to feel pain. Because they experience these lower-level needs, animals and inanimate objects are sometimes compared to humans.

Folk-psychology models of anthropomorphism highlight "the ways in which perceptions, beliefs, goals, intentions, and actions relate, and how people in everyday talk explain behavior in terms of such 'inner states'"

(Persson, Laaksolahti, and Lonnquist 2000). When animals and inanimate objects seem to display instances of folk psychology, they seem to show a belief-desire reasoning process, making inferences about the desires and intellectual reasons that guide human and nonhuman behaviors. The traits level of an anthropomorphic system, on the other hand, provides a way to summarize impressions of an individual's attributes or dispositions, such as shy, aggressive, or selfish. Persson, and his colleagues assert that "in contrast to the mental terms in folk-psychology, traits are considered to be more enduring and stable features," but they also may be closely linked with "complex processes on the folk-psychological level."

Other levels of anthropomorphism include social roles (in which situations are understood in terms of social schemas from occupancy roles to family roles and social stereotypes) and emotional anthropomorphism, which extends connections between human and nonhuman nature "into the affective realm" (Persson, Laaksolahti, and Lonnquist 2000). From a positive perspective, all these levels of anthropomorphism may help make sense of complex behaviors in the world around us "by projecting a host of expectations about human life onto aspects of that environment." They also illuminate the multiple ways insects are anthropomorphized in *The Hellstrom Chronicle* and *Beetle Queen Conquers Tokyo*.

The Hellstrom Chronicle: Turning Insects into Monsters

With the 1971 Academy Award for Best Documentary, *The Hellstrom Chronicle* connects amazing micro-documentary footage with a horrific voice-over from a fictional character, Dr. Hellstrom (Lawrence Pressman). The film's faux documentary stance, however, is complicated by its confusing rhetorical message. It warns of mass elimination due to environmentally disastrous practices performed by insects at the micro level. But it also suggests their survival will not be threatened. Such a complex perspective may draw on the expertise of the documentary's filmmakers: codirector and co-cinematographer Walon Green also cowrote the screenplay for Sam Peckinpah's hyperviolent *The Wild Bunch* (1969). The documentary's screenwriter, David Seltzer, was also the author of *The Omen* (1976) and *Prophecy* (1979), and the producer, David L. Wolper, also produced *Appointment with Destiny* (1971), a pseudo-documentary television series. The series used grainy film stock and chiaroscuro lighting to simulate the appearance of actual documentary footage from pre-cinema eras to enhance episodes such as one highlighting the shootout at the O.K. Corral.

Reviews of *Hellstrom* were also mixed, primarily because the film combined a fictional narrator with authentic documentary footage. Roger Ebert (1971) states, for example, that the film "has hypnotically fascinating color photography of insects. The camera becomes so intimate with insects, indeed, that at times we are actually in bed with copulating spiders. . . . Precisely because the photography of insects is so astonishingly good, the narration is annoying." DVD reviewer Glenn Erickson (2011) maintains that the film "has top-level docu credentials" and "uses excellent footage of insect life" but also thinks the voice-over weakens the film.

Other reviewers note the conflicting messages the film espouses about insects' connection with humanity. Erickson notes, for example, that Hellstrom warns that insects dominated Earth from the Big Bang, "the brutal violence of rape," forward, not only because they "had a 300 million year head start," but also because they share some of humanity's best and worst characteristics. Vincent Canby (1971) of the *New York Times* argues that the film "purports to be an ultimatum . . . to the effect that if we don't watch out, the insects will inherit the earth," but he also states that it turns its insect subjects "into monsters of anthropomorphic dimension." These reviewers highlight the consequences of anthropomorphism. If insects are like humans, then both may be monstrous.

Perhaps in an attempt to warn humanity about the negative consequences of its own exploitation of the natural world, the film constructs insects as monsters first by highlighting characteristics that Stephen R. Kellert suggests promote fear in humans. But those traits may also draw on the qualities shared by the most horrific versions of ourselves. According to Kellert, insects have "vastly different ecological strategies, spatially and temporally." They rely on an "extraordinary multiplicity" rather than "individual identity and selfhood," and their "shapes and forms appear 'monstrous'" (quoted in E. C. Brown 2006b, xi). But insects are also "often associated with notions of mindlessness and an absence of feeling," as with the link between insects and madness, a link that explicitly connects the insect and human worlds. And they also possess a radical "autonomy . . . from human will and control" (Kellert quoted in E. C. Brown 2006b, xi), a disposition also associated with

humans who resist subjugation. Their incredible fecundity seems to generate the most fear in humans, according to Kellert, a stereotype associated
with some humans, as well.

By emphasizing these fear-inducing characteristics, the film seems not
only to warn humanity about insects seeming invulnerability but also to
attribute their possible dominance on Earth to humanity's own mistreatment of the natural world. If we continue to destroy our environment, the
film suggests, our species will be usurped by the insect world. Despite the
film's attempts to separate humans and insects, however, its narrative and
film footage suggest that insects will inherit the Earth not because they are
superior to humans but because they are just like us.

Ultimately, insects become monstrous in *The Hellstrom Chronicle* because
they resemble humans at their worst, as, what Eric C. Brown calls "humanity's
Other" (2006b, xi). Drawing on all levels of anthropomorphism proposed
by Persson and his colleagues, the film constructs insects as monsters by
highlighting their primitive psychological qualities, their connection to
human folk psychology, their traits and "dispositions," the social roles they
play, and the emotions they both display and produce.

The film first applies the primitive-psychology level of anthropomorphism, highlighting that insects' drive to fulfill their basic needs aligns with
that of humans. Hellstrom claims, "In fighting the insect we have killed
ourselves, polluted our water, poisoned our wildlife, permeated our own
flesh with deadly toxins. The insect becomes immune, and we are poisoned.
In fighting with superior intellect, we have outsmarted ourselves." Yet that
so-called immunity is based on one element that humans and insects share:
"only humans and insects as species are on the increase." Humans radically
change the Earth, and insects adapt to any changes they can make, Hellstrom
declares. Yet his attempts to separate humans from the insect world fall flat
because he bases his arguments that insects will inherit the Earth on their
similarity to humans.

Even when making claims about differences between these two worlds,
Hellstrom grounds his arguments in demonstrations of their similarities. For
example, he discusses insect traits in relation to those of humans, maintaining
that the society of bees is perfect because it is based on cooperation rather than
competition and "individual need," so that "in [this] cooperative society, the

fate of each is the destiny of all." Since both individuality and cooperation are human traits and dispositions, connecting them to insects anthropomorphizes them on the level of traits, a higher level than that of primitive psychology.

Hellstrom also draws on the folk-psychology level of anthropomorphism when describing the cooperative behavior of insects. At the same time he separates bees from humans because of their perfect cooperative culture, he connects the cooperative harvest of fungi by ants to human farmers when he suggests they were "the first to take steps toward agriculture," a parallel that aligns with folk psychology. Hellstrom draws on both traits and folk-psychology anthropomorphism when he maintains that these insects' "instinct to harvest is an instinct of greed," just as in the human world. He makes similar comparisons with a termite-mound society, "one of the first experiments in social order" that he visually compares to a computer at the California Institute of Technology.

Hellstrom contradicts himself in similar ways when exploring warring elements of nature, elements that again apply a traits level of anthropomorphism. He calls insects and carnivorous plants "macabre masterpiece[s] of revenge," explaining that flying insects spread contagious diseases to human populations, while we observe carnivorous cobra plants capturing and eating insect victims. He anthropomorphizes other carnivorous plants, as well, using primitive, traits, folk-psychology, and emotional levels of anthropomorphism to make his points about their villainy: a Venus flytrap has "gaping jaws" and a "menacing hunger" that "beckons with gentle perfume." The sundew is "beautiful," "a murderess in disguise." Other insects "become instrument[s] of death," as well, Hellstrom declares, connecting their violent behavior to that of humans. At the same time, however, he maintains that insects' violence is not based in the greed and revenge he pointed to previously. Hellstrom declares, "Man will point to nature, claiming war was meant to be. But here they died with reason—through selflessness, not greed."

Near the film's end, footage and voice-over again contradict this claim, combining images and commentary that illustrate folk-psychology and traits levels of anthropomorphism. Images of insect violence, including those of ants from *The Naked Jungle* (1954), illustrate these anthropomorphic levels. Ants use their bodies as bridges, build trenches to prepare for war, and act as sentries and guards to launch attacks and bring back their kill. Hellstrom proclaims that these driver ants are a "mindless unstoppable killing machine, dedicated to the destruction of everything that stands in its way. Each of them is completely blind, driven forward through the darkness by a single demanding need within—the need to kill and plunder." Through pillaging their young are fed, Hellstrom tells us, and an ant-covered lizard is shown being dragged back into their fortress. Other animals and insects are also brought back to share with the rest of the colony: a snake, a caterpillar, a scorpion, and a butterfly.

Hellstrom ends the film with the diatribe, "The true winner is the last to finish the race," but his narrative and film footage suggest that insects will inherit the Earth not because they are superior to humans but because they are us. By integrating multiple levels of anthropomorphism, *The Hellstrom Chronicle* turns insects into monsters possessing the worst human traits and exploiting them for the most destructive reasons. The film also lays the groundwork for future insect documentaries such as *Microcosmos: Le peuple de l'herbe/ Microcosmos* (Nuridsany and Pérennou 1996) and *Beetle Queen Conquers Tokyo*.

Microcosmos illustrates how the human world is mirrored by an "unseen" insect world in a categorical documentary constructed by the filmmakers. With little voice-over narration, the film is a powerful argument for the conservation of insects because they so resemble us. Within the film's context, however, the images of insects' everyday activities become poetry as well as rhetoric, subtly revealing connections between our worlds and providing an opening for empathetic responses from viewers that may lead to changes in environmental politics. As ecocritic Mitman asserts in his discussion of elephant conservation, "While an appeal to numbers has often shored up the authority and expertise of scientists in the political realm ... anthropomorphism and emotion, more than numbers, have lent greater credence to science in the public sphere" (2005, 176).

What is missing from *The Hellstrom Chronicle* is at least a partial nod toward the interdependence and biotic community of organismic approaches to ecology. As Canby (1971) suggests in his review of the film, "Anyone who has ever lived more than a week in a New York apartment already knows, for example, that an entente with insects must be reached if the world is to survive." By constructing insects as monsters, the film connects them to the human world without inducing the sympathy that might save both.

Insects as Captives and Queens in *Beetle Queen Conquers Tokyo*

In contrast to *The Hellstrom Chronicle*, *Beetle Queen Conquers Tokyo* examines the insect world from humanity's point of view, focusing specifically on the worldview and behaviors of insect collectors in Tokyo. Jason Solomons of the *Observer* states, "It speaks of harmony, nature and the national culture, touching on the quintessentially Japanese philosophical notion of Mono no aware (and I hope I've got this right): a feeling of gentle sadness experienced at the inevitable fading of transient beauty." In *Beetle Queen* insects are anthropomorphized even more explicitly than in *Hellstrom*, however, with specific comparisons between insects and human characteristics on multiple levels made throughout the film by various experts commenting on Japanese culture. Despite references to the monster movie *Mothra* (1961), *Beetle Queen* goes beyond merely evoking emotions by humanizing insects of various species. The unequivocal comparison between the human and insect worlds promotes positive results in the film, encouraging a more interconnected relationship between humans and their environment that may manifest in real environmental preservation and restoration for the benefit of both humans and nature, at least within the parameters of the film. As *Beetle Queen*'s director, Jessica Oreck explains in *Don't Panic Magazine*, "I want to share the immediacy of nature—not the idealized, simplified, and anonymous version we see in nature programs on TV, but a nature populated with human characters and personal connections" (Mokoena 2011).

The opening of *Beetle Queen Conquers Tokyo* immediately establishes its human perspective on insects as an anthropomorphized commodity. Two men in a forest hunt insects with nets and other tools, collecting caterpillars and pulling beetles from a knothole. One stamps a tree trunk. The other looks at the ground for falling insects and extends a net to catch them as they fall. This pastoral scene is contrasted with an urban sequence that introduces the motivation for this beetle collection: selling beetles as pets. After a blur of city lights, urban music, and whizzing cars, the film shows a child in a beetle store attempting to purchase a beetle. He is deciding between two species: the king beetle and the rainbow beetle, which cost from forty-seven to fifty-seven dollars. Plastic versions of these beetles and other insects flow from gumball machines near the store's front door, highlighting the attraction these beetles have for children of multiple social classes.

But the film takes care to demonstrate that the lure of the beetle transcends childish fascination and, instead, drawing on folk-psychology models of anthropomorphism, signifies humanity's connection to the natural world. According to one of the film's experts, author and scientist Takeshi Yoro, it symbolizes "the simple pleasure of existence," the essence of being Japanese established in the eighteenth century. While caterpillars crawl from their eggs, the narration highlights Japanese philosophies regarding beauty. "Insects are essential," he explains, "and life and nature are cohesive. The cocoon may signify independence." To more broadly compare Japanese culture and the insect world, the film shows multiple parallel images of insects and the Japanese urban centers of humanity. As Peter Rainer (2010) of the *Christian Science Monitor* explains of Oreck, "She visually contrasts, for example, pedestrians' multicolored umbrellas with beetles' protective shells."

Folk-psychology and emotional anthropomorphism underpin the treatment of these insects from their capture or cultivation to their captivity. Because insects have become precious symbols of essential nature, each species is nurtured and collected with careful attention. In what looks like a beetle farm, an insect cultivator digs in a rotten log, picking out eggs and placing them in film containers. "This is the season when they begin to emerge," he explains, and beetles climb out of the soil in a literal demonstration. Noel Murray (2010) of *A.V. Club* calls these harvesting sequences "stunningly gorgeous and eerie scenes of bug-harvesting and cultivation, including long shots of a nighttime hunt involving damp screens and floodlights, and a fascinating sequence where a man gently pulls apart a chunk of wood to find a tiny egg." Another beetle farmer reveals how he raises caterpillars in soil with homemade containers in which they can dig.

The traits level of anthropomorphism is also underlined in these humans' interaction with insects. Crickets, too, are reared as pets, and their roar illustrates their nickname, "crying insects." The narrator explains that some species have weak wings and cannot cry, but there are more than 118 species of crickets in Japan, and their capture spread across Japan after a food vendor began feeding crickets and caged one as a pet. A shop showcasing a variety of beetles illustrates the extent of this tradition. Celebrities sign autographs in the shop while other hug merchandise and an insect-driven videogame reinforce the culture's appetite for insects.

The presentation of Japanese philosophy and aesthetics highlights the interaction between culture and nature signified by this love of insects. It also demonstrates anthropomorphism on the level of traits and dispositions, emotions and social roles. According to the film, haiku from the seventeenth century highlights a Japanese aesthetic of nature that encourages this love of captive beetles and crickets. A poem about dragonflies accompanying an image of a mechanized dragonfly reinforces the narrator's claim: "Poetry eternally captures mundane reality. Haiku, like nature, is about transience, creating an intimate relationship with nature without intermediaries. Man is nature." Night views of the city look like poetry. We see fighting beetles in a video game, on a crowded street, and in a mall. The narrator even assigns specific human traits to the insects to emphasize humanity's connection with the natural world: "A dragonfly is the emblem of strength, courage, and bravery. . . . Fireflies are unrequited love." Workers wearing illuminated vests look like fireflies and underline the message.

Other scenes specifically highlight social-role anthropomorphism by illustrating how families and schools continue the tradition of insect glorification. Family members feed cucumber slices to caged crickets. Children and their parents chase butterflies and other insects with nets in "an ancient ritual." Shops sell accessories for insect collectors. A Zen garden presents humanity's interaction with nature as a shrinking of worlds similar to that of both bonsai and insects. "They hold all the truths of nature in their ergonomic bodies," the narrator tells us. Even though classes teach butterfly and beetle pinning, and children are rewarded for their skills, families primarily seek to interact with living nature. The narrator asserts that people look at nature in everyday life as a way to connect and combat natural disasters. *Beetle Queen* demonstrates how songs in the trees mesh with statues of human faces and symbols of Buddhism and Shintoism, representatives of nature's harmony as in anima and animus that evoke folk-psychology models of anthropomorphism.

This folk-psychology level of connection between human and nonhuman nature is illustrated by a comparison between feet in a pair of socks and an insect in a cocoon. According to the narrator, Shintoism and Buddhism emphasize reincarnation in nature's seasons, an animistic view of birth, death, and rebirth. Those who follow these philosophies cannot destroy even a blade of grass. Even though human language is a fixed vision of culture, emphasizing the lack of change in culture, individuals do change. "The present day is fixed," the narrator tells us, but "if you plant a tree, it grows. It always changes." This philosophy of interconnectedness between human and nonhuman nature is illustrated by parallel images of fireflies in a willow and fireworks over the city.

As the film portrays it, the devotion to nature inspired by Japanese philosophy, aesthetics, and connection to insects moves beyond a surface belief system to actions that conserve and replenish the natural environment. Because, as narrator Takeshi Yoro tells us, rice paddies are good for dragonflies, their disappearance was detrimental to both dragonflies and human culture. With less need for rice fields to feed people, rice paddies turned into cities, but the narrator explains, this loss motivated the Japanese to begin preserving streams and ponds around the city, rejuvenating the environment and community for national pride. "We learn from insects," he explains. "If we open our minds to the insects, they will teach us. To learn is to change, so insects are more than pets. They represent an entire culture." As the sun rises over the water, Takeshi Yoro highlights the interconnected relationship that humans share with the insects and their natural world: "Observing change in insects connects with changes in nature. Their numbers are much fewer now, because the world is being destroyed."

In *Beetle Queen Conquers Tokyo*, Oreck tells us she seeks to "remind the audience that humans are animals" to help us remember "it is impossible to separate ourselves from nature" (Mokoena 2011). As she tells *Independent Lens* blog contributor Shelby Biggs, "It seems that a lot of the environmental messages our society is pumping out are getting lost, either because we are preaching to the choir or because the scare tactics are working too well—and people come away feeling disheartened instead of inspired" (Biggs 2011). For Oreck change occurs when people begin to look at nature—not just glance at a picture or watch some aerial view of a world they have no connection to—but pick up a leaf or a bug in their own city and really take the time to look at it, to understand it, to realize its place in the extraordinary complex system that makes up our environment (Biggs 2011).

Although critic Mike Hale (2010) of the *New York Times* claims that the film "says less about Japan than it does about America's continuing fascination with modern Japanese culture," *Beetle Queen Conquers Tokyo* seems to move beyond the anthropomorphism found in *The Hellstrom Chronicle*, giving it a unique environmental purpose. By illuminating connections between humans and nature based on dispositions, emotions, roles, and philosophies of Buddhism and Shintoism, *Beetle Queen Conquers Tokyo* seeks to demonstrate how anthropomorphism may have positive results for both human and nonhuman nature.

The attitudes toward insects documented in *Beetle Queen Conquers Tokyo* suggest that despite negative connotations still associated with anthropomorphism, it may encourage conservation of a variety of animal species, at least in some instances. The purpose behind anthropomorphizing differs in each of these documentaries, however. *The Hellstrom Chronicle* anthropomorphizes insects in order to highlight their "monstrous" qualities, perhaps as a warning to humanity about its own destruction of Earth's environment. The resulting images in the film, however, recall horror movies of the 1950s and 1960s such as *Them!* (1954), *The Deadly Mantis* (1957), and *The Blood Beast Terror* (1968). With Hellstrom's cautionary narration, these visions of horror incite fear more than empathy, even though the micro-cinematography of insect habitants alone could encourage more positive responses.

Beetle Queen Conquers Tokyo expands on this argument because its filmmaker deliberately seeks to build connections between humans and nature to change attitudes toward the environment and encourage sustainable environmental policies. In a blog interview with *Independent Lens*, Oreck laments hearing "more kids asking if a butterfly is 'broken' than asking if it is 'dead,'" commenting, "I think that's a real indication that there's a rather potent problem in the human-nature interaction" (Biggs 2011). For Oreck documentary filmmaking offers a place in which humans can interact with an insect in the natural world and, perhaps, "understand it, realize its place in the extraordinary complex system that makes up our environment" in order to eventually "make a change."

Beetle Queen Conquers Tokyo: Insect pet store entices children with bright packaging

Oreck's goals align well with those of nature documentary filmmaker Sarita Siegal, who asserts, "As science becomes increasingly accepting of filmmakers' needs to communicate with broad audiences via vivid and accessible language that contains metaphors and analogies, which are or may be anthropomorphic, we should see increased cooperation between science and media in aid of conservation efforts" (2006, 221). Siegal filmed her documentary, *The Disenchanted Forest* (2002), to "bring ... audiences intimately into the world of orangutans in hopes that it may be useful in the care and conservation of this magnificent species in the remnants of rainforest that endure in Borneo and Sumatra" (221).

If anthropomorphism "is the nearly exclusive method for describing, explaining, and predicting animal behavior—whether the animals are kept as pets, visited in the zoo, or observed in nature" (Horowitz and Bekoff 2007, 24), perhaps it can also serve as a conservation tool for animals and the plant life that sustains them. When wondering if "even mosquitos have emotional lives," Bekoff also concludes, "knowledge about animal passions should make a difference in how we view, represent, and treat our fellow beings" (2007, 2). *Beetle Queen Conquers Tokyo* suggests that providing images of insects that anthropomorphize them in relation to primitive psychology, folk psychology, traits, emotions, and social roles may help audiences understand the place of insects in a biotic community and facilitate positive environmental change.

Within the context of *Beetle Queen Conquers Tokyo*, this goal seems to be fulfilled since streams and ponds around the city have been preserved to rejuvenate the environment and its insect life. Within the world outside these films, however, "the difference between the known number of species and the total number of species out there in the world—the biological unknown—walking, flying, and crawling around, is somewhere between 2.8 million species and, at the opposite extreme, ten million or even tens of millions of species" (Dunn and Fitzpatrick 2012, 217). This ignorance makes us ill prepared to address species extinction associated with climate change and other forms of environmental degradation. We can hope, however, that viewing documentaries such as *Beetle Queen Conquers Tokyo* will help audiences understand the insect world and "realize its place in the extraordinary complex system that makes up our environment" in order to eventually "make a change."

2

"As Beautiful as a Butterfly"?

Monstrous Cockroach Nature and the Horror Film

A key center scene in Guillermo del Toro's 1993 horror debut, *Cronos*, introduces conflicting views of insects like those in *The Hellstrom Chronicle* and *Beetle Queen Conquers Tokyo* from a fictional film perspective. According to a dying industrialist, De la Guardia (Claudio Brook), a coveted device prolongs life because a cockroach trapped inside it is working like a "living filter" attesting to the power of insects. As De la Guardia asks the film's hero, Jesus Gris (Federico Luppi), who has activated the device, "Who says insects aren't God's favorite creatures?" They have survived from almost Earth's beginnings, even when other species have disappeared. More to the point, De la Guardia suggests insects may have qualities that transform them from vile creatures into gods, declaring, "Christ walked on water—just like a mosquito."

Animal studies scholar Marion W. Copeland provides a context for this reaction in her "Voices of the Least Loved: Cockroaches in the Contemporary

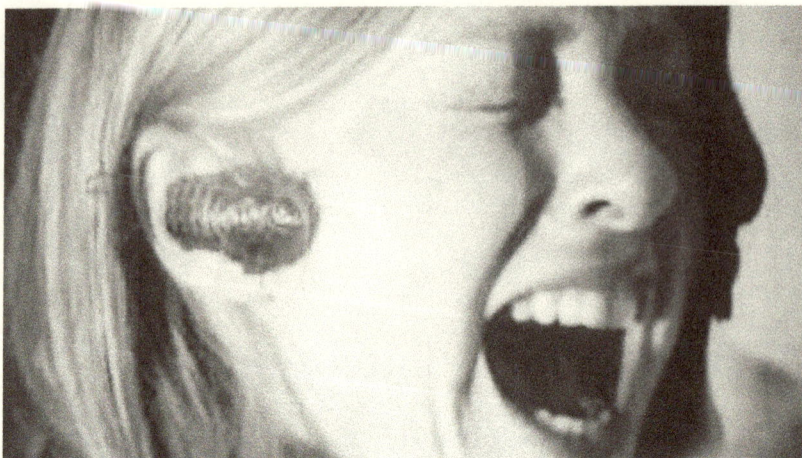

Bug: A deadly cockroach attacks.

American Novel" in *Insect Poetics*, asserting, "The symbolic value of the cockroach to marginal literatures comes from the insect's reputation as both survivor and victim" (2006, 155). Characteristics like these anthropomorphize the cockroach in relation to both positive and negative perspectives on humanity. In the horror genre, this symbolic value also sometimes leads to explorations of how that reputation may transform cockroaches into both monsters and saviors when humanity intervenes either deliberately or by accident. Marion Copeland and evolutionary biologist Marc Bekoff emphasize the usefulness of anthropomorphizing, and entomological consultant James W. Mertins declares that "almost all of the well-treated movie arthropods are at least somewhat anthropomorphized" (1986, 86). Yet in the cockroach horror film, representations of the cockroach highlight characteristics that Stephen R. Kellert suggests promote fear in humans while also drawing on the qualities shared by the most horrific versions of ourselves.

As computer scientists Per Persson, Jarmo Laaksolahti, and Peter Lonnquist (2000) declare, anthropomorphism is "a way of simplifying and thereby making sense of the environment by projecting a host of expectations about human life onto aspects of that environment." Such anthropomorphized qualities of the cockroach underpin the narratives of cockroach horror films whether or not cockroaches are presented as survivors or victims, and whether or not they are constructed as benefactors or destructive forces of nature. The suggestion that the cockroach will outlast all other life forms, including humans, permeates popular film, including positive appearances as the only friend of the hero in WALL-E (2008) and negative portrayals as villain in *Men in Black* (1997) and *Starship Troopers* (1997).[1]

In the horror films *Bug* (1975), *Damnation Alley* (1977), *The Nest* (1988), *Cronos*, and *Mimic* (1997), however, their "villainy" is a product of transformation, either through deliberate genetic alterations or chemical or nuclear environmental disasters. *Mimic* and *Bug* examine the destructive repercussions of genetic engineering meant to alter cockroaches for human benefit but move beyond historian William M. Tsutsui's suggestion that "these cinematic big bugs [represent] ambivalence about science and technocratic authority, and repressed Freudian impulses" (2007, 1). *Cronos* advances these points, emphasizing the symbolic survival value of insects to examine the implications of humanity's drive for immortality by transforming its hero into an insect not unlike the cockroach source of this change. Despite this seemingly positive association, however, *Cronos* also projects a negative view of the cockroach and all it represents. As James W. Mertins asserts, "Arthropod features rarely project positive images of arthropods, entomologists, or science" (1986, 86).

Typically, then, altered and enhanced roaches are presented as horrific monsters that must be destroyed, perhaps because they too closely resemble the monstrous side of humanity. *Damnation Alley* illustrates how cockroaches might transform into killers after a nuclear holocaust, and *The Nest* explores the possible disastrous consequences of a biological experiment that turns roaches into flesh-eating fiends. *Mimic* and *Bug*, on the other hand, examine the destructive repercussions of genetic engineering meant to alter cockroaches for human benefit, a more positive result that corresponds with the level of anthropomorphizing on the screen. *Mimic* explores the long-term effects after entomologist Susan Tyler (Mira Sorvino) creates a mutant breed of cockroach, the Judas Breed, to offset an epidemic spread by the common cockroach. *Bug* also examines the ramifications of developing a new breed of cockroach, in this case both the positive growth in intelligence and in destructive force. *Cronos* more explicitly highlights the symbolic value of the cockroach as a seemingly immortal survivor. All these films, however, demonstrate a similar perspective on the cockroach, suggesting that manipulating nature, even for beneficial results, ultimately leads to destructive results.

The Cockroach Mythology

According to interdisciplinary scholar Eric C. Brown's introduction to *Insect Poetics*, "Cockroaches routinely outrank other animals as the most repulsive species, and reality television shows like *Survivor* and *Fear Factor* exploit disgust at protein-laden arthropods to draw ratings" (2006a, x). Marion W. Copeland, on the other hand, highlights how metaphors surrounding the cockroach draw on anthropomorphic tendencies. For example, she demonstrates how associations of the cockroach with chthonic elements affect their literary and filmic reputation. For her, these works are "rooted in world traditions that draw on the cockroach's tendency to prefer dark and hidden places, both linked in the modern mind to the chthonic, the early powers associated with the feminine as well as with eroticism and fertility" (2006, 155). In a similar vein, golden cockroaches in the Mexican tradition were associated with fertility and rebirth. As literary scholar Christopher Hollingsworth suggests, "To Mexicans, the cockroach is more than a pest. Celebrated in folklore and song, this durable creature is associated with survival and successful opposition to oppression" (2006, 273).

Copeland notes other positive associations with cockroaches in her book-length *Cockroach*, as well. Because "of its predilection for the dark" (2003, 81), Copeland suggests, the cockroach has become associated with "the unconscious and the power of the id" (81). In Thailand, Australia, South America, and French Guiana, cockroaches serve as food, medicine, and folktale source. Copeland suggests that studies by anthropologists and explorers reveal that "rather than racking their brains for effective ways to destroy cockroaches, these cultures found the cockroach a useful neighbor, rich in protein and effective for many human diseases. They also seem to have recognized how useful they were to the environment" (81–82). Copeland also notes that cockroaches contribute to cancer research (131).

Other studies of cockroaches highlight their physical and intellectual strengths by making explicit connections between cockroaches and humans.

According to Copeland, "as in humans, female cockroaches have stronger immune responses than males and the very young and very old have weaker responses than mature adults" (2003, 131). As early as 1912, studies at Summer Teacher's College in St. Louis showed that cockroaches could learn to "overcome their innate aversion to light" (135). They were also found capable of running a maze, even without their heads, a feat few animals could manage (135).

Because of these strengths, Copeland believes we can learn from cockroaches. She suggests in "Voices of the Least Loved," for example, that "the necessity of humans drastically altering our current cultural and personal assumptions about ourselves and the rest of the living world (and, of course, of altering the behavior such assumptions foster) is critical if we hope *Homo sapiens* is to enjoy anything approaching the long, successful life story of the cockroach" (2006, 170). In *Cockroach* Copeland amplifies this view, arguing, "Our survival as a species may depend on discovering a saviour who looks at us from many-faceted eyes that replace our own myopic human view with the cockroach's 'very long view indeed'" (2003, 168).

Despite these positive associations with cockroaches, however, at least in Western culture they continue to promote fear and aversion in humans. In Hollywood films, insects, and cockroaches in particular, embody characteristics that social ecologist Stephen R. Kellert suggests promote fear in humans, but those traits may also draw on the qualities shared by the most horrific versions of humanity. For example, insects are "often associated with notions of mindlessness and an absence of feeling," as with the link between insects and madness, a link that explicitly connects the insect and human worlds. And they also possess a radical "autonomy ... from human will and control" (Kellert 1993, 58), a disposition also associated with humans who resist subjugation. Their incredible fecundity seems to generate the most fear in humans, according to Kellert, a stereotype associated with some people, as well.

In many ways cockroaches are, as Eric C. Brown claims, "humanity's Other" (2006b, xi). Entomologist Edward O. Wilson's foreword to *Cockroaches: Ecology, Behavior, and Natural History* illustrates well the revulsion humans feel toward the cockroach, an aversion illuminated by the cockroach horror film. As Wilson explains, "Most of us, even the entomologists in whose ranks I belong, have a stereotype of revolting creatures that scatter from leftover food when you turn on the kitchen light and instantly disappear into inaccessible crevices. These particular cockroaches are a *problem*, and the only solution is *blatticide*, with spray, poison, or trap" (2007, ix)

Horror films from *Damnation Alley* to *Mimic* reinforce this stereotype as they highlight humanity's ambivalence toward cockroaches. *Damnation Alley* and *The Nest* clearly construct cockroaches as monsters with no redeeming qualities. *Mimic*, *Bug*, and *Cronos*, however, draw on positive qualities associated with cockroaches, including their contributions to human health, their intelligence, and their longevity. Yet these films also turn these strengths into detriments and, consequently, turn cockroaches into horrific monsters, an "Other" whose humanlike qualities grow into a monstrous nature not only because this is a convention of the horror genre but also because their transformation is either a product of a genetic, chemical, or nuclear eco-disaster or a violation of human and nonhuman nature alike.

Damnation Alley and *The Nest*: Cockroach Horror

Based on a novel by science fiction writer Roger Zelazny ([1969] 2004), *Damnation Alley* (1977) shows us an Earth that is tilted off its axis after a third world war, covered in radioactive dust, and surrounded by bizarre red clouds and spasmodic flames. Like the iconic "big bug" movie *Them!* (1954), one of the new realities is monstrously transformed insect life. According to the film's narrator, the climate has gone insane. Once the radiation settles down, all that is left for the few humans who remain is a struggle for survival and dominance, the film tells us, a struggle nearly thwarted by the monstrous insects created by nuclear war.

The first set of insect monsters in the film are giant blue scorpions that surround a compound where ex-military personnel now live. The scorpions attempt to attack a motorcycle rider, Tanner (Jan-Michael Vincent), who is returning from town with a stuffed life-size female doll. His roommate, Keegan (Paul Winfield), first believes that Tanner has sacrificed a woman to the scorpions, but when he looks through his binoculars, he realizes it is a department store mannequin.

This comic scene in some ways separates *Damnation Alley* from earlier insect horror films with primarily serious tones. In an essay suggesting that these "big bug" movies were responding to "growing misgivings about the safety and effectiveness of modern insecticides," historian William M. Tsutsui argues, "Critics and historians have invariably interpreted these cinematic big bugs as symbolic manifestations of Cold War era anxieties, including nuclear fear, concern over communist infiltration, ambivalence about science and technocratic authority, and repressed Freudian impulses" (2007 abstract). Despite the comic effect, however, these scorpions are portrayed as monsters that must be avoided and destroyed, even though humanity's addiction to war produced them.

The second set of insect monsters show up later in the film, after the military compound near Tanner and Keegan's refuge explodes when a cigarette ignites a gas leak, and only two of the officers housed there survive, Maj. Eugene Denton (George Peppard) and Lt. Tom Perry (Kip Niven). The new insect monsters emerge in Salt Lake City, Utah, where the group encounters large formations of killer cockroaches while collecting supplies. The first evidence of the roaches appears when they find a human skeleton picked completely clean by radioactive cockroaches emerging from the sewers. To emphasize their monstrous nature, the film shows the roaches attacking Keegan, who is overwhelmed and killed in seconds. Tanner and love-interest Janice (Dominique Sanda) encounter hordes of cockroaches in a department store as well, but they escape on their motorcycle. "The whole town is infested with killer cockroaches," Tanner exclaims, an insight proven when we see bare human bones throughout the town.

Cockroaches are constructed as monsters throughout these battles within the community, with little attempt to anthropomorphize them. As the survivors head toward the hope of sanctuary in Albany, New York, insects become monsters, even when they defy all accurate natural laws. Radiation serves as the culprit causing changes in insect life, alterations that don't appear in any other species in the film. Ultimately Tanner, Janice, and Denton successfully combat all the insect monsters they encounter and find fellowship in Albany, with what we presume are the only remaining humans in the United States. The transformed cockroaches presumably live on as monstrous nature that must be eradicated or avoided.

The Nest (1988) copies *Alien* (1979) with its focus on the corporate science connection, ultimately leading to the discovery of a queen and her brood hidden deep in a cave outside an idyllic California coastal town.

The film serves as a warning against genetic modifications of cockroaches, a transformation that turns bugs into horrifically anthropomorphized monsters. Negative associations with the insects heighten their monstrous qualities as they take center stage from the film's opening until its closing denouement. These cockroaches are first established as pests that must be eradicated but transform into monsters that may ultimately destroy humanity instead.

The film opens in the small harbor town of North Port, where Sheriff Richard Tarbell's (Franc Luz) switchboard officer has been getting strange calls about missing animals, calls that are immediately connected to insects when Tarbell finds a cockroach in his coffee at a diner counter. The presence of cockroaches is also reinforced when the librarian reveals that something—mice or insects—has eaten all the binding of her library books. The central cockroach drama, however, intertwines with a subplot of the film, a love triangle Tarbell creates between himself and two women, the diner's owner Lillian (Nancy Morgan) and his previous girlfriend Beth (Lisa Langlois). The reigniting of Tarbell and Beth's romance begins to solve the mystery broached by the cockroach evidence. When Beth takes a walk toward the hideout of their youth, she finds a "no trespassing" sign labeled "Intec Development." A German shepherd's cries of agony stop her, and when she reaches the dog, its flesh has been eaten down to the bone. Tarbell investigates and retrieves something that looks like insect droppings on the dog, yet village mayor Elias urges Tarbell to hold off on searching the Intec property for more evidence. He claims Intec is building condominiums to bring revenue to the island.

The Nest also constructs scientists as monsters when Intec sends an entomologist, Dr. Morgan Hubbard (Terri Treas), to the island to examine the devoured dog. Hubbard serves as a typical representative of the inhuman and perhaps "mad" scientist seen in most classic monster movies. Hubbard's response to these incidents emphasizes the negative portrait of science and scientists in the film. Instead of the fear felt by the rest of the community, Hubbard seems enamored of the roaches and explicitly anthropomorphizes them. For example, when the cockroaches attack a trapped cat, she exclaims, "Very brave, very strange creatures," a point emphasized by the few predators that can threaten the cockroach. These strengths add to the town's danger but also draw on cockroach mythology.

Because they have been genetically modified in an Intec lab, the roaches have developed new powers, more concretely illustrating human and godlike-qualities associated with them. Because she has produced them, Hubbard embraces these new superior but deadly qualities, naming them nymph cockroaches. She lauds their ability to reproduce without the contributions of male counterparts, but when she puts her gloved hand near them in a large lab container, they quickly bite it, highlighting their move from human prey to predator. As a "mad" scientist, however, she seems sexually excited by the mangling of her hand, refusing to remove it until Elias pulls it out before the roaches devour it. Despite these warning signs, Hubbard tells Elias she can control the roaches and asks for twenty-four hours to solve the problem.

Beth's examination of Elias's papers begins to reveal the truth about these cockroaches' genetic alteration. Instead of condos, Intec has built a research facility where, according to Hubbard, her experiments are benevolent rather than destructive and meant to create cockroaches that will destroy all other roaches and then die without reproducing. Instead the cockroaches have grown so powerful that even a lethal pesticide can't destroy them. A solution arises when they realize the roaches have become social animals and must have a nest and a queen to guide them.

The final sinister scenes of the movie emphasize a possible solution to the horror of this now monstrous nature. As Beth explains, if they destroy the caves, they will destroy the nest, suggesting that if they destroy the horror setting, the monstrous insect horror will also disappear. The roaches all go toward the queen in the caves like "a collective unconscious," making an overt connection to an anthropomorphized cockroach mythology. In the cave where the nest is hidden, Hubbard is destroyed by a roach figure built out of multiple human skeletons. Tarbell and Beth escape the cave before it explodes, and the two kiss, an ending that perhaps satisfactorily resolves the insect conflict in the film but leaves gaps in the love triangle connecting with it. In *The Nest* both science and the cockroach become monstrous, but only the bugs and the mad scientist die, perhaps signifying the need to destroy our worst selves.

Bug and Mimic: Transforming Cockroaches for Human Good

Although both *Bug* and *Mimic* anthropomorphize roaches and other insects on a higher level, neither the insect nor the scientists that transform them are well treated. Based on the novel *The Hephaestus Plague*, William Castle's final film, *Bug*, highlights what happens when a scientist tampers with nature: roaches that belch flames remain vulnerable and easily destroyed until another entomologist, James Parmiter (Bradford Dillman), attempts to mate them with other roaches. The roaches then become more like humans as they gain intelligence and grow deadly as they breed, producing carnivorous offspring. Eventually these offspring also mate and kill, creating a flying burning insect that drags Parmiter and the science he represents to hell.

Despite the heightened anthropomorphism, then, in *Bug*, both cockroach and scientist are constructed as monstrous. Although the film's scientist, Parmiter is a biology teacher who explains many things, he is also, as entomologist James W. Mertins explains of the scientist image, "shown . . . as detached from reality," a "psychotic" (1986, 86). Parmiter tells his students, "Earth, soil, wind, temperature are all part of an exact pattern." He mesmerizes a squirrel. He tells them about a Florida beetle that scalds its enemy. But when a farm boy shows him his dead cat, burned by the flaming cockroaches, the teacher is intrigued, so much so that he makes the roach his life work, even after the roaches kill his wife by crawling into her hair and lighting her up like a human torch.

Aided by the insect photography of Ken Middleham, who also filmed the documentary *The Hellstrom Chronicle* (1971) and the science fiction thriller *Phase IV* (1974), *Bug* provides an authentic portrayal of the cockroaches, at least until breeding ignites their intelligence to such an extent that they can read and write. The prehistoric roaches that appear after the quake, for example, produce sparks not unlike the bioluminescence of the South American cockroach, called "pronatal headlights" in William Bell and his colleagues' *Cockroaches* (2007). As critic Bill Gibron (2004) of *PopMatters* declares, close-up shots of these roaches' mandibles also "make their actions seem almost plausible."

The monstrous nature of these roaches is shown in a variety of scenes before Parmiter decides to breed a new species. His friend Mark's (Alan Fudge) wife, Sylvia (Patty McCormack), is killed by a roach attack, for example, and a roach also climbs in another woman's ear (Jamie Smith Jackson) and destroys her. Although we do not see her killed onscreen, the death of Parmiter's wife, Carrie (Joanna Miles), is gruesome. But as Mark explains, these new roaches live very short lives and cannot reproduce, at least without intervention, so the danger associated with them should be finite.

The horror of the film becomes amplified when Parmiter even more extensively anthropomorphizes the roaches by facilitating their reproduction. In a dark and deserted farmhouse setting, the now-reclusive Parmiter breeds this new species of roach with what looks like an American cockroach specimen, a process that will transform a dying species into a menace. When Parmiter sees the roaches write "We Live" on the wall with their bodies, he knows he has created unbeatable humanlike monsters and is helpless against their assault. After their flames engulf him, we see him burning, but in an odd twist that emphasizes the parallels between the roaches and their creator, Parmiter, the offspring of the original breed drag him into the crevice left by a second earthquake. The fissure's bottom looks like the bowels of hell, with fire and brimstone deep below, and the earth explodes and covers them, closing off the opening.

This sudden ending turns horror into camp but demonstrates negative associations with both science and anthropomorphized insects found in most bug features. It also serves as a not-too-subtle moral attack on science and the cockroach monsters it could create. As Bill Gibron (2004) states, "Naturally, whenever you wander onto God's domain, things get out of hand and more people die. And it takes an unexplainable divine intervention (a second earthquake and a noble individual sacrifice) to end the debacle." Because the evolutionary transformation Parmiter attempts involves a cockroach pest, however, his violation of nature becomes even more monstrous.

As in *The Nest*, *Mimic* illustrates some of the negative repercussions of genetic engineering, even with good intentions. To eradicate a deadly disease spread by roaches, entomologist Dr. Susan Tyler (Mira Sorvino) creates the Judas Breed, a roach hybrid designed to kill the common American cockroaches carrying the virus. What fails in Tyler's design, however, is the genetic change meant to kill off this new strain. Although Tyler has constructed this new species without the ability to reproduce, they mutate over a three-year period and not only multiply but also grow to an enormous size allowing them to mimic their human prey in an explicit act of anthropomorphism.

Drawing on their mythology, however, the filmmaker constructs cockroaches as monsters early in the film when they are connected with the deaths of hundreds of children in New York City.[2] An opening shot of pinned cockroaches parallels photos of deceased children, also pinned like insects. Close-ups of the eyes and other body parts of departed children amplify this connection. We learn the death toll has reached one thousand, but the Centers for Disease Control has been unable to halt the epidemic of "Strickler's Disease" until Tyler creates the Judas Breed.

Despite their benefits to the city's young population, however, the Judas Breed's impact on the biotic community remains unclear. Three years after the breed's creation, the disease has been eradicated, but evidence that the new breed has become monstrous begins to appear. We see a man running from something and falling to his death from a painting scaffold while an autistic boy, Chuy (Alexander Goodwin), watches from his window and recites names of different kinds of shoes. He also provides the first indication that the predator is the Judas Breed when he makes the sound of an insect with his two spoons and exclaims, "Funny, funny shoes." When Tyler receives an intermediate-sized specimen, she begins to realize that her genetic experiment has failed. Instead of dying off, the Judas Breed has evolved, growing into a powerful predator. The Judas Breed has found a way to reproduce despite genetic engineering and has become a threat to the city instead of its savior.

Tyler's role as a "mad scientist" is complicated in *Mimic*, however, when she and her partner, Peter (Jeremy Northam), decide to "undo" the monstrous genetic mistake she has produced. Here help from Chuy's father (Giancarlo Giannini), Tyler, and a subway cop (Charles S. Dutton) brings tension to the conflict between human and nonhuman nature. After a long and suspenseful battle with the Judas Breed "Mimics" in the subway tunnels, an abandoned train station, and an antique train car, Tyler escapes with Chuy, and Peter destroys the Mimics' nest by lighting gas in the subway tunnels and escaping through a waterway beneath it. Tyler destroys the male Judas Breed by leading him to a train that crushes him, and Peter walks out of a tunnel, reuniting the family, with Chuy added to the bunch. Brute force, not genetic manipulation, seemingly destroys the Judas Breed.

Despite its initial traditionally negative construction of both scientists and the mutant bugs they create, the film concludes with a more sympathetic portrayal of entomology and a more nuanced critique of humanity's exploitation of the natural world. As Stacy Alaimo notes, humans also mimic the Judas Breed when they cover themselves with their odor for protection. According to Alaimo, "In this underground world where homeless live as 'moles,' and all people become prey to this man-like insect, the boundaries between humans and nature threaten to become imperceptible" (2001, 287). Both the Judas Breed and Tyler save the city, as well. The Judas Breed eradicates the carriers of Strickler's Disease. Tyler destroys the Judas Breed, so her seemingly "mad" science goes unpunished.

Although, as Janet Maslin (1997) states in her *New York Times* review, the film "exploits a dual fascination with morbidity and rogue science," this traditional horror film, drawn from installments such as *The Relic* and *Alien*, gains force under the direction of Guillermo del Toro, who infuses a stale plot with stylistic elements that emphasize the disastrous environmental consequences of such genetic alterations. As Roger Ebert suggests, for example, del Toro creates "tactical suspense" with Chuy's clicking spoons. Del Toro also constructs both the Judas Breed and its habitat with an eye toward Gothic horror and suspense.

The Judas Breed, too, moves beyond typical horror monsters, with help from both del Toro and production designer Carol Spier. According to Maslin (1997), "The bugs move with scary agility, and the sounds are highly evocative, even if histrionic music too often suggests that the Phantom of the Opera may be in the wings." Shots of the breed mimicking humans also transform a commonplace horror into a fresh Gothic film. Because the breed is a mutant insect (a mixture of termite and mantis), however, its monstrous qualities also draw on the cockroach's strengths and stereotypes. Ultimately the Judas Breed must be destroyed, and entomologist Tyler must correct the deadly mistake she made despite its initial benefits. With these qualities in mind, the film demonstrates well (with both narrative and aesthetic elements) that manipulation of the natural world may have dangerous repercussions.

Cronos and Humanity's Search for Immortality

Like *Mimic*, *Cronos* argues against manipulating nature and transforming insects. But it also draws on the more positive aspects of the cockroach mythology and anthropomorphism, stressing the roach's ability to survive as a way to explore humanity's urge to live forever. Told from the perspective of a revisionist vampire, Jesus Gris (Federico Luppi), and his not-so-innocent grand-daughter, Aurora (Tamara Shanath), the film normalizes this urge, as well, by highlighting its universality. Jesus unwittingly reactivates a cockroach-shaped gold device built by a sixteenth-century alchemist, Uberto Fulcanelli (Mario Iván Martínez), who craved eternal life. When the device reappears in Jesus's antique shop more than four hundred years later, it prompts the primary struggles of the film; Jesus must overcome inner conflicts between life and death, and between the human and monstrous forces driving his actions. He must also battle a dying corporate magnate, De la Guardia (Claudio Brook) and his American nephew, Angel (Ron Perlman), who will do anything to get the device. The resolutions of these conflicts, however, draw on the same ideology as other cockroach horror films: Because the Cronos device exploits the mythologized sense of permanence associated with the cockroach to transform a mortal human into an enduring insect-like vampire, the natural order has been defied and can only lead to failure, death, and devastation.

Cronos illustrates and explains the source of the device in an opening scene that introduces the first conflict of the film, that between life and death. The device is created in 1536 by an alchemist seeking eternal life who lives until 1937, when the device is rediscovered. Brad O'Brien reinforces this connection between life and death, suggesting that *Cronos* adapts both the Dracula and the Frankenstein myths. As O'Brien asserts, "Although Fulcanelli is a vampire, first he is a mad scientist playing God, a postmodern version of Prometheus, a late twentieth-century take on Frankenstein.... Del Toro has combined the myths of Dracula and Frankenstein in order to form his own creation myth" (2007, 173). For us, however, the film concentrates more fully on the drive for eternal life associated with both the insect that operates the device and the vampire Jesus becomes.

This exploration of immortality as both a blessing and a curse is presented in two contrasting settings that emphasize these and other dualities: the

Gris home and antique shop, and the De la Guardia industrial complex and residence. As Roger Ebert (1994) declares, "This is the stuff of classic horror films, and *Cronos* ... combines it with a colorful Latin magic realism." And Desson Howe (1994) of the *Washington Post* calls it "an enormously enjoyable gothic yarn from Mexico [that] transfuses the genre with wry grotesquerie, but retains respect for the old classic films." The light and color choices made by del Toro accentuate this respect for the classic horror film, while also drawing on elements of both the Gothic horror of literature and the alienation created by the modern industrial world.

The contrast between the color palates in these two settings amplifies the conflicts Jesus confronts. Although the sixteenth-century past of the alchemist is shot in sepias with smooth light that provides a neutral view of this world, the world of the Grises is warm and inviting despite, as del Toro explains in his notes, "a stylistic connection between the alchemist and Jesus" (1993, 16) attached to shots of the interior of the device. According to del Toro, in the Gris home and antique shop there should be "no cold tones" and "blues, grays, purples, etc." (16) should be avoided. The cinematography, del Toro explains, "should be filtering toward an almost golden light" (16). This use of warm colors connects both the home and the antique shop with life rather than death, and good rather than evil, complicating traditional views of the vampire once the device transforms Jesus, endowing him with youthful drives and eternal life. Del Toro accentuates this warmth with soft and fluffy textures, as well, from puffy pillows to the comfy towel Aurora offers Jesus when he returns home after Angel attempts to murder him.

Angel provides the catalyst for Jesus's transformation, as well as the multiple conflicts of the film, as he introduces both the Cronos device and the roaches that "operate" it inside an archangel statue with a missing eye. Shaped like a cockroach, the Cronos device is gold, evoking images of golden cockroaches, the fertility symbol of Mexican folklore. According to Marion W. Copeland, golden cockroaches in the Mexican tradition were associated with "the golden maize used in their ritual observance of the sun's power over the biotic community. They had revered the roaches as one of the chthonic powers" (2006, 157).

The film introduces the negative associations with cockroaches and eternal life when Angel learns of the archangel statue and seeks to retrieve it for his dying uncle and benefactor, De la Guardia. Angel also initiates the change from the warmth of the Gris home and antique shop to the cold lifelessness of the De La Guardia factory and residence, where his uncle lives in a germ-free environment lit like a horror setting, a change that draws on the chiaroscuro of Gothic film, according to del Toro's production notes.

Jesus's first encounter with the Cronos device begins to disrupt the warmth of his home and shop as it begins to transform him from human to immortal insect vampire. Although it looks like a windup toy, instead of a playful display, the device pierces Jesus's palm, leaving a pool of blood. Jesus seems to react with thirst to the sting, drinking nearly a pitcher of water directly out of the refrigerator. When he sees a plate of meat, he seems aroused. The meat seems to glow and turn even more blood red. This hunger grows so powerful that he uses the device again, exposing the cockroach mechanism that controls it. Aurora watches from the head of the stairs as the device begins to work, and Jesus recites the Lord's Prayer. We see the inner workings of the device as it penetrates him. Clock gears turn and fill a cockroach with fluid. When it finishes, the device disconnects, and the next morning he awakens feeling and looking younger, even shaving off his mustache. When he enters the kitchen, though, he lowers the blinds because the light bothers him, underpinning the repercussions associated with eternal life.

Jesus's renewed life force, however, seems to trigger a counterattack from De la Guardia. When a revived grandpa Jesus goes to his shop, the lock has been broken, and the shop is in shambles. A card has been left there with Angel's name on it and a note, "We are open all night." When Jesus enters the De la Guardia factory, he leaves the warmth of his antique shop and home behind. It is almost as dark and gray as De la Guardia's enormous room. Because he is dying, De la Guardia will do anything to get the device and prolong his life, even with his own cancerous body parts in jars around him, but now that he has tasted its results, Jesus will not relinquish it. Instead, he again applies the device, broaching cockroach mythology as he anthropomorphizes its contents: "Who are you, little one?" he asks. "A god?" not acknowledging his own transformation into the insect from which he draws eternal life.

At a New Year's party, however, the disastrous repercussions of Jesus's transformation become clear. Jesus and his wife, Mercedes (Margarita Isabel), act like young lovers until another guest gets a nosebleed and rushes to the restroom. Jesus follows and focuses intently on the man's blood, nearly licking it off the sink before another guest cleans it. More blood is on the floor, so Jesus kneels down and begins to lick it slowly. Insect noises seem to accompany his thirst, suggesting he is turning into a man-sized cockroach like the one inside the device. Angel disturbs his feeding when he knocks him unconscious. When Jesus awakens, he is at the wheel of a car, and Angel pushes it over a cliff. At the bottom, Jesus exclaims, "I don't want to die today" and thinks of Aurora, even after his body is carted off to a funeral home and he escapes before being cremated.

The final battle between warm and cold, good and evil, and the life-giving and treacherous qualities of the cockroach occurs because Jesus wants to escape the horror he has become. To better use the device to stop his pain, Jesus must find the alchemist's book in the De la Guardia factory. Aurora follows and finds the book, but the relevant pages are missing. De la Guardia has eaten them and declares that Jesus has been reborn. To illustrate this rebirth, De la Guardia peels off Jesus's old, useless skin, revealing the new white skin beneath it. Jesus needs human blood, De la Guardia explains, and now can survive like any bloodsucking insect. When Jesus gives De la Guardia the Cronos device to be free of the curse it contains, De la Guardia attacks him with the sharp end of his cane. "You don't even bleed right," he says, but before he can pierce Jesus's heart, Aurora smashes his head, killing him.

The battle between the two opposing forces connected with the device and its insect center are resolved when Jesus defeats Angel during the fight's climax. To save himself and his family, Jesus falls with Angel off the factory's neon sign, suggesting a merging of the warmth of the neon and the cold of the factory. Angel is dead, but Aurora revives Jesus with the device. When Aurora seems ready to sacrifice herself for him, giving him her blood with one word, "Grandpa," Jesus draws on the humane qualities deep within him and smashes the device, freeing himself and his family from his curse. The last shot of the film shows him in his new skin, lying in bed with Aurora beside him. Mercedes enters the room, and they share

a loving family moment before his death. In these last scenes, immortality
and the cockroach device that produces it are constructed as immoral and,
as Del Guardia presents it, evil, even though Jesus becomes a literal Christ
figure with his ultimate sacrifice for the common good because he has also
merged with the cockroach from which he draws his longevity. As Roger
Ebert (1994) suggests, "There is always something shameful . . . about being
unwilling to die when your time has come." *Cronos* adds a religious edge
to this moral claim, demonstrating perhaps that an Earthly immortality is
a "greater punishment" than death, since our role in this world is "to prepare for the next." Because this immortality is associated explicitly with the
cockroach—both the golden cockroach exterior of the device and its inner
insect workings—it too must be destroyed.

Ultimately, however, *Cronos* and the other cockroach horror films discussed
here also make a larger statement about humanity's exploitation of the natural
world. In these films such exploitation turns insects into monsters, creating
a monstrous nature that must be eradicated. Although the level of anthropomorphizing in these films coincides, to a certain extent, with the quality
of treatment the insects receive, whether the film in question highlights the
positive or negative qualities of cockroaches seems to have no impact on
this lethal conclusion. Unlike insect horror films highlighting less repulsive
bugs like butterflies and moths, cockroach horror films anthropomorphize
roaches to reveal their monstrous human qualities. As noted earlier, Per Persson, Jarmo Laaksolahti, and Peter Lonnquist define anthropomorphism in
relation to different phenomena and schools of thought outlined in these
categories: primitive psychology, folk psychology, traits, social roles, and
emotional anthropomorphism.

Although aligned with these levels, the anthropomorphism included
in the cockroach films explored here does not, as Mertins suggests, lead to
positive representations. Although *Damnation Alley*, *The Nest*, and *Mimic*
blame humanity for transforming the lowly cockroach into a flesh-eating
monster, none of these films suggest that humanity should be destroyed, no
matter how adroitly the insects are anthropomorphized. *Damnation Alley*
includes little or no anthropomorphizing, but both *The Nest* and *Mimic*
anthropomorphize on several levels: primitive psychology, folk psychology,
traits, and social roles. In *Mimic* the Judas Breed's protective stance toward its

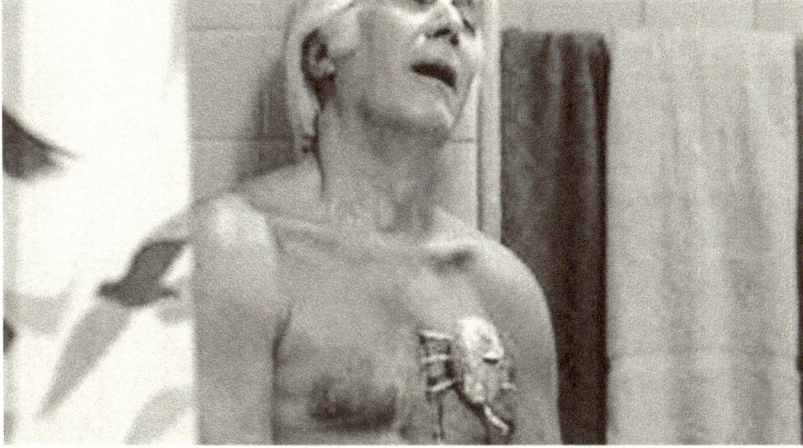

Cronos: Jesus activates the "golden cockroach" device.

offspring might also indicate a social level of anthropomorphism. Despite this anthropomorphizing, all these films illustrate the monstrous qualities of these cockroaches so that their destruction becomes not only feasible but also desirable.

Bug and *Cronos* take a more individual approach to cockroach monsters, illustrating, perhaps, what happens when humanity embraces the cockroach and its strengths so vehemently that both cockroach and human are transformed. The levels of anthropomorphizing are amplified in both these films because of the integral connection between the roaches and their human counterparts. One might argue that Jesus, for example, becomes a humanized version of the cockroach. In *Bug*, on the other hand, the roaches gain such a high degree of human intelligence that they not only become literate but also responsibly rid the world of its dangerous mad scientist.

In spite of this anthropomorphizing, in these films both the human "scientist" or "victim" and the cockroach must be annihilated to eliminate their "evil" influence, a destruction that signifies, perhaps, a desire to eliminate the most monstrous elements of human and nonhuman nature. When monstrous nature becomes anthropomorphized, it may become too human, making it too easy to see us in them.

37

2

Human Ecology and
the Horror Film

The Pack: Charlotte's blood feeds the vampire "miners."

3

The Earth Bites Back

Vampires and the Ecological Roots of Home

Hurricane Sandy and its aftermath highlight the negative effects that environmental exploitation can have on humanity. As the deadliest hurricane of 2012 and the second most costly storm in U.S. history, Sandy killed over one hundred people (*New York Times* 2012) and left thousands of residents homeless in New York, New Jersey, and New England. It was also at least "enhanced by global warming influences" (Trenberth 2012), according to climatologists. This connection between human-caused climate change and the devastating hurricane that ravaged the East Coast highlights the irrevocable connection between humanity and the natural world that moves beyond anthropomorphism. An August 2013 *National Geographic* article "Sugar Love" demonstrates how our exploitation of the natural world may come back to bite us in unexpected but direct ways. An addiction to sugar spread by Western imperialism destroyed natural environments and enslaved indigenous populations from Hispaniola to Barbados, where, "you can see the legacies of sugar: the ruined mills, their wooden blades turning in the wind, marking time" (R. Cohen 2013, 87). According to the article, however, that destruction of environments and their people led to a sugar diet that destroys consumers. As Dr. Richard Johnson explains, "It seems every time I study an illness and trace a path to the first cause, I find my way back to sugar" (R. Cohen 2013, 87). This same connection is explored in films from mountaintop-removal-mining documentaries such as *The Last Mountain* (2012) to postapocalyptic science fiction films like *Tank Girl* (1995) but reaches terrifying levels in the horror genre.

This direct relationship between environmental exploitation and a destructive nature comes to the fore in the vampire film, when the living dead literally arise from the grave. For us, in at least a few horror films, human desecration of the Earth may create the very monsters that drink their blood. The French black comic–horror movie *The Pack* (2010) and the British/Romanian satirical vampire film *Strigoi* (2009) explicitly illustrate what might happen when an environment "bites back." Vampires have typically been associated with sexuality, power, evil and the Antichrist, the fluid boundaries between humanity and the monstrous, and intimacy as conquest. In these two comic-horror films, however, vampirism most readily compares with consumption, a greed for resources, land, and blood that separates humans from the natural world that provides their home. This separation from Earth's ecology and the home it represents has monstrous repercussions in *The Pack* and *Strigoi*, transforming the eco-trauma associated with a lost connection with nature and a shattered human ecology into horror. Drawing on the work of early twentieth-century human ecologist Ellen Swallow Richards and environmental psychologist Tina Amorok, we argue that these films amplify the real trauma humans experience when their earthly home is destroyed, illustrating the sometimes horrific effects environmental degradation may have on humanity. In *The Pack* and *Strigoi*, however, a damaged Earth fights back, turning humans into vampires and ghouls, literal monsters that concretize monstrous treatment of the natural world and magnify the actual consequences of environmental exploitation.

At least since the 1897 publication of Bram Stoker's *Dracula*, the need to sleep in native soil has been an integral part of the vampire myth. For example, one of the novel's narrators, real estate representative Jonathan

Harker, remarks on the "earth placed in wooden boxes" (54) and that on "a pile of newly dug earth lay the Count!" (Stoker [1897] 2000, 54), as he explores Dracula's castle. Later we learn that the count has transported "fifty cases of common earth" (244) to his new home in England and that it is best to attack Dracula at certain times when he has "limited freedom" (258). As the journal entry asserts, "whereas he can do as he will within his limit, when he have his earth-home, his coffin-home, the place unhallowed, as we saw when he went to the grave of the suicide at Whitby, still at other times he can only change when the time has come" (258). These comments in the novel emphasize the importance of home and earth in the Dracula narrative.

This connection between vampires and their native soil continues in films from adaptations of the novel such as *Nosferatu* (1922), *Dracula* (1933), *The Vampire Returns* (1944), *The Horror of Dracula* (1958), *Dracula Has Risen from the Grave* (1967), and *Bram Stoker's Dracula* (1992), to genre stretches such as the popular *Van Helsing* (2004, 2012) and *Underworld* (2003, 2006, 2009, 2012) films, the coming-of-age tale *Let the Right One In* (2007), or the comedy *Vamps* (2012). As in the Dracula novel, these vampire films underline the connection between soil and home and consequently emphasize their link to ecology, literally the study of homes. Although some popular media representations of vampires eschew traditional vampire mythology altogether, many do include some version of native soil, even, as in novelist Chelsea Quinn Yarbro's *Saint Germain Chronicles* (1983) series, placing it in a hidden compartment within the heels of vampires' shoes.

Early in the novel *Dracula*, however, Count Dracula broaches another connection with native soil that moves beyond his need to become reinvigorated in his nation's earth. When describing some of the "strange things of the preceding night" on the journey to his castle, Dracula connects soil with blood, declaring to Harker, "There is hardly a foot of soil in all this region that has not been enriched by the blood of men, patriots or invaders" (Stoker [1897] 2000, 25). This direct relationship between blood, soil, and vampires is overlooked in most representations of vampires in popular culture, despite its origin in Stoker's novel.

The Pack and *Strigoi* examine this interconnected relationship between blood, soil, and vampirism, highlighting the environmental underpinnings of the vampire myth in relation to a shattered ecology or home.

This connection between ecology and home illuminates the truly inter-dependent relationship between human and nonhuman nature illustrated by both *The Pack* and *Strigoi*. The roots of that connection rest with the human ecology movement, which grew out of the work of human ecologist Ellen Swallow Richards. Destroying that human ecology may lead to what clinical psychologist Tina Amorok calls an "eco-trauma of Being" (2007, 29). In both *The Pack* and *Strigoi*, vampires rather than eco-trauma are the product of this devastated home, a soil desecrated by the blood of war or exploitation of human and nonhuman nature. In *The Pack* and *Strigoi*, a mistreated Earth bites back.

Reading the Vampire

The vampire has served as one of the most prevalent monsters of focus since the inception of the horror film genre: in silent versions of the Dracula novel and the successful stage play based on the novel in the 1920s, Universal's great success in 1931 with Bela Lugosi in the lead, and Hammer Studio's 1950s revisions of the count's narrative. Some subgenres of vampire films have explored sexuality, while others have merged with other genres, including comedy, science fiction, and the blaxploitation film. *Love at First Bite* (1979) and *Dracula: Dead and Loving It* (1995) highlight the comic turn in the genre. *Rabid* (1976) and *Red-Blooded American Girl* (1990) illustrate the merge with science fiction, and *Blacula* (1972), *Scream Blacula Scream* (1973), and *Ganja and Hess* (1973) serve as blaxploitation representatives, for example.

Research on the horror genre reflects the popularity of the vampire film and its multiple manifestations. Book-length explorations of the horror genre typically include references to the vampire film. The pioneering work of Noel Carroll examines representations of Dracula and other vampires in *The Philosophy of Horror* (1990). Studies of pre–World War II horror films such as Reynold Humphries's *The Hollywood Horror Film, 1931–1941: Madness in a Social Landscape* (2006) again discusses Dracula and the Dracula films in detail, as well as exploring the vampire myth. Melvin E. Matthews Jr.'s *Fear Itself: Horror on Screen and in Reality during the Depression and World War II* (2009) suggests that the horror cycle began with *Dracula* and *Frankenstein* (1931). Dracula is also included as one of the monsters George Ochoa examines in his *Deformed and Destructive Beings* (2011).

Vampires are also examined in relation to their subgenres. Carol J. Clover's *Men, Women, and Chainsaws: Gender in the Modern Horror Film* (1992) explores Kathryn Bigelow's *Near Dark* (1987) from a gendered perspective. Bruce G. Hallenbeck (2009) examines comic vampire films such as *Blood for Dracula* (1974) and *Love at First Bite*. *Monstrous Adaptations*, an anthology focused on film adaptations of literary work also includes a study of the vampire myth in Brad O'Brien's essay, "Fulcanelli as a Vampiric Frankenstein and Jesus as His Vampiric Monster: The Frankenstein and Dracula myths in Guillermo del Toro's *Cronos*." And an examination of the horror film as a cultural experience, Ian Conrich's edited anthology, *Horror Zone* (2010), includes explorations of Dracula and Van Helsing in multiple media. Yet none of these explorations addresses environmental concerns associated with the vampire.

The resurgence of the vampire in film, television, comic books, and other media has also encouraged a plethora of scholarly studies of their media representations. Research exploring the *Buffy the Vampire Slayer* film and TV series, the *Twilight* films, and the *True Blood* HBO series provides a glimpse of the diverse lenses through which vampire identity is examined. *Buffy the Vampire Slayer* resulted in a new area of research, "Buffy Studies," which has prompted multiple volumes and conferences, including Lorna Jowett's 2005 book, *Sex and The Slayer: A Gender Studies Primer for the Buffy Fan* and an annual International Slayage Conference. The focus of research here, however, excludes ecocritical readings of the series, highlighting instead gender issues, aesthetics, family structure, and media and popular culture.

This exclusion of ecological readings continues in recent work addressing the *Twilight* series. Maggie Parke and Natalie Wilson's edited volume, *Theorizing "Twilight": Critical Essays on What's at Stake in a Post-Vampire World* (2011), for example, highlights the film adaptations as pop-cultural artifact; explores the film adaptation series as fairy tale, romance, and coming-of-age narrative; and underscores the film series as texts open to readings from multiple critical perspectives, including patriarchy, white privilege, heteronormativity, rape culture, and religion. None of the chapters includes ecocritical readings of the films, despite their environmental leanings. Melissa A. Click's edited volume, *Bitten by "Twilight": Youth Culture, Media and the Vampire Franchise*, "gives crucial attention to the cultural, social, and economic aspects of the

Twilight phenomenon. Building upon the work of feminist cultural scholars who examine girls' and women's relationships to the media, [the contributors'] overall goal in this collection is to examine Twilight's themes, appeal, and cultural impact" (2010, 8). Again the volume highlights theology, romantic love, gender and sexuality, race, and heteronormativity without a nod toward environmental issues broached by the novels and films.

True Blood studies also avoid exploring environmental issues. In "Lesbian Desires in the Vampire Subgenre: *True Blood* as a Platform for a Lesbian Discourse" (2012) for example, Eve Dufour argues that *True Blood* addresses human fears of "the Other" and reveals the complexity of human sexualities and sexual desires. Maria Lindgren Leavenworth's "'What Are You?' Fear, Desire, and Disgust in the Southern Vampire Mysteries and *True Blood*" (2012) suggests that the sympathetic vampires in contemporary narratives "are modeled on the early 19th-century Romantic instantiations created by John Polidori and Lord Byron." In Brigid Cherry's edited volume, *"True Blood": Investigating Vampires and Southern Gothic* (2013), Cherry explores *True Blood* as cult television. Part 1 of the volume centers on genre and style in the series, examining, for example, the southern Gothic milieu in the series (see essays by Caroline Ruddell and Brigid Cherry). Part 2 focuses on myths and meanings in the series, discussing the series as fairytale (Mikel J. Koven), a reworking of the Christ myth (Gregory Erickson), and a minoritarian Romantic fable (Dennis Rothermel). Part 3 explores character and identity in the series, and part 4 highlights marketing and fandom associated with the series. None of this research, however, broaches environmental issues attached to vampires, the vampire genre, or the series in particular.

Environmental Themes in Vampire Films

Although not often noted, both the *Twilight* films and the *True Blood* series are ripe for ecocritical readings. Most obviously in *Twilight*, the Cullen vampire family shuns human blood, claiming they are vegetarians because they drink only nonhuman blood. In *True Blood* vampires are able to coexist with humans, at least initially, because a synthetic blood source has been developed. The cause of vampirism in these films is also sometimes tied to the natural world as a plague or virus. An early version of this virus as origin of vampirism theme can be found in *The Last Man on Earth* (1964), the first of at least three adaptations of Richard Matheson's *I Am Legend* (1954), which also include *The Omega Man* (1971) and *I Am Legend* (2007). The three *Blade* films (1998, 2002, 2004) also play on this theme, as does the more recent *Daybreakers* (2009) and *Stake Land* (2010).

Other vampire films highlight the power of the blood transfusion either as a cause of vampirism or its solution. In Chan Wook-Park's *Thirst* (2009), for example, Sang-hyun (Kang-ho Song), a priest working for a hospital, selflessly volunteers for a secret vaccine development project intended to eradicate a deadly virus. However, the virus eventually takes over the priest. He nearly dies but makes a miraculous recovery by an accidental transfusion of vampire blood. *Dark Shadows* (2012) uses this transfusion of vampire blood to comic effect. In Kathryn Bigelow's *Near Dark* (1987), on the other hand, a transfusion restores a young vampire to humanity.

The Pack: When Earth Fights Back

Unlike most vampire films with environmental leanings, the comic-horror *The Pack* explicitly connects vampirism and its desire for blood with humanity's exploitation of the natural world. *The Pack* highlights the sometimes horrific and blood-sucking consequences of mistreating the Earth in relation to exploitative mining techniques, which destroy both the land and its human laborers. The film begins as a road movie with illusory romantic possibilities between a lone driver, Charlotte (Emilie Dequenne), and a hitchhiker, Max (Benjamin Biolay). Both genre and mood change when a drive ends at a café owned by Max's mother, La Spack (Yolande Moreau), who hides a deadly secret that connects human and nonhuman nature. In *The Pack* vampire miners and the slagheap that transformed them seek revenge.

Set around an abandoned postindustrial mine similar to the Lorraine mines of filmmaker Franck Richard's childhood, *The Pack* connects vampirism to a ravaged Earth and a desecrated home. In *The Pack* vampire-like ghouls are not only produced from a mine's slagheap but also become an integral part of its byproducts, illustrating the need for interconnection between human and nonhuman ecologies. They arise only when they and the Earth they inhabit are fed human blood. Unlike *Strigoi*, however, *The Pack*'s attempts at comedy conflict with any serious message the film may be making about mining, miners, and the environment they exploited.

The Pack fuses dark humor with multiple genres in its sometimes ineffective attempts to highlight that message. The opening scenes of *The Pack* provide little evidence of the grim ecological and human disaster revealed by the film. Instead the film's introductory "road movie" scenes focus on lone driver Charlotte, who plans to go as far as her many CDs of music will allow. The film enters a simulated Wild West, however, when ridiculous outlaws riding motorcycles instead of horses chase Charlotte down a wind turbine–lined lane.

The conventions of the comic road movie and the Western turn monstrous when Charlotte picks up the hitchhiking Max to discourage the bikers. Music and setting changes reinforce this break with the introduction of Max, who is played by Benjamin Biolay and recognizable by most French and Belgian viewers as a singer and songwriter of songs such as "Bloodbath." This song ties him to the horror genre and foreshadows *The Pack*'s blood-drinking ghouls, especially with the song's line, "He tells me, 'You're a vampire.'"

Horror conventions are cemented when they reach La Spack, the dilapidated café at the end of a dark country lane, where any efforts to infuse the narrative with comedy end. The tone grows even more foreboding when Max disappears into the café restroom and does not return. When Charlotte tries to find him behind a hidden door, La Spack assaults and captures her, locking her into one of the animal cages in the middle of a back room. In a makeshift torture chamber that takes Edgar Allen Poe to extremes, Charlotte and another prisoner, Tofu (Ian Fonteyn), are even force-fed their own blood to prepare them for their sacrifice to the vampires on the slagheap.

Connections between humanity and the Earth are made explicit when this nightmare turns into eco-horror. At nightfall the reason for Charlotte and Tofu's blood diet is revealed: they have been prepared to feed monsters rising from the earth. Now helplessly weak, Charlotte and Tofu are flung into a coal car and pushed toward a slagheap, where they are chained by their ankles. Cuts in their calves drip blood into the earth, luring vampire ghouls dressed in mining clothes out of the soil. Eyeless, fanged, and carrying mining tools, they seem to gasp for air but drink the dripping blood frantically, licking Charlotte's leg and ripping off Tofu's arm to drain his arteries. These monsters survive only in an earth fertilized with human blood.

The source of these horrific monsters clearly connects human and nonhuman ecologies, however, moving the narrative beyond the extreme gore of the slagheap. As Max explains to Charlotte the next morning, "[My mother] hasn't always been like this. But when my brothers died, she went mad. The authorities would rather see them die in the mine than risk a firedamp explosion. . . . The village elders talked about a creature born of mud and the blood of the dead, miners who died underground. That always made us laugh. . . . I think they dug too deep." Max continues talking as the scene changes to an external shot of power lines crossing a large field lined with winter trees, illustrating his claim: "My mother says the earth wants blood. And we can't refuse it." Charlotte's discovery of a photo album of the La Spack family miners killed in a mining accident reinforces La Spack's claim. On a page adjacent to photos of La Spack's now-dead sons, a newspaper clipping declares, "We raped the earth. It's sending us monsters."

The horror reaches a climax at the slagheap during a battle between La Spack and a gang that includes Charlotte, Max, and the motorcycle club that followed Charlotte to the café. After a gruesome fight that leaves La Spack dead, her blood draining into the slagheap, the ghouls return, slaughtering everyone but Charlotte, who escapes the now-burning house through a window, exclaiming, "So the earth wants blood. I'll give it some" as she shoots. When she reaches a field, however, the vampire ghouls rise up from the mist and follow her, feeding on her until the moon fades into morning.

The horror of this scene suggests a tragic end for Charlotte and Max and a resolution in favor of monstrous nature. Instead, Charlotte seems to survive, appropriating the now now-dead La Spack's role, with Max resuming his own function as a handsome hitchhiker luring drivers in to feed the vampire ghouls they now protect. Quickly, however, the film switches from this dream sequence to a shot of Charlotte hanging on chains over the slagheap, where a vampire ghoul drinks her blood. The wind rocks the chain, and Charlotte's blood drips into the soil. The sun comes up, and blood seems to cover the light with a hiss and red clouds. Bluegrass music ends the film, with the line "I'm down in that old coal mine," lightening the frightening mood with perhaps ineffective humor.

This ending effectively illustrates the conflict between genre mixing and environmental message in the film. The appearance of the monstrous vampire rising from the slagheap reinforces the negative consequences associated with exploiting both human and nonhuman ecologies. But the film's genre transformation from dreamlike resolution in the café to comic horror above the deserted coal mine dilutes this message, turning eco-horror into "an amusing hodgepodge" that is, as Jordan Mintzer (2010) of *Variety* states, "too uproariously modeled on every late-night classic under the sun to feel fresh or dramatically apt." The movie may, as Mintzer asserts, soon "be unshouldered to rest alongside its home-video ancestry."

Despite its weak ending and lack of originality, *The Pack* highlights the terrible consequences of eco-disasters associated with mining. The slagheap broaches not only the filmmaker's childhood memories but also the real horrors of the mining industry and its exploitation of resources and labor. In Franck Richard's own region of Lorraine, industrial medicine studies found an increased mortality rate from lung and stomach cancer in Lorraine iron miners (N. Chau et al. 1993, 1017). Coal mining in the region also had disastrous repercussions. According to a February 26, 1985, *Los Angeles Times* article, "an explosion [in February 1985] in a coal mine in France's eastern region of Lorraine killed 22 miners and injured about 100." The article explains, "The blast, 3,450 feet underground in the Forbach mine near the West German border, was thought to have been caused by fire damp, a gas given off by coal and constituted largely of methane. When it explodes, it immediately ignites coal dust nearby." *The Pack* turns these real instances of monstrous nature into biting horror.

Strigoi and the Blood of War

Like *The Pack*, *Strigoi* also connects vampirism and its desire for blood with humanity's mistreatment of the natural world, but this time war and its violent repercussions initiate a monstrous response. In *Strigoi* a young medical school dropout, Vlad (Catalin Paraschiv), returns to Romania from Italy and, after discovering town drunk Florin's mysterious death, investigates secret post-Communism land deals, forgery, and corruption. This conspiracy of silence has led to the presence of strigoi. According to *The Vampire Book*, the strigoi of the film is closely related to the Romanian word *striga* (a witch), which in turn was derived from the Latin *strix*, the word for screech owl that was extended to refer to "a demon that attacked children at night" (Gordon 1999, 586) and drank their blood. In *Strigoi* vampirism has its origin in blood, but it is the blood of war over land rather than romantic or sexual desire that transforms some citizens into strigoi mort, or dead vampires.

Although Dracula typically survives only in his native soil, *Strigoi* amplifies this connection between the earth and humanity, demonstrating powerfully the ecological roots of home. As Andrew Dowler (2009) of *Now* magazine suggests, "This is a serious and seriously black comedy about land, heritage in the blood and the rape of the country and people from the Nazis onward." With a comic tone that comes close to satire, *Strigoi* draws parallels between literal vampirism and struggles for land, struggles that comment on the greed of dictators such as Romania's Nicolae Ceaușescu that destroys both human and nonhuman nature.

Strigoi both sets its comic tone and establishes its critique of such greed from its opening title card humorously declaring the film's setting: "Podoleoi Village, Romania—last Wednesday." As punishment for crimes against the village, local leaders murder the owners of a large estate, Constantin Tirescu (Constantin Barbelesku) and his wife, Ileana (Roxana Gutman), thinly disguised representatives of the Ceaușescu family. An unofficial trial led by the village leaders, including their priest, Tudor (Dan Popa), and mayor, Stefan (Zane Jarcu), sentences the Tirecu's to death for the murder of Florin for his land, but an executioner's misfiring gun shifts this violence to comedy. Constantin exclaims, "You're acting like animals . . . like peasants. I can still buy you though. You've never had trouble taking my money," reinforcing the joke. The scene also initiates the connection between the earth, their disrupted home, and vampirism when the blood of a violent death meets the village soil. Blood remains after the Tirescus are buried, as if it has drained into the soil, ultimately transforming them into the strigoi of the film's title.

The Tirescus' change into strigoi mort also connects to an earth flowing with blood. The scene reinforces this connection by paralleling the end of the 1989 Romanian revolution, a conflict between rich and poor that culminated with the overthrow and execution of long-term dictator Nicolae Ceaușescu and his wife, Ileana. As director Faye Jackson explains, "The initial concept of the film was inspired by the Romanian revolution of 1989 and the [overthrow and execution of Nicolae Ceaușescu]. The idea in *Strigoi* was that this village would kill their leader because he was corrupt, but by doing so, they become complicit in his corruption" (quoted in Savlov 2009). The greed associated with this era connects explicitly with the strigoi of the film, vampires driven by an insatiable hunger.

As if to illustrate this transfer of greed, the villagers celebrate the symbolic overthrow of power in the Tirescu manor house. Instead of the violent deaths forced on Florin and, in retaliation, the Tirescus, these villagers hope for an end for themselves that ensures their rise "to the spirit of the sky," echoing the song accompanying their plundering of the Tirescus' consumer goods, an end that will leave the earth unbruised and their homes reclaimed. The looting of the Tirescu manor also corresponds with vampirism in the film, as well as the multiple repercussions of greed it represents. Multiple metaphorical images illustrate this greed, including the feast that Vlad's neighbor Mara Tomsa (Camelia Maxim) prepares for him. This gluttony is intensified by Vlad's explanation for his decision to quit work at an Italian fast-food restaurant called The Chicken Hut: "All I did was fry chicken," he tells her, as she piles food in front of him.

Vlad's uncertainties about Florin's death expose the villagers' beliefs about vampirism, as well as connecting that vampirism with corruption and desire for land and home. When they toast Florin during the three days they guard his body, however, the villagers on watch introduce the real horrors he survived: the Nazis, the Russians, and finally the Communists. Vlad may believe Constantin has bribed them to ensure Florin does not awaken as a strigoi, but as Matt McAllister's *Sci-Fi Bulletin* DVD review (2011) explains, the film's exploration of "how life in post-Ceausescu Romania hasn't entirely escaped the bureaucracy and corruption that blighted the former regime" expands genre expectations. As Dennis Harvey (2010) of *Variety* asserts, the film "is a witty and unpredictable upending of genre tropes." Despite the comic tone maintained throughout *Strigoi*, the film's references to Ceaușescu and the multiple wars and class conflicts Romanians endured raises a new approach to vampirism that moves beyond conventional Dracula-based narratives.

The blood of war is manifested in several ways in the film. Most obviously, the violent murders of the Tirescus transforms them into strigoi, a transformation that further connects them with Ceaușescu. The villagers watching Florin's body offer a different perspective on stolen land and home when Vlad asks them about the deed to Florin's land, reasserting the battle between rich and poor on which the 1989 Revolution was built. One of the villagers explains, "One day you were working on your own farm. Then you were working on it, but it wasn't yours any more. After the revolution, everyone was supposed to get their land back, but they didn't have the papers."

Most importantly, the connection between blood, earth, and home demonstrates how violent treatment of both a land and its people breeds vampirism. In this post-Communist village, community members must fight to keep their homes, even hiding the deeds to their property to counter corrupt government officials and avaricious capitalists like the Tirescus, a point made concrete by Florin's murder. Octav (Vlad Jipa), the town cop, connects that evidence with earth more explicitly: "I can't make a case with dirt under fingernails. Everyone has dirt under their nails, and it's all the same dirt." The fights over land produce strigoi in a variety of ways, the film suggests. As Mara explains, "Some people are born strigoi, and some become strigoi after death. We created [the Tirescu strigoi]. We knew they murdered Florin. We gave them a violent death."

This fight over property even extends to blood relatives, including Vlad's relationship with his grandfather Nicolae (Rudy Rosefeld). Nicolae shows Vlad the papers he has hidden, saying, "It's my land. Mine!" Ultimately Vlad discovers that Constantin and Tudor, the priest, have been working together to acquire deeds to the villagers' property. Constantin wants the land for money and power. Tudor wants a new tower for his church. They both demonstrate greed and gluttony like that of the strigoi mort, vampires born out of the bloodied earth around them.

The desecrated home has also transformed Vlad's grandfather into a strigoi, as Vlad discovers when he awakens from a nightmare to find his grandfather drinking his blood. "It's my blood. I gave it to you," Nicolae explains ominously. His grandfather's struggles through multiple wars and across war-torn lands have transformed him into a vampire:

> I went to Russia, to Stalingrad. I had to fight for the Germans. When the Russians won, I had to walk all the way home. Then the Russians occupied Romania. They were even worse than the Germans. And there was a terrible famine. I lost my son. . . . Then the Communists took my land. I still had to work on it. I still had to work on the same land with the same horses, but it wasn't mine anymore. I was born on this land. My father was born here. My children were born here. I died here.

He is a living strigoi.

The battle for Florin's deed serves as the climax of the film as it connects the mythical strigoi with its earthly manifestations: the Tirescus, Stefan, and the village priest. As Vlad explains to Constantin, "Strigoi hate the living. You were always strigoi." In *Strigoi* the battle for land and home turns violent, with the blood of what Constantin calls "peasants" transforming villagers into vengeful living strigoi who fight back, reclaiming their land and their heritage from dead strigoi like the Tirescus. Ultimately, Vlad and his grandfather reclaim the villagers' right to their land from those in power in the village—Constantin, Stefan, and the priest. Once Vlad realizes his own connection with the village and its violent legacy, the celebration that opened the film can resume. Vlad may claim he knows nothing about strigoi, but Mara, his grandfather, and the other villagers do, because they have suffered the violence to both human and nonhuman nature caused by greed for land. With at least a temporary end to this desire, they dance, rejoicing even more with the added knowledge that Vlad is now one of them. To illustrate his own transformation, Vlad returns to Constantin's grave and digs up his body, seemingly prepared to cut out his heart to finally restore their land and reconnect them with the earth, an ecology they can now truly call home. *Strigoi* offers a different take on the vampire, offering a horrific version of humanity's response to a war-ravaged land. In *Strigoi* vampires' greed for blood is both literal and figurative.

The drive to reconnect with the earth as home highlights the interdependent relationship between human and nonhuman nature illustrated by both *The Pack* and *Strigoi*, a relationship that in the horror setting may produce monsters instead of monstrous eco-trauma. This connection brings us back to Ellen Swallow Richards, who viewed humans as part of nature and considered urban problems like air and water pollution as products of human activity imposed on the environment and, subsequently, best resolved by humans. The human ecology movement eventually evolved into home economics, but its grounding in conservation had lasting effects, including environmental justice movements, health ecology, and urban renewal, according to C. R. Palamar. As Palamar explains, "Richards . . . saw the degradation of the urban environment as a distinct threat to human life" (2008, 84).

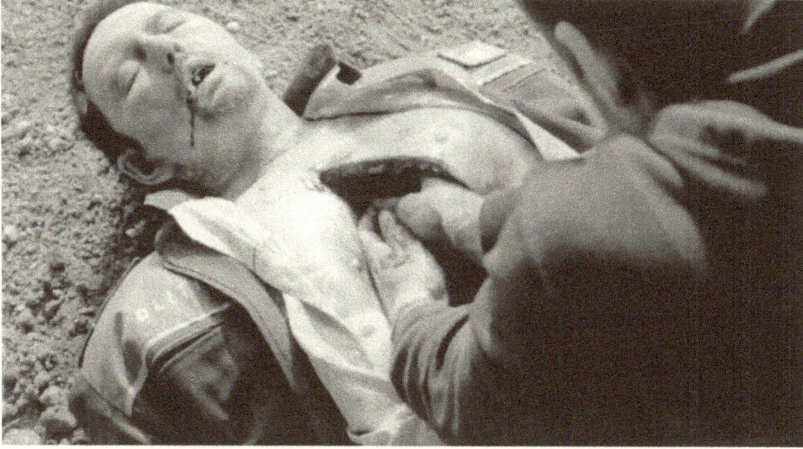

Strigoi: Vlad uses his medical training against strigoi.

According to clinical psychologist Tina Amorok, this threat is both physical and psychological and amounts to an "eco-trauma of Being" (2007, 29), which includes urban, rural, and wilderness ecologies. "When humans are forcibly torn from their family, culture, and land, a violent disruption to and deficit in the realm of Being—individually, collectively, ecologically, and spiritually—are created" (30). Amorok suggests that we must "connect to the pain of the world" (37) to regain a sense of well-being. For Amorok and eco-psychologists such as Eduardo Duran, eco-trauma "is in a state of constant retraumatization with the continual devastation of the land" (30). Amorok also asserts that eco-trauma originated in "harmful effects" of "aberrant human violence" (30), a violence that continues in our methods of protecting ourselves from despair caused by our separation from the environment.

The most powerful of these protections is war, a force that not only destroys human and nonhuman nature but also disrupts our connection with the natural environment. As geographer A. M. Mannion asserts, "War and terrorism have a considerable environmental impact by altering urban and rural landscapes to leave a variety of legacies which bear witness to past and recent conflicts" (2003, 2). The Zaatari refugee camp, about ten miles across the border from Syria in northern Jordan, illustrates the ongoing environmental and humanitarian consequences of war. With a population of more than 120,000 people as of September 2013, the camp "is now the second largest refugee camp in the world—and that has put a strain on nearby communities in Jordan, where water is often scarce," according to a September 7, 2013, PBS *Newshour* report from Kristen Gillespie. In another report *IRIN* explains, "Supplying adequate drinking water, toilets and washrooms to this huge and rapidly growing camp for Syrian refugees in the Jordanian desert . . . is proving to be a challenge" ("Vandalism Hampers Sanitation" 2013). These conditions broach some of the questions that feminist film critic Barbara Creed asks regarding the cinema of eco-trauma: "Are we either too aggressive or too fearful to share the planet and its resources? Another more disturbing possibility is that humankind is drawn not to life, but to the dark side of its evolutionary history—to warfare, decay, death, and extinction" (Narine 2015, 26). *The Pack* and *Strigoi* draw on this possibility.

The both literal and figurative war-torn landscapes in *The Pack* and *Strigoi* bear witness to a variety of environmental conflicts, providing a space in which to explore eco-trauma and human ecology through metaphors of vampirism. Although these views of such landscapes to a certain extent draw on the ideals of European Romanticism, by fusing these ideals with vampire horror we hope to have at least begun to turn them on their head. Instead of admiring the natural world from afar or demonizing it in order to exploit it, *The Pack* and *Strigoi* at least implicitly illustrate an ecology (a home) that includes humans as part of the monstrous nature they create.

Although *The Pack* may vilify a landscape that transforms miners into monsters, it blames humans, not the earth, for the change, reinforcing the interdependent relationship we share with the environment. Attempts to separate from nature are futile in *The Pack*. *Strigoi* challenges Romantic notions even more, exploring the idea of ecology or home through Vlad's return to his native land, which reconnects him to both the village and the natural environment. In *Strigoi* mort and living strigoi provide a corporeal connection between human and nonhuman nature. But the earth of the comic horror film may bridge the separation from nature caused by humans in gruesome ways. In both *The Pack* and *Strigoi*, an ecology abused by the blood of war or greed for mining resources turns monstrous.

4

Through an Eco-lens of Childhood

Roberto Rossellini's *Germany Year Zero* and
Guillermo del Toro's *The Devil's Backbone*

The horrific results of war illustrated by *Strigoi* reach terrifying heights when children are involved. The refugee crisis resulting from the recent "apocalyptic civil war" (Salopek 2015, 48) in Syria illustrates the dire consequences children face when confronted by war and its aftermath. According to *National Geographic* correspondent Paul Salopek, "By the end of 2013, more than 51 million people world-wide were displaced because of warfare, violence, and persecution. More than half were women and children. Among Syrian refugees in Turkey, the proportion of women and children zooms to 75 percent. The men stay behind to fight or protect property. The women and children become destitute wanderers" (58). Children suffer greatly because of war, according to a March 2015 *National Geographic* photo essay. Mothers marry off their daughters at thirteen to protect them from sexual predators (58). Eleven-year-old boys use their bare hands to clean chemical-covered cups and teapots (69). The pain these images evokes gains even more force

Germany Year Zero: Edmund succumbs to a war-torn environment.

in war films focusing on childhood, such as *Germany Year Zero* (1948) and *The Devil's Backbone* (2001).

The opening scenes of West Berlin in *Germany Year Zero* and of war-torn Spain in *The Devil's Backbone* showcase the horror children face when traumatized by the terror and environmental devastation that violent combat leaves behind. In *Germany Year Zero* Berlin is in ruins, filled with collapsed buildings and adults eagerly dismembering a fallen horse lying in the middle of a wide avenue. The film's twelve-year-old hero, Edmund (Edmund Moeschke), passes these activities after failing to hold a job at a cemetery digging graves. He is too young and weak for such work and is kicked off the job site by hungrier and older men and women. When he returns home empty handed, he confronts his failure to support his father (Ernst Pittschau); sister, Eva (Ingetraude Hinze); and older brother, Karl-Heinz (Franz Cruger). When Eva asks him, "Did you get the Number 2 Card?" a ration card that would increase their food supplies, Edmund replies, "No. They kicked me out because I'm not fifteen yet." Although Edmund's father declares, "That's too much work for a boy your age," Edmund disagrees: "But it would have meant more to eat. For Karl-Heinz, too." In the post–World War II Berlin of *Germany Year Zero*, children lose their innocence, doing anything to survive, including acts a former teacher calls monstrous.

The Devil's Backbone heightens the trauma a war-torn environment causes children by including the ghost of a murdered orphan. The opening voice-over of the film introduces this connection between a scarred environment and the fiends it may construct. While we watch fighter planes drop a bomb into an orphanage courtyard, we hear the narrator, Dr. Casares (Federico Luppi), ask, "What is a ghost? A tragedy condemned to repeat itself time and again? An instant of pain, perhaps. Something dead which still seems to be alive. An emotion suspended in time. Like a blurred photograph. Like an insect trapped in amber." In *The Devil's Backbone*, the monstrous is more explicitly connected with the eco-trauma surrounding it because ghosts literally are defined as tragedies and instances of pain. Suffering attached to the toxic environment left by the Spanish Civil War turns children into monsters, the film suggests. Ultimately, as in *Germany Year Zero*, the monster is not the ghost but a human: the former orphan student Jacinto (Eduardo Noriega), who condemns the ghost Santi (Junio Valverde) to repeat his pain forever. Both films demonstrate that, as ecocritic Anil Narine suggests, "a traumatized earth begets traumatized people" (2015, 13).

The Eco-horrors of War

Despite this clear interaction between war and human and nonhuman ecologies of childhood, however, few historians have examined the environmental consequences of war. As environmental historians Richard Tucker and Edmund Russell explain, "Rarely have we explicitly considered the ecological consequences of warfare as a central, distinctive element of humans' historically evolving relation to the natural world" despite the fact that "twentieth-century wars have made momentous contributions to the global environmental stress and deterioration of our contemporary world" (2004, 1). Tucker and Russell's 2004 edited volume begins to fill this research gap, with chapters examining the environmental repercussions of warfare from ancient to contemporary periods. World War II was especially detrimental to the natural world according to several chapters, facilitating massive timber cutting and promoting overuse of chemicals, including DDT. Most devastating was "the radioactive aftermath at Hiroshima and Nagasaki [which] would have sweeping implications, even long after the end of the conflict" (Tsutsui 2004, 195).

Other works provide strategies for mapping the multiple negative environmental consequences of war. In a 2003 article, geographer A. M. Mannion asserts, for example, that "war and terrorism have a considerable environmental impact by altering urban and rural landscapes to leave a variety of legacies which bear witness to past and recent conflicts" (2). According to Mannion, "The immediate impacts of war, and of terrorism, are usually sudden and dramatic, and can be either direct or indirect. Direct impacts include bomb and blast damage to settlements, rural areas and communication networks. Defoliation and ecosystem destruction, the dumping of the machinery of war and the destruction of resources such as oil fields also occur" (2). During the Spanish Civil War and World War II, for example, bombing raids "substantially altered" hundreds of European cities, from London, Coventry, and Warsaw to Berlin, Rotterdam, Dresden, Moscow, Stalingrad, and Guernica. *Germany Year Zero* and *The Devil's Backbone* illustrate the negative environmental effects of such bombing. Other environmental impacts of war are less direct, however. As Mannion explains, "These indirect impacts . . . include the construction of various camps such as refugee camps and the distortion of population composition as young males join the conflict; in countries where agriculture is a major activity this may result in land abandonment and degradation may ensue" (2). Mannion outlines other indirect impacts, as well, including wildlife destruction. Mannion also notes the environmental effects of refugee camps, as well as prisoner of war and internment camps during World War II and the hundreds of concentration camps in Germany, Poland, and Austria "constructed to house and kill European civilians who were considered to be undesirable to the Nazis" (15), a horrific monstrosity of the war that connects explicitly to environmental and human degradation.

Geographer Steve Dutch (2010) outlines four different classes of military effects on the environment: "Collateral Effects" such as cratering, injury to plants and animals, and chemical contamination, and "Use of Environment as a Weapon" such as the dam-busting raids on the dams in the Ruhr Valley during World War II and Germany's 1945 destruction of the Roer Dam's spillways and machinery, which created massive floods. He then explores "Environmental Modification to Aid Own Operations or Impede Enemy" such as canal cutting and road building, and "Eco-Terrorism" such as Hitler's "scorched earth" order in 1945, "which was fortunately disregarded by his subordinates. His order would have destroyed Germany's infrastructure and returned Germany to the Middle Ages." The Russians also used scorched earth warfare in 1941–42, just as they successfully employed such tactics against Napoleon in 1812.

Clay Risen (2010), managing editor of *Democracy: A Journal of Ideas*, examines the continuing effects of eco-horrors of war, noting, "In the waning days of World War II, the retreating Japanese army left millions of chemical weapons scattered across northeastern China. To prevent the Allies from capturing them, units buried the shells—containing chemicals including mustard gas, phosgene, and lewisite—in fields, lakes, and streams. The result has been a slow-motion public health disaster," with more than two thousand deaths and countless injuries due to leaking toxins. Whole cities were also destroyed through "strategic bombing" in Europe and Asia throughout the war, culminating in the destruction of Japan's key cities through "unconventional" means, the unprecedented dropping of atomic bombs on Hiroshima and Nagasaki.

Although these disastrous incidents all focus on the negative environmental repercussions of war, they also reinforce the interconnected relationship humans have with their environments. Yet according to law professor Rosemary Rayfuse, it was not until 2012 that the International Law Commission began considering "protection of the environment in relation to armed conflict" (2014, 157). The Battle of Berlin nearly flattened the city, destroying what had been standing after air raids by the Allies near the end of the war. In a battle lasting from April 7 to May 2, the city was annihilated, leaving hundreds of thousands of Soviet, Polish, and German soldiers and civilians dead and wounded, according to historian Antony Beevor's *The Fall of Berlin, 1945* (2002). Beevor also notes that at least one hundred thousand women were raped in Berlin during and after the battle, exacerbating the connection between war and human ecology. When war destroys elements of nonhuman nature, it also harms the human nature that relies on nature's resources for survival. This human approach to ecology will help illuminate the impact a war-torn environment has on children in *Germany Year Zero* and *The Devil's Backbone*.

The interconnection between human and nonhuman nature becomes most evident when one examines ecology in relation to the human ecology movement. The human ecology movement grew out of the work of Ellen Swallow Richards, who translated Ernst Haeckel's work from its original German and, according to Robert Clarke, introduced the concept of ecology in the United States. Richards, an MIT chemist, defined human ecology as "the study of the surroundings of human beings and the effects they produce on the lives of men" (1907). According to Palamar, Richards "used the term [ecology] to refer not only to the great expanses of the natural world, but also to the urban environment" (2008, 85). Richards's work also influenced the achievements of environmentalists such as Rachel Carson (85) and contributed to the environmental justice movement.

Richards examined the negative effects that a shattered and polluted environment has on the family and its children in her multiple explorations of human ecology at the turn of the twentieth century and defined and analyzed human ecology in practical ways throughout her works. Her *Sanitation in Daily Life* (1907), for example, provides an explicit definition and strong arguments for addressing environmental problems effecting humanity. According to Richards, human ecology includes the features of the environment that humanity should combat: "noise, dust, poisonous vapors, vitiated air, dirty water, and unclean food" (v).

Richards not only delineated the harmful environmental features to which humans contributed, she also promoted their eradication to ensure that all humans, especially children, obtain their basic needs, or what Richards called "essentials," which include clean air, water, soil, and food (1908, 49–50). As Richards declares in *The Cost of Cleanness*, "The one thing we are sure of is that it is our duty to give the child a fair chance. Twentieth century civilization belies itself if it does not. Knowledge of what clean air, water, and food may do for the race is now at hand. Why not use it?" (1908, 78). Richards provides scientific evidence that we all need clean water and air and nutritious food to thrive, elements missing for the characters in *Germany Year Zero* and *The Devil's Backbone*, an absence that proves fatal for Edmund and the ghost of Santi because their worlds are doubly disrupted. The war has shattered not only their homes but also their childhoods. According to Richards and Alpheus Woodman, "There is a law of conservation of human energy. The human body, in order to carry on all its functions to the best advantage, especially those of the highest thought for the longest time, must be placed under the best conditions and must be supplied with clean air, safe water, and good food, and must be able to appropriate them to its use" (1909, 2).

Several recent films interrogate the eco-traumas associated with war from various perspectives and levels of violence to highlight human rights and environmental justice violations, sometimes at monumental levels. In Riki Stern and Anne Sundberg's documentary, *The Devil Comes on Horseback* (2007), marine-turned-military-observer Brian Steidl snaps away with his telephoto lens as he watches Janjaweed raiders shoot children, rape women, massacre men, and burn entire villages to the ground in Darfur, Sudan. Steidl serves as a witness to the horrific crimes on display, offering his photographic evidence as a powerful rationale for intervention when, as an observer, he could shoot only pictures instead of the cruel Janjaweed. Steidl's return to a Chad refugee camp highlights the massive losses suffered by those who survive the unspeakable atrocities of the Janjaweed. Their homes and villages are gone. Their land is unfit for farming, not only because the Janjaweed have burned their crops but also because oil production and transport have destroyed soil and watersheds. Their family members have been murdered or mutilated. And their only home is a crowded tent camp.

Claudia Llosa's *Milk of Sorrow* (2009), a fictionalized account of the repercussions of the Peruvian civil war, centers on a woman's struggle to cope with her mother's experiences with rape as a tool of war, a traumatic experience passed on to her through her mother's songs and, perhaps, breast milk. To protect herself from a similar sexual assault, Fausta (Magaly Solier) inserts a potato as a shield, gingerly cutting off growing vines. Fausta's displacement is twofold. She must leave her village home when her mother dies and transport her mother's body to her uncle's home in a Lima ghetto. To earn money to bury her mother, however, she also leaves her uncle's home and the ghetto community to work as a maid in a walled compound where a concert pianist tosses a grand piano out a window and steals Fausta's songs in exchange for the promise of pearls. The post–civil war Peruvian settling clearly bifurcates both rural and urban and rich and poor, but it also illustrates the repercussions of the traumas of war, placing the rape of women, landscapes, and cultures on display in relation to both colonial and postcolonial exploitation.

Kim Nguyen's Academy Award–nominated *War Witch* (2012) explores the consequences children face during civil war in sub-Saharan Africa. Told from the perspective of a fictional fourteen-year-old girl, Komona (Rachel Mwanza), the film illuminates the results of childhood eco-traumas. Kidnapped by rebels and forced to kill her own parents, Komona survives by joining their cause as a "war witch" who can predict when and where the enemy will attack. It is only when the ghosts of her parents begin haunting her that she finds the courage to escape the rebels, bury her parents, and return home with help from an albino "magician" (Serge Kanyinda). Komona's story becomes even more powerful once we realize we are overhearing her telling her story to her unborn baby.

Germany Year Zero and the Eco-trauma of Childhood

Germany Year Zero also highlights eco-traumas of childhood. The interchange of Edmund's family members at the beginning of the film illustrates the goal of *Germany Year Zero* as the third film in Roberto Rossellini's War Trilogy, a moral imperative "to see clearly," according to Mary Lee Grisanti in her 2010 review of the first film in the trilogy, *Rome, Open City* (1945). *Germany Year Zero* and, to a certain extent, *Rome, Open City* and *Paisan* (1946) strive to help us see "a generation of children who lived in the streets and rewrote the rules of growing up." Ultimately, all three films focus on the effects World War II and the smashed environment left in its wake had on children. These films show the reciprocal relationship between humans and their environment, but they advance this human ecology approach by emphasizing the double threat war holds for children, who must cope not only with a literally shattered urban and home environment but also with a fractured childhood landscape. As the narrator of *Germany Year Zero* states,

> This movie, shot in Berlin in the summer of 1947 aims only to be an objective and true portrait of this large, almost totally destroyed city where 3.5 million people live a terrible life, almost without realizing it.

They live as if tragedy were natural, not because of strength or faith, but because they are tired. This is not an accusation or even a defense of the German people. It is an objective assessment. Yet if anyone, after watching Edmund Kohler's story, feels that something needs to be done—that German children need to relearn to love life—then the efforts of those who made this movie will be greatly rewarded.

Rome, Open City highlights children who are fractured by their landscape and join the resistance. These boys go on late-night sabotage attacks against the Nazis only to be beaten by their parents in the morning for being out without their permission. Although their explosions result in violent retaliations from the Fascists, the boys endure hardships and witness extraordinary violence that forces them into a false maturity. The film's final shot of the children walking together down a dusty road after witnessing the execution of their parish priest seems to suggest that they will replace the dead and dying if necessary.

Paisan (1946) documents six distinct stories set in six distinct parts of Italy during World War II. The second story is set in Naples, a port city traumatized by war and now teeming with Allied supply ships, thousands of troops, and numerous displaced refugees, along with countless street urchins hustling to stay alive in this war-torn environment despite their fractured childhoods.

Germany Year Zero amplifies this goal, powerfully demonstrating the detrimental effects that an environment destroyed by war has on children. The eco-horrors illustrated in all three films shatter both human and nonhuman nature and fracture childhood landscapes, reinforcing the lasting environmental effects of warfare and the relevance of human approaches to ecology.

In *Rome, Open City* and *Paisan*, Rossellini spends some focused time on children without clean air, safe water, and good food living in war-torn environments that unsurprisingly affect them detrimentally. But it is *Germany Year Zero* where all his concentration is on the effects of war on the young. Here Edmund translates a destructive human ecology into a fractured and war-torn landscape of childhood.

Although the film title *Rome, Open City* draws on an agreement to spare the city of Rome from multiple bombing raids to preserve the ancient art and architecture throughout its streets, the characters in the film suffer from a violent environment in which their basic human needs cannot be adequately met. Although much has been written about *Rome, Open City* as a groundbreaking introduction to Italian Neorealism of the post–World War II era, few if any critics address the city as an eco-horror with dangerous ramifications for its citizens.

Sidney Gottlieb, for example, asserts, "The connection between *Open City* and neorealism is . . . both inevitable and problematic, enlightening and potentially darkening" (2004, 31). According to Peter Bondanella, the film "continued many of the stylistic characteristics of cinema produced during the Fascist era, but it embodied at the same time, a clear antifascist ideology that attempted to reconcile all of the different and conflicting political positions of the various groups making up the Italian antifascist Resistance" (2004, 43), an ideology associated with neorealism. And Marcia Landy's exploration of gender, melodrama, and neorealism in *Open City* examines the film "as a test case for rethinking the premises of neorealism through examining its emphasis on and treatment of cliché, particularly in relation to representations of gender and sexuality" (2004, 85).

For us, however, *Rome, Open City* serves as an example of how an eco-horror caused by war and occupation also destroys the internal and external landscapes of children and those who represent them. The film contrasts the normative landscapes of these children with their fractured reality in a long shot that provides an establishing shot of Rome from above highlighting its beauty without revealing the Nazi occupation and its effects on the city and its inhabitants below. Citizens sing as they march. But the scene quickly reveals trucks filled with armed German soldiers knocking on doors looking for rebels.

The narrative highlights the struggles of these rebels, but it also showcases the effects of starvation on women and their now-fractured children. In one scene, for example, women storm and loot a bakery. "They even had pastries," a woman tells a city official. Single mother and bride-to-be Pina (Anna Magnani) is there to avoid starving to death, and a Roman officer (Eduardo Passarelli) escorts her back to her apartment complex, and to reinforce the need to stave off hunger, she gives him some bread for his troubles.

Children are negatively affected by the disastrous environment around them, an environment that destroys their childhood and transforms them into pseudo-adult partisans who deposit a bomb in a Nazi truck. The successful blow to the occupiers initiates the boys' loss of innocence, a loss that fractures their childhood landscapes. In this desperate environment, even Pina breaks down, calming only when she and her fiancé, Francesco (Francesco Grandjacquet), talk privately about days before the war took hold. "When is it going to end? Sometimes I just can't go on," Pina declares. But Francesco reassures her that things will be "more beautiful than ever because we're free. . . . And our children especially will see it," a claim that seems baseless in this fractured environment.

On Pina and Francesco's wedding day, the conflict reaches a climax, amplifying the loss of childhood enforced by this environment. Germans and Fascists surround their building, and in another move away from innocence, the boys and priest must try to help and run back into the building to protect those in hiding and those unable to leave. Marcello (Vito Annichiarico), Pina's son, dresses as an altar boy and helps his priest, Don Pietro (Aldo Fabrizi), perform last rites for an invalid man. And when Pina runs after Francesco when he is hauled away by the Nazis, her son watches helplessly as she is gunned down.

The boys' help demonstrates their forced pseudo-maturity, but it also may trigger others to embrace a reality that, with hope, could be changed. Don Pietro is captured and witnesses the torture of partisan leader Manfredi (Marcello Pagliero) during his interrogation. In a tragic parallel to the earlier scene with a soccer ball, Don Pietro is shot in the head by an SS officer when the Italian firing squad refuses to shoot him. The boys watch beside a fence, mourning his loss but walking away along a road, perhaps as the new hope for a future free of war, as Francesco has explained to Pita, but also as evidence that childhood has become as shattered here as the environment surrounding them.

Paisan (1946) unfolds like a travelogue, divided into six distinct stories, set in six distinct geographical places. All but one of the settings demonstrates the horrific environmental effects of war and the terrible impact of a war-torn environment on its inhabitants, especially its children. While many admirers were and remain awed by Rossellini's inventive style, wedded to content that was fresh and unseen in Italy for most of its twenty years of living under Fascist control, others note the director's sensitivity to landscape. In *Paisan*

we move from the rocky countryside of Sicily through the southern port of
Naples to the relatively undamaged Rome, the bitter inner-city fighting in
Florence, the serene monastery of Romagna untouched by battle or history,
and, finally, to the grim marshes of the Po River Valley.

The impact of war on children is seen most clearly in a scene set in
Naples. A drunken GI is being guided by a young boy, eager to steal his
belongings. The boy takes the soldier to a puppet show, and when the
soldier passes out, the boy leaves with his boots. A few days later we see
the soldier, now as an MP, driving his jeep through the clogged streets. He
sees the boy, grabs him, and demands his shoes back. The boy takes him
to his neighborhood, and the man is stunned by the gruesome number of
homeless families living in squalor. Women and children hover over open
fires, cooking whatever is at hand. Because the MP seems to understand this
world, he loses all interest in shoes and leaves the area as the story stops.
Although brief, the scene highlights the devastating effects that a war-torn
environment has on its children. The boy suffers not only because, as a
human ecology approach explains, his environment has become a shattered
wasteland of hunger and thirst but also because his landscape of childhood
has become a fractured memory.

If *Paisan* was created in part to give us a feeling of being in the center
of the action, it succeeds. The film stills feel fresh and contemporary. If the
concept of "neorealism" is ever to be understood, *Paisan* is the film that helps
explain it in the most concrete fashion. In *Paisan* neorealism includes environmental degradation, shattered human ecology, and, to a certain extent,
a fractured landscape of childhood.

In *Germany Year Zero* Rossellini intensifies the effects an eco-horror caused
by total war and occupation has on innocence, especially the innocence of
children whose external and internal landscapes have become broken. The
film opens on a devastated city, and a long pan from a car window reveals
a war-torn urban landscape broken by motorcycles and automobiles. Every
building seems shattered by the 1945 battle. Nothing, including magnificent
cathedrals throughout the city, is exempt.[1] An overhead shot of a cemetery
shifts focus from the ruined buildings, connecting their devastation to human
loss. The cemetery offers one of the few jobs in this disaster area. Women
workers talk about bread and jam as they dig. Other workers complain, but

Edmund begins digging with relish and protests when run off because of both his age and the competition for a job.

Germany Year Zero demonstrates how the disastrous consequences of this war-torn city affect all aspects of the survivors' lives. More importantly for us, however, the eco-horror that has inundated the city most powerfully affects its most innocent, the children, and Edmund serves as their representative. Although Bosley Crowther argues that "what might be a terribly touching story of the ruin of a 12-year-old boy ... becomes, in the cold accumulation by the camera of sordid details, little more than a literal (and depressing) presentation of an objective case" (1946), this literal presentation provides a concrete and powerful image of the devastating effects of an environment where basic needs are barely met and only with great effort. In this disastrous environment, human ecology is shattered and childhood is splintered.

Edmund convincingly illustrates the consequences of a fractured landscape of childhood. Because both his urban and family environments have failed him, he has taken sole responsibility for ensuring his family attains its basic needs, a burden too heavy for a twelve-year-old to bear. The maturity he is forced to embrace is tenuous at best, so when Edmund follows a starving crowd to a dead horse in the middle of the avenue, his youth interferes, and he is pushed away by larger adults. Fuel for cooking and heating homes is also scarce, but because he is too young for work, Edmund can only scavenge for coal behind a delivery truck. The original score by Renzo Rossellini rises to accentuate the boy's desperation as he walks down damaged streets. Despite the sense of normality signified by streetcars and passing trucks, the building Edmund enters is also dilapidated, a home where ten people share a small apartment and argue about electricity and water usage, utilities they maintain only with bribes of cigarettes to the neighborhood meter readers.

In this horrific environment, despite Edmund's sick and starving father's attempts to conserve and support his three children by selling everything he owns, Edmund must bear the weight of the family. His father declares that he won't "kick the bucket in a POW camp" and encourages elder brother Karl-Heinz to do his duty as a soldier and help support them despite his paranoia about being arrested because he fought the Russians all the way to the doorstep of their home. Karl-Heinz refuses to work and register for a ration card because he fears reprisal for his war acts, arguing he was a "victim of Fascism." The boy's sister, Eva, calls Karl-Heinz a selfish coward because he refuses to register, but she earns only cigarettes and affection from the occupying forces she meets at taverns late at night. She tells Karl-Heinz they can't let Edmund tow the load, but neither she nor Karl-Heinz seems able or willing to find more lucrative work to help him. A shattered human ecology has left them helpless, leaving Edmund, despite his fractured childhood, to provide for them.

Edmund's childhood landscape has become broken not only because of the bomb-battered city and demolished building in which he lives but also because of the adult roles forced upon him in his discordant home environment. To ease tensions between families in the apartment, for example, he agrees to try to sell a neighbor's scale for at least three hundred marks. He also cares deeply for his sister, Eva, and worries about her nightly romps with foreign soldiers. A scene in a bar illustrates why Edmund is concerned. While Eva collects cigarettes, a friend tells her she should go further, taking the opportunity established by their growing connection to acquire more. Although Eva does not proposition the soldier in this scene, the danger remains because her family is still hungry, and young women are a valuable commodity, especially among the soldiers and businessmen of the victorious Western Sector occupiers. Edmund's childhood has become a landscape as decimated as the war-torn environment around him.

The dire eco-horror around Edmund and his family is intensified in scenes where starving women stand in line for supplies, their ration cards and inadequate stock limiting their prospects. Their hunger is real, but conversations reveal even more devastating causes for Eva's nightly visits to taverns. Her boyfriend, Helmut, is in a POW camp. With nothing to hold onto except the possibility of reconciling with her when he returns, Eva suggests she will stick with cigarettes instead of pillow talk for Helmut's sake.

Edmund's fractured landscapes transform him into a pseudo-adult. For Edmund war has destroyed both the landscape of Berlin and the landscape of childhood. While Eva hopes for food, Edmund works to fulfill his family's basic needs by looking in the city for a buyer for the neighbor's scale. On a busy avenue, a large man gets out of a car and grabs the scale, and when Edmund demands three hundred marks, he gives him only two cans of tinned meat before driving off. Edmund protests, but another boy tells him, "You're a dumb ass," impelling Edmund to move on.

These losses highlight for Edmund the consequences of a landscape of childhood splintered by war. Shattered and lost between childhood and maturity, Edmund walks through the city to find some physical and psychological relief. A former Nazi schoolteacher he meets at a crumbling fountain seems to provide the adult support he needs. He asks Edmund about his father and brother and touches the boy's shoulder, rubbing his arm and neck as he invites him up to his apartment to keep him company.

Instead of providing the help Edmund needs to perhaps heal his shattered childhood landscape, the teacher, like Edmund's family, seeks support from Edmund. The streetcar they ride passes workers digging up rubble, emphasizing the toxic environment surrounding them. This environment has turned his teacher into a predator who laments the loss of the great Third Reich. The teacher's dilapidated apartment building illustrates a variety of immoral excesses exacerbated by the environmental horrors of war. Women lounge in a sitting room and paint their nails. The teacher asks furtively, "Is he around?" and sneaks Edmund into his apartment. He asks Edmund to tell him stories while sitting him on his lap and continuing to rub his neck. Edmund talks about what he has gone through to provide for himself and his family, seeking some solace from an adult. Instead of parental guidance and support, however, the teacher sends him off on a black market job selling recordings of a Hitler speech to occupying soldiers at the chancellery.

The wrecked state of Edmund's childhood is reinforced when he and two older children get a tour of the ruined city on their way. The images they view conflict with the fantasy Edmund reveals to his new friends. "When I grow up, I'm going to buy a car," he tells them. The sampling of Hitler's speech meant to entice soldiers to buy the recording shatters this dream and again emphasizes the environmental catastrophe Edmund faces: both the city and his childhood landscape have been destroyed. As more evidence of his loss, even though the children collect two hundred marks for the record, Edmund receives only ten. Edmund's failure to secure his and his family's survival needs even include interactions with other children. An older boy, Jo (Jo Herbst), sells him a bar of fake soap, for example, but he does give him potatoes and provides another friend, Christl (Christl Merker), to keep him company through the night.

Edmund's exhausting attempts to help his neighbor and his family and secure a successful human ecology prove inadequate. The neighbor resents receiving canned meat instead of money. And Edmund's family has nothing but potatoes to eat that night. The only reprieve the family receives is from a sympathetic doctor who prescribes a hospital stay for their father where he brags about having two full meals a day of soup, meat, potatoes, and milk. When the short stay revives his health, the father must return home to short rations, and Edmund again must find a solution to the family's survival.

Displaced between a splintered childhood and maturity, Edmund looks for work but can find little, so he again seeks out his teacher for another job. The teacher is picking up another young boy, but Edmund asks him to help him find food because his father is in poor health. Instead, the teacher offers philosophy that ultimately drives Edmund to his end: "Everything dies," he tells Edmund. "Don't be selfish. Look at nature [not] the weak. It's all about saving ourselves," he explains. Because Edmund takes these words literally, he believes his teacher has offered him a piece of practical advice, so when he visits his father in the hospital, he pockets a bottle marked poison to keep his father from becoming "the burden" he expects to become.

Edmund's family still faces the same degradation in their small apartment, without the "essentials" they need to survive. Without Karl-Heinz's ration card, for example, the family has no oil, flour, or tea now, only bread. Edmund hears his father argue that he feels "the misery of watching and not being able to help . . . but being condemned to live." According to his father, they are "paying for [their] own mistakes" and must "acknowledge [their] responsibility" to "set things right." These words reinforce those of his teacher, so a distraught Edmund makes his father a cup of hot, poisoned tea to free him from his misery and help the family. His father drinks the tea, saying it "tastes odd" but "does a man good."

The disastrous consequences of Edmund's broken childhood landscape climax after his father drinks the poison. The police raid the building and force Karl-Heinz to register. And after his father dies, tenants and other family members show Edmund sympathy instead of the admiration he believes he deserves, even as they scavenge the father's sweater and woolen socks. When Karl-Heinz returns after successfully registering with the police without facing arrest, Edmund realizes the depth of his failure. "You should have thought of that before I walked the streets for you," he tells Karl-Heinz. Karl-Heinz attempts to console him, saying, "You made [father's] wish come true. That's the main thing." Edmund asks him, "Is he free now?" and Karl-Heinz agrees, yes, "completely free."

Now nearly as ruined as the city, Edmund wanders in the rubble instead of leaving with Eva and Karl-Heinz. When his female friend Christl refuses to accompany him, Edmund again seeks help from his teacher, telling him, "I did it" and hoping for a reinforcing response from him. Instead, his teacher accosts him: "I didn't tell you to do anything, you monster! I never told you to do such a thing. Never!" Edmund's rejection is hyperbolic and emphasized by a group of children refusing to let him join their soccer match. He is alone, a war victim of "nature," his childhood landscape as broken as the city surrounding him. As a solitary victim, he plays hopscotch on scorched streets, kicks a can down a sidewalk, and climbs high into a dilapidated building from which he watches his family. He pretends to shoot himself with a hammer and hears a neighbor say, "Someone should tell the children."

But it is too late for Edmund. He sees Karl-Heinz and hears him call for him, but when Edmund doesn't answer, he and Eva walk away. Edmund slides down a beam and looks out on the eco-horror surrounding him. He sees his old home and cries, remembering his father. Then he jumps. A woman screams and goes toward him. Edmund is dead, sacrificing himself for his family and, perhaps, the sins of war. Although Dennis Schwartz claims Edmund serves as a "symbol of German loss, Nazi brainwashing, hopelessness and national guilt" (2006), he most significantly serves as an illustration of the importance of a safe, secure, and clean human ecology, an environment not racked by war but supported by hope. Without it Edmund's childhood landscape is destroyed.

The Devil's Backbone and the Origin of Ghosts

The horrific opening scenes of The Devil's Backbone also highlight the eco-traumas of childhood associated with war and fascism. According to del Toro, the Spanish Civil War was "the precursor of all the fascist conflicts in Europe" (quoted in Kermode 2013). As in Germany Year Zero, the film connects war with "monsters," in this case not only through the doctor's narration but also through a series of seemingly unrelated images: a bomb dropping and a boy hit in the head, an underwater scene of Santi's body, and spike-backed fetuses in glass jars, the devil's backbone of the film's title. As film critic Ellen Brinks explains, as a Gothic film, *The Devil's Backbone* "rewrites Spanish Civil War history in respect to its traumatic impact on intelligibility, to a coherent sense of self, and to the possibility of catharsis or closure" (2004, 293).

The short opening scene explicitly juxtaposes the ghost of the horror genre with the real horrors of war, demonstrating genre expectations: ghosts in horror films usually are a product of trauma. In *The Haunting* (1999), for example, the ghosts haunting a mansion are the souls of orphaned children exploited in unsafe workhouses. In the more recent *Mama* (2013), the ghost is a Down syndrome woman who died escaping from a mental hospital with her baby. Both of these haunted-house movies highlight the fear and disgust that Noel Carroll (1990) asserts defines "art horror."

The Devil's Backbone, on the other hand, combines art and natural horror. This alliance between what Carroll calls art horror (the ghost) and natural horror (the Spanish Civil War) underpins the narrative and mise-en-scène of *The Devil's Backbone.* We learn more about the source of this alliance when another boy—Carlos (Fernando Tielve)—arrives at what we discover is an orphanage and school for children whose parents have died in the Spanish Civil War. A wounded man escorts Carlos to the school's headmistress, Carmen (Marisa Paredes), who laments the added mouth to feed. The fighting has terrible ramifications for both soldiers and the women and children they leave behind. But this natural horror is immediately connected to art horror when Carlos adds a slug to his collection near the kitchen where Santi was murdered and sees his ghost.

The juxtaposition between natural and art horror is reinforced in multiple scenes in the film. As Santi's ghost watches Carlos through a window, we hear about more comrades killed at the war front. When Carlos is assigned to Santi's bed in the dormitory, Santi's ghost appears as "the one who sighs" and knocks over water pitchers that must be refilled in the kitchen, where Santi died. Carlos and the older Jaime (Íñigo Garcés) pass the bomb in the courtyard on the way and seem to hear it tick. Santi tells Carlos, "Many of you will die" in a scene before Carmen and Dr. Casares discuss the fall of Catalonia, declaring, "Sometimes I think we are the ghosts," while boys erect a huge Catholic cross.

Ultimately, however, it is natural horror rather than art horror that proves monstrous in *The Devil's Backbone*. The ghosts of Santi and—in the end—of Dr. Casares are heroes rather than fiends. Instead, former student Jacinto, who now works for the orphanage, transforms into the monster of the film, a terrifying product of the horrific environment of war. As Carlos again interacts with Santi's ghost, we learn that Jacinto had killed him because Santi witnessed his attempt to steal the school's gold that Carmen is saving for the rebel cause. Jacinto's greed is also connected with the war when Dr. Casares takes rum to the town market, sees a firing squad, and discovers that the army now knows the school supports the rebels. When Dr. Casares returns, he urges Carmen and the boys to leave. But Jacinto is determined to steal the gold, and after being caught and thrown out, he returns to destroy the orphanage by rigging a gasoline bomb. The massive explosion kills Carmen and most of the boys, as well as mortally wounding Dr. Casares.

In the final battle, however, the remaining boys and the ghosts of Santi and Dr. Casares destroy the real monster, Jacinto, forcing him into the same cistern where he stowed Santi's body. Kermode argues del Toro "saw clear parallels between the plight of the orphans and that of Spain, abandoned by Europe 'in the middle of nowhere, in the hands of fascism'" (2013). Yet *The Devil's Backbone* offers a way out for these orphans, with help from the ghosts eco-traumas create, that demonstrates, as Kermode declares, "the irrepressibility of the innocent human spirit." The film ends with the same question that opened the film, "What is a ghost? A moment of pain perhaps? ... An emotion suspended in time like a blurred photograph?" Yet because Santi's ghost avenges his death, the remaining boys can try to move on. But their escape from the ruins of their only home is a harsh landscape miles from any stable, nurturing place of safety. In *The Devil's Backbone* it is not the ghosts that are the monsters but the war and its horrific offspring, Jacinto.

Although *Rome, Open City* and *Paisan* demonstrate to differing levels the negative consequences of a war-torn environment, *Germany Year Zero* and *The Devil's Backbone* personalize this connection. In *Germany Year Zero*

Edmund represents the interconnected relationship between humans and their environment. As José Luis Guarner notes, "The environment denies Edmund any possibility of remaining a child by reminding him all the time of the need to lie, steal and defraud in order to feed himself and his family" (1970, 31). *Germany Year Zero*'s narrative and setting draw on some of the negative consequences of the eco-horror Berlin faced after the war. The film demonstrates the struggles faced by families that historian Antony Beevor explores. Beevor explains, "Over a million people in the city were without any home at all.... Smoke from cooking fires emerged from what looked like piles of rubble, as women tried to re-create something like a home-life for their children amid the ruins" (2002, 419). Despite the psychological and physical repercussions of widespread rape, women served as the backbone of the community. Beevor notes, "The most common sight in Berlin became the *Trummerfrauen*, the 'rubble women,' forming human chains with buckets to clear smashed buildings and salvage bricks. Many of the German men left in the city were either in hiding or had collapsed with psychosomatic illnesses as soon as the fighting was over" (416). The film's focus on the plight of multiple families living in a small apartment in a shattered building originates in the devastating conditions of postwar Berlin.

The Devil's Backbone also illustrates the negative effects that war has on those most innocent. Because they have lost their families and homes, the children in del Toro's "experiment in antifascist super-naturalism" (J. Hoberman 2001) face even worse eco-trauma than does Edmund. As Antonio Lazaro-Reboll explains, "The children inhabiting Santa Lucía are the children of imprisoned, murdered, and exiled Republicans ('rojos cuidando hijos de rojos,' as Carmen bluntly puts it), as well as those children abandoned as a consequence of the casualties of the civil war" (2007, 48). These abandoned children also illuminate the victims of the Spanish Civil War and Franco-era Spain. As recently as 2009, Spain was struggling with how to address the 350,000 deaths and over 30,000 children "forcibly removed from their parents, given to childless pro-Franco couples or put into institutions where they were brainwashed and cruelly abused" (Roberts 2009). *The Devil's Backbone* provides hope that is missing from this historical memory.

Germany Year Zero and *The Devil's Backbone* illuminate the direct connection between environmental devastation and the physical and psychological

The Devil's Backbone: A bomb introduces Carlos to the monstrous effects of war.

state of children, personalizing that relationship with Edmund's and Jacinto's inevitable destruction. This same interconnection is broached in the last entry in *A Woman in Berlin*, an anonymous diary of a woman coping with life during and after war in Berlin: "Yesterday I experienced something comic: a cart stopped outside our house, with an old horse in front, nothing but skin and bones. Four-year-old Lutz Lehmann came walking up holding his mother's hand, stopped beside the cart, and asked, in a dreamy voice, '*Mutti*, can we eat the horse?'" (anonymous 2005, 261). With no mother to provide support, Edmund attempts to become such a mother figure for his family but fails, his fractured childhood landscape leading to his ultimate fall into the rubble that destroys him. It is only when the natural horror of war meets the art horror of ghosts that children can overcome eco-trauma. With help from the ghosts of Santi and Dr. Casares, Carlos and the other boys escape the monster.

3

Evolution and Monstrous Nature

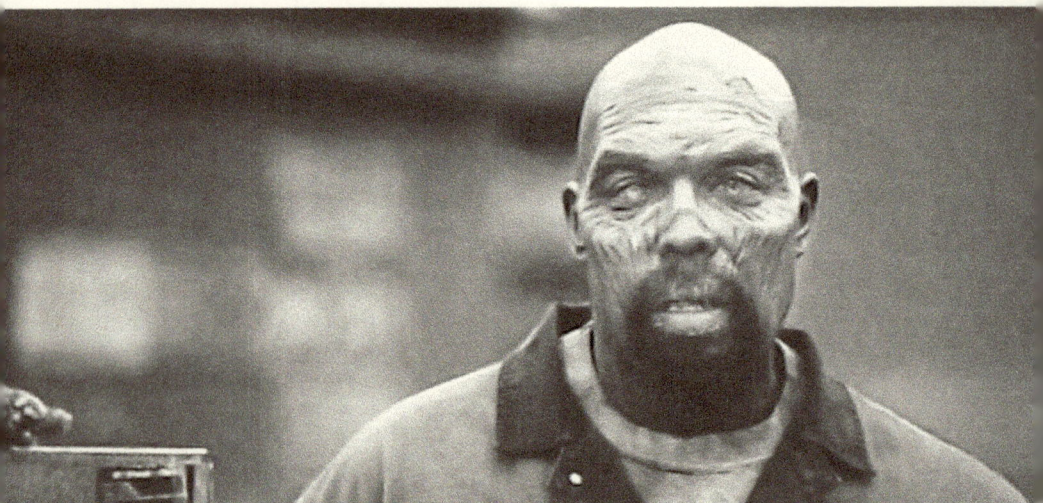

Land of the Dead: An evolved Big Daddy no longer stops for fireworks.

5

Zombie Evolution

A New World with or without Humans

RILEY: [about the fireworks] Put some flowers in the graveyard.
CHARLIE: Put some flowers in the graveyard. How come you call them that,
    Riley? I don't get it. These here ain't the kind of flowers you lay on the ground,
    these here are sky flowers. Way up in heaven . . .
RILEY: That's why I love you, Charlie, 'cause you still believe in heaven.
—*Land of the Dead* (2004)

Other monstrous nature films stress interdependence over human ecology,
emphasizing a biotic community over human-centered worldviews. Zombie
films such as *Land of the Dead* and *Warm Bodies* reinforce this vision. During
a supply run in George A. Romero's *Land of the Dead*, Mike (Shawn Roberts),
one of the human militia members, reacts with surprise when he sees zombies outside their mall-like stronghold donning aprons, carrying wrenches,
pumping gas, and exclaims, "They're pretending to be alive!" a response
that suggests the resemblance to humans these zombies are attempting is
superficial. In his reply, however, the team's leader, Riley (Simon Baker),
expands on this connection between humans and zombies. "Isn't that what
we're doing? Pretending to be alive?" a question that transforms surface
similarities into deliberate cognitive choices.

A similar connection occurs in Jonathan Levine's *Warm Bodies* (2013)
when one of the zombies, R (Nicholas Hoult), has a much closer encounter

with humans inside their walled city. Trying to blend in, R says, "H-hi" to people he meets, but a voice-over provides insight into the thought behind his words: "Say something human," the voice-over tells us, and R responds, "How . . . are . . . you?" perhaps illustrating Mike's claim in *Land of the Dead* that zombies may "pretend to be alive." But the voice-over asserts that R thinks he "nailed it," a conclusion that assumes an intellectual decision rather than mere modeling, a move that gives a sense that pre–*Night of the Living Dead* (1968) zombie films don't exist. Unlike these earlier films, in both *Land of the Dead* and *Warm Bodies*, zombies don't just pretend to be alive. They live, expanding definitions of humanity and adapting for survival in a postapocalyptic world that ideally includes both species.

Both *Land of the Dead* and *Warm Bodies* explicitly address evolutionary narratives of survival and reproduction that broach ethical questions about humanity's place on Earth that we previously raised in a reading of *28 Days Later* (2002) and *28 Weeks Later* (2007): If humanity's destruction is an inevitable product of a constructed virus, then is it our presence or our absence that is a natural part of Earth's evolution? And how can humanity best ensure its survival, through extermination or accommodation? For us *28 Days Later* highlights a comic evolutionary narrative that reinforces community over individual pioneers. This same comic narrative is explored in the blockbuster *World War Z* (2013) when former UN employee Gerry Lane (Brad Pitt) helps find a cure for the zombie virus in order to save his family. *28 Weeks Later*, on the other hand, emphasizes a tragic evolutionary narrative, which ends in destruction rather than species survival. All three films separate humanity from zombies, stressing separate evolutionary paths for each.

But unlike *28 Days Later*, *28 Weeks Later*, and *World War Z*, the evolutionary narrative in *Land of the Dead* and *Warm Bodies* includes both humanity and the zombies they battle and may serve as a source of instruction. According to sustainability-studies scholar and political philosopher Leslie Paul Thiele, this evolutionary narrative "is the grandest (nonteleological) story at our disposal. It is appropriate that we co-opt it for moral instruction. . . . An ecological ethics situates us within interdependent social and biological relationships and prescribes action to sustain this web of life" (1999, 34). Even though June Pulliam's "Our Zombies, Ourselves: Exiting the Foucauldian Universe in George A. Romero's *Land of the Dead*" (2009) argues that zombies, not humans, form class-consciousness and can reorganize society in their own interests, we assert that *Land of the Dead* and *Warm Bodies* teach us that the most successful evolutionary narratives include both.

Reading the Zombie Film

Scholarship examining zombie movies typically depends on whether the films come before or after George A. Romero's *Night of the Living Dead*. Research on films prior to 1968 explores the cultural contexts of the films in various ways. Jennifer Fay's "Dead Subjectivity: White Zombie, Black Baghdad," for example, asserts that zombies are not only "monstrous symptoms of a manipulative, exploitative society" but also, with their destructive cannibalism, "remedies for its ills" (2008, 87–88), despite a scientist's claim in Romero's *Dawn of the Dead* (1978) that zombies aren't cannibals because they are a different species. The essay focuses on *White Zombie* (1931) and connects the U.S. occupation of Haiti with the culture of occupation in Iraq. Elizabeth McAlister's "Slaves, Cannibals, and Infected Hyper-Whites: The Race and Religion of Zombies" explores zombies as the first monsters and posits, "Embedded in a set of deeply symbolic structures that are a matter of religious thought Zombies are used in both ethnographic and film contexts to think through the conditions of embodiment, the boundaries between life and death, expression of freedom, and the racialized ways in which humans construct other humans" (2012, 457–58). Kyle Bishop's "Raising the Dead" (2006) explores the roots of zombie folklore and voodoo traditions, unearthing the nonliterary origins of zombie cinema. And Jean and John Comaroff's "Alien-Nation: Zombies, Immigrants, and Millennial Capitalism" (2002) compares colonial zombies to compromised immigrant workers in a postcolonial economy.

Research examining *Night of the Living Dead* explores the contexts of the film in multiple ways, including in terms of the filmmaking process and the film's distribution. Matt Becker's "A Point of Little Hope: Hippie Horror Films and the Politics of Ambivalence" highlights the impact that George Romero's hippie youth had on his choices in *Night of the Living Dead*. According to Becker, the identity of the youthful hippie filmmaker mapped out the zombie genre with conflicted character types, depictions of worlds in which people rather than fantastic creatures are monsters, and where realistic graphic violence prevail (2006, 42). Kevin Heffernan's "Inner-City Exhibition and the Genre Film: Distributing *Night of the Living Dead* (1968)" also responds to the film's violence, calling it a pornographic reaction to horror and science fiction films and fictions, as well as the race-themed topical dramas, of the 1950s and 1960s. According to Heffernan, "issues of audience, text, and industrial context intersected during a period of immense change in both popular culture and the film industry" (2002, 75).

Other post-1968 zombie film research explores race and class issues in various zombie movies. For example, Justin Ponder's "Dawn of the Different: The Mulatto Zombie in Zack Snyder's *Dawn of the Dead*" (2012) highlights what he calls "seeds of interracial hope" that undermine the North American nightmare of the black and zombie child. Kyle William Bishop's "The Idle Proletariat: *Dawn of the Dead*, Consumer Ideology, and the Loss of Productive Labor" sees Romero's zombies not only as a metaphor for consumerism but also as a "catalyst for the true problem infecting humanity—pervasive consumerism" (2010, 235). For Bishop the film provides a grim outlook for humans because they can only consume and cannot do anything else. Still other research explores style in zombie films in multiple ways. Amy Rust's "Hitting the Vérité Jackpot": The Ecstatic Profits of Freeze-Framed Violence" (2011) proposes that the conspicuous appearance of freeze-frames in commercial cinema of the late 1960s and early 1970s figures the popularization of ecstatic fantasy in American culture during this period. Allan Cameron's "Zombie Media: Transmission, Reproduction, and the Digital Dead" highlights how "film grains, distortion, and digital pixilation" align with "bodily phenomena of death, decay, and dismemberment" in the zombie film to "explore the breakdown of bodies, images, and meaning" (2012, 66).

A few scholars also address how the zombie film and its style evolve, a focus that hints at an ecocritical approach to the genre. Meghan Sutherland's "Rigor/Mortis: The Industrial Life of Style in American Zombie Cinema" explores zombie remakes "as an element of the style and a bearer of the textual meaning that accrues that meaning precisely through repetition, which is to say, through an infrastructure of re-production" (2007, 66). According to Sutherland, "The mainstream zombie remake signifies as it does ... because the themes and subjects it narrates intersect with the political and industrial institutions that produce it in unexpected and ultimately very instructive ways" (76). Robin Wood's "Fresh Meat: *Diary of the Dead*" argues that the film may be "the summation of George A. Romero's Zombie Cycle (at least Until the Next Installment)" and that "what we used to think of as our civilization" or "human life itself in all its confusions and unsatisfactoriness" or "all of the above," (2008, 28) but not about punishment for sin.

Our work comes closest to intersecting with Wood and Sutherland, especially in conjunction with the more ecocritical work of Michael Newbury's "Fast Zombie, Slow Zombie: Food Writing, Horror Movies, and Agribusiness Apocalypse," which argues that in zombie films such as *28 Days Later* the "yearning for the pastoral, for the local, for slow food tend[s] to be crushed" (2012, 91). Whereas contemporary critics of agribusiness "fashion to varying degrees an idealized return to the 'natural' as a solution to the corporate remaking of food, zombie films insist in their imagery of the apocalypse on the problematic provisionality of any such reference to the 'natural,' offering instead a world and food that are always and inescapably made by culture and economic power" (91). For us these scholars' evocation of evolution aligns most closely with the narratives of zombie films, especially those of *Land of the Dead* and *Warm Bodies*.

Evolutionary Narratives and the Zombie Film

At least since George Romero's *Night of the Living Dead*, the modern zombie movie has explored humanity's drive for survival and reproduction, two mainstays of Darwinian views of evolution. As Charles Darwin convincingly demonstrates, "species have changed, and are still slowly changing by the preservation and accumulation of successive slight favourable variations" ([1859] 2001, 425). Some of the causes for the change from human to zombie may illustrate the preponderance of evolutionary narratives. Although prior to Romero's *Night of the Living Dead*, in most films zombies were a product of voodoo, other causes are more environmental than based in ritual.[1] Mathias Clasen's "Vampire Apocalypse: A Biocultural Critique of Richard Matheson's *I Am Legend*" draws on work of evolutionary critics such as Joseph Carroll and Brian Boyd to label the novel a speculative account of what happens when basic human needs are suppressed—an evolved psychology (2010, 315). According to Clasen we fear not just any old thing but things in our evolutionary pasts (316). In this case we fear death caused by nuclear and biological warfare. In the novel vampires are also driven by their basic needs (321), and vampirism has its origins in a prescientific explanation for infectious disease (323).

Toxic waste, radiation, and war serve frequent environmental causes for the zombie change. In most of these films, zombies seem to supersede humanity as a species (or at least as individuals).[2] Some of these films, however, emphasize more-complex views of evolution. In Peter Jackson's *Dead Alive* (1992), another comic take on zombies, New Zealanders become zombies when bitten by a rare rat monkey. Unlikely hero Lionel Cosgrove (Timothy Balme) must defeat them and destroy his monstrous zombie mother to win the heart of his love, Paquita (Diana Peñalver). In an unusual turn, however, one of the zombies, Nurse McTavish (Brenda Kendall), is impregnated by another, Father McGruder (Stuart Devenie), and produces a zombie child. And in *Deadheads* (dir. Brett Pierce, Drew T. Pierce, 2011), zombies are created by the military, but at least two of the dead are injected with a different virus that maintains their intelligence. One of these smart zombies, Mike Kellerman (Michael McKiddy), remembers his girlfriend, Ellie (Natalie Victoria), and searches for her cross-country with the help of another cogent undead, Brent (Ross Kidder). After numerous battles with militia and an ex-con African American seeking his freedom, Thomas (Thomas Galasso), Mike is reunited with Ellie, despite her father's attempts to stop him, and the two actually kiss, so a zombie and human literally connect.

Zombie viruses most often prompt these evolutionary changes. In *28 Days Later* (2002), for example, an anger virus turns humans into ultra-fast zombies. In *Colin* (dir. Marc Price, 2008), the film presents protagonist Colin's (Alastair Kirton) viral infection from a first-person point of view, highlighting how he and other zombies survive and reproduce by spreading the zombie virus. There, we see zombies from Colin's human perspective first, but once he contracts the zombie virus, the perspective is maintained, even though Colin is now "changed." As the "virus" spreads through Colin, we see him deteriorate, no longer able to open a door, for example. Eventually Colin bites his sister, so she too becomes a zombie and is locked up with him in a kitchen, but unlike her brother, she maintains the ability to open the door. The film's ending suggests that zombies, not humans, will survive this transformation: Colin, the zombie, sits with his eyes closed, as if he is remembering the moment of his change.[3] In Romero's *Survival of the Dead* (2009), another viral attack and zombie outbreak occurs, but a chance for zombie evolution sets the film apart from other zombie movies. On Plum Island one of the two warring Irish families attempts to teach zombies to eat something other than humans and ultimately succeeds, but the survivors don't notice the change. Audience members see the zombies begin to eat a horse instead of humans in a concluding example of dramatic irony.

Although most zombie-virus films imply that this new zombie species will overpower and drive humanity to extinction, a few of them stress interdependence. *Fido* (dir. Andrew Currie, 2006) and *Shaun of the Dead* (dir. Edgar Wright, 2004), for example, suggest that both zombies and humans can evolve to live interconnected lives. With a setting reminiscent of *Pleasantville* (1998) or *All That Heaven Allows* (1955), *Fido* highlights gray (black and white–like) zombies who serve their human masters and mistresses, but when an unusual family buys a zombie servant, their son, Timmy (Kesun Loder), befriends him and names him Fido (Billy Connolly). After a series of mishaps, Timmy's mother, Helen (Carrie-Anne Moss), and the rest of the neighborhood respond to Fido's charms and become friends instead of prey and predator. The other zombie servants seem to see that Fido no longer wants to eat Timmy or Helen, and they and the remaining humans react positively to the change. *Shaun of the Dead* emphasizes the possibility of friendship between a human, Shaun (Simon Pegg), and his now-zombie best friend, Ed (Nick Frost). Grace Lee's *American Zombie* (2007) moves humor into a mockumentary "documenting" the everyday lives of cogent undead in Los Angeles, but here the drive to assimilate into human culture seems to deteriorate after the undead and their filmmaker followers attend "Live Dead," an annual zombie-only retreat.

Zombie films such as *Land of the Dead* and *Warm Bodies* take these evolutionary narratives further, demonstrating a need for interdependence for species survival. As Charles Darwin explains, "All past and present organic beings constitute one grand natural system, with group subordinate to group, and with extinct groups often falling in between recent groups" ([1859] 2001, 433). Changes within and among species may preserve them, if they respond to the needs of the "one grand natural system." For Darwin, these elaborately constructed forms, so different from each other, and dependent on each other in so complex a manner, have all been produced by laws acting around us. These laws, taken in the largest sense, being Growth with Reproduction; Inheritance which is almost implied by reproduction; Variability from the indirect and direct action of the external conditions of life, and from use and disuse; a Ration of Increase so high as to lead to a Struggle for Life, and as a consequence to Natural Selection, entailing Divergence of Character and the Extinction of less-improved forms. ([1859] 2001, 433)

Groundbreaking organismic ecologist Aldo Leopold connects the ethics of theorists like Thiele and Darwin in his *Sand County Almanac*. Leopold explains that extending ethics to include nonhuman nature "is actually a process in ecological evolution" (1949, 202). For Leopold "all ethics so far evolved reset upon a stable premise: that the individual is a member of a community of interdependent parts" (203).

We see this focus on ecological evolution as moving the narrative beyond bioethics toward a comic view of evolution, an evolutionary narrative that might, as Leslie Paul Thiele suggests, "inform moral reasoning and facilitate the cultivation of certain moral sentiments [and] might legitimate an ecological ethic" (1999, 7–8). Like Thiele we draw on Thomas's suggestion that we need a new story, "a story that will educate us, a story that will heal, guide, and discipline us" (2006, 124). This story may, as Thiele explains, address philosophical concerns that "can be gleaned from the 'transfer' of certain biological concepts to humanistic concerns" (1999, 8). Thiele provides a useful definition of such a narrative that draws on its etymology. According to Thiele, "The word *narrative* derives from the Latin *narrare*, which means to relate, and the Greek *gno*, which refers to knowledge" (2011, 189, emphasis Thiele's). This emphasis on relationships highlights how, as Thiele explains, narratives or "stories allow us to discover meaning because they reveal action in terms of its antecedents, its effects, and its side effects" (189). Stories lend actions and reactions "significance" (189), providing them with meaning. In the end, we do not so much "discover values in nature as read values into nature" (8). As Thiele asserts, the moral codes "we propagate may persist over millennia with astounding fidelity" (33). For Thiele "propagating mores that facilitate ecological sustainability becomes a very reasonable endeavor indeed" (33).

A comic evolutionary narrative like that proposed by human ecologist Joseph Meeker moves us closer to this new story. Although a comic evolutionary narrative of accommodation most ensures a species survival, according to Meeker humans typically embrace a tragic evolutionary narrative that counters the climax communities of plants and animals, which are "extremely diverse and complicated" (1996, 162). But this position comes at a price and may cost humanity its existence. Meeker asserts, "We demand that one species, our own, achieve unchallenged dominance where hundreds of species lived in complex equilibrium before our arrival" (164). This attitude may lead to the destruction not only of other species but of humanity itself. Meeker believes humanity has "a growing need to learn from the more stable comic heroes of nature, the animals" (164). At least one of the evolutionary narratives of *Land of the Dead* illustrates the consequences of continuing down a tragic pioneer path.

Primarily, however, the evolutionary narratives of *Land of the Dead* and *Warm Bodies* explore what might happen if both zombies and humanity did learn from these more stable comic heroes, since, according to Meeker, "Evolution itself is a gigantic comic drama, not the bloody tragic spectacle imagined by the sentimental humanists of early Darwinism" (1996, 164). Meeker asserts: "Nature is not 'red in tooth and claw' as the nineteenth-century English poet Alfred, Lord Tennyson characterized it, for evolution does not proceed through battles fought among animals to see who is fit enough to survive and who is not. Rather, the evolutionary process is one of adaptation and accommodation, with the various species exploring opportunistically their environments in search of a means to maintain their existence. Like comedy, evolution is a matter of muddling through" (1996, 164).

For Meeker successful evolution encourages communal action to ensure survival: "Its ground rules for participants (including man) are those which also govern literary comedy: organisms must adapt themselves to their circumstances in every possible way, must studiously avoid all-or-nothing choices, must prefer any alternative to death, must accept and encourage maximum diversity, must accommodate themselves to the accidental limitations of birth and environment, and must always prefer love to war—though if warfare is inevitable, it should be prosecuted so as to humble the enemy without destroying him" (1996, 166). Ultimately, in spite of the films' horrific plotlines, they embrace evolutionary narratives that move beyond zombie films highlighting evolutionary changes that elevate humans or zombies over other species. As in 28 *Days Later*, the primary narratives of *Land of the Dead* and *Warm Bodies* are based in a comic and communal view of survival, rather than a tragic view that equates survival with extermination, but in *Land of the Dead* and *Warm Bodies*, ideals of community extend to include zombies and the nonhuman nature they represent.

Multiple Evolutionary Narratives in *Land of the Dead*

Land of the Dead showcases a zombie assault on Pittsburgh, Pennsylvania, where a feudal-like government exists. The survivors in the film have fled to the Golden Triangle area of downtown Pittsburgh, and the wealthy have transformed a skyscraper into a prosperous haven called Fiddler's Green. *Land of the Dead* at first seems like most post-1968 American zombie films, with an opening that illustrates the cause of the film's zombie infestation, a virus that turns humans into flesh-eating undead shown in a montage of disturbing images from "some time ago." As a disheveled newscaster explains, "We must not be lulled by the concept that these are our family members or our friends. They are not. They must be destroyed on sight." But the opening also foreshadows how this film moves beyond most virus-driven zombie films with a warning about the consequences: "if these creatures ever develop the power to think, even in primitive ways," the world will be theirs, a newscaster cautions.

This prediction highlights both the evolution of the Romero zombie film and the evolution of the zombie species. From *Night of the Living Dead* forward, Romero's zombies have had a rudimentary ability to use primitive tools in their drive for survival. If a rock will bring them closer to human "food," they "learn" to use it. In *Dawn of the Dead* zombies come back to the mall where humans have escaped, as if they "remember" shopping there. One picks up a dropped gun. Another uses a tire iron to smash a window in the beginning of cognitive changes. Later Romero films illustrate more substantial evolutions, as when Bub in *Day of the Dead* (1985) seems to respond to training meant to domesticate him and when zombies eat a horse instead of humans in *Survival of the Dead*. But it is in *Land of the Dead* that this evolution becomes the centerpiece of the film.

The prediction also connects with zombie evolution in *Land of the Dead,* a comic evolutionary narrative, according to Meeker, "of adaptation and accommodation," in which zombies explore "opportunistically their environments in search of a means to maintain their existence" (1996, 164). The first example of such adaptation occurs after the opening flashback, when the crew of humans seeking supplies notices a group of zombies "trying to be us." A lone zombie walks down the street carrying a briefcase. In a park gazebo a "quartet" of zombies blow on brass instruments and shake tambourines. Another zombie hears the cling of a bell at a gas station, comes out, and picks up a gas hose. As Manohla Dargis of the *New York Times* states, "Here, in a wasteland called Uniontown, next to a diner sign emblazoned with the word 'EATS,' Riley and his sidekick, Charlie (Robert Joy), watch as Big Daddy, dressed in a gas-station attendant's uniform, tries to go through the work motions" (2005).

These images not only demonstrate the accuracy of the earlier warning. They also illustrate the beginning of comic evolutionary adaptations that may or may not include humanity. In the new world of cogent zombies, humans who refuse to change may, as the newscaster warned, be left behind. Although critics suggest only zombies evolve in *Land of the Dead*, we assert that the film explores multiple instances of evolutionary adaptations among both humans and zombies: the successful "comic" evolutionary narratives of the zombies led by Big Daddy (Eugene Clark), a human crew led by Riley and, perhaps, the human proletariat led by Mulligan (Bruce McFee), and the unsuccessful "tragic" evolutionary narrative of Kaufman (Dennis Hopper), the upper-class owner of the exclusive residence for the rich, Fiddler's Green, and the walled off humans even he leaves behind.

Illustrating the comic nature of both Riley and the zombies' evolution, the evolutionary narrative of the zombies is primarily told from the perspective of Riley, who notices and responds sympathetically to their changes. During the opening supply run, for example, Riley observes that the zombies "are communicating. They're thinking." As Riley explains, "Things are changing," and humans must "be careful" to survive in this new world. Big Daddy most explicitly illustrates these changes and shares what he learns with his zombie family, the new humanlike species adapting for survival and reproduction in this new world. When Riley's group sets off fireworks to distract the zombies, for example, Big Daddy doesn't look up and tries to stop the others from staring. And when one of Riley's most rebellious crewmembers, Cholo (John Leguizamo), shoots down zombies in the street, Big Daddy screams in pain.

The empathetic connection Big Daddy makes with his fellow zombies begins an evolutionary narrative that combines comic and tragic elements. Although Big Daddy at first seems to represent a pioneer species of the tragic narrative, ultimately he proves more collaborative than individually driven in his choices. To preserve his species, Big Daddy must build a cooperative community that learns collectively both to protect one another and to destroy the humans who seek to destroy them. After Cholo and his men destroy zombies in his community, Big Daddy leads his fellow zombies to the walled city, seemingly to avenge the brutal slaughter executed by the humans. Mike even calls it "a freakin' massacre" before zombies attack him at a liquor store.

A zombie evolution becomes most evident once the zombies reach the city. Big Daddy first teaches one of the zombies how to use his meat cleaver to knock down a barrier. Together the zombies knock down a fence and attack the military security guards at "the Mouth" as well, and Big Daddy discovers how to use a gun to explode a gas tank, nearly halting the soldiers' defense. This setting also reveals changes in other zombies. They not only mimic Big Daddy; they also move toward a goal together, destroying Fiddler's Green, the origin of the zombie massacre. When they see the Green's lights, they stop feeding and move on. As Riley explains, "They're learning how to work together," a point illustrated most powerfully when the zombies overcome their fear of water and cross the river, with Big Daddy leading them toward Fiddler's Green.

The battle at Fiddler's Green seems to align with a tragic rather than comic evolutionary narrative that supports extermination and warfare rather than accommodation. As if seeking retribution for the slaughter of his zombie family, Big Daddy teaches a female zombie to shoot; as a result, soldiers blocking their way to access Kaufman's haven for the rich are killed. When the soldiers retaliate, Big Daddy even shoots wounded zombies to end their suffering.

All the zombies pick up weapons to fight their human enemies, replacing tambourines with clubs. Together, they knock out the glass doors securing Fiddler's Green and attack the rich residents hiding there. Ultimately, Big Daddy tracks down Kaufman and strategically executes him, as if punishing him for his crimes. He fills Kaufman's car with gasoline and leaves but returns to roll a fireball through the gas for a spectacular underground explosion.

Yet once Kaufman and the rich from Fiddler Green are destroyed, the zombies leave the rest of the humans unscathed before marching slowly over a hill away from the city. "They're looking for a place to live," Riley explains. They are also constructing a comic evolutionary narrative of accommodation and adaptation in which both humans and zombies survive. Their narrative contrasts starkly with Kaufman's tragic narrative of extermination at any cost, a narrative that leaves him and the rich he fails to protect behind. According to Darwin their tragic choices have led "as a consequence, to Natural Selection, entailing Divergence of Character and the Extinction of less-improved forms" ([1859] 2001, 433). By choosing to act like a pioneer species to dominate zombies and humans different from themselves, Kaufman and the Fiddler's Green group have, within the film's context, driven themselves to extinction.

Riley and his crew of misfits and, to a certain extent, Mulligan and the city's survivors, however, at least potentially have chosen a comic evolutionary narrative from which we all might learn. Instead of walling out zombies and preserving only themselves, Riley, Charlie, and his other crewmembers, Slack (Asia Argento), Pretty Boy (Joanne Boland), and Pillsbury (Pedro Miguel Arce), prefer to find a home where barriers are unnecessary. As Riley explains to Mulligan, "I can't think we're not all locked in. I'm looking for a world with no fences." Instead of leaving once he has retrieved "Dead Reckoning" from Cholo, however, Riley goes back to the city to help Mulligan and his street people escape a city where fences and rivers "block them in." The final battle saves those whose social and economic class makes them unacceptable for Fiddler's Green. Zombies feast on the rich, but they leave the poor to, as Mulligan suggests "turn this place into what we always wanted it to be." Riley and his crew, however, choose to leave the now-open city. In a push for a new home parallel to that of Big Daddy, they travel away from their old lives to a new world where they can build a community. Like the zombies Riley, Charlie, Slack, and Pillsbury have chosen a comic evolutionary narrative of adaptation and accommodation. The narrative of Mulligan and his followers, however, remains ambiguous.

Comic Evolutionary Narratives in *Warm Bodies*

The comic evolutionary narratives in *Warm Bodies* demonstrate most powerfully how a new story might "heal, guide, and discipline us" (Berry [1988] 2006, 22). *Warm Bodies* aligns even more powerfully with Meeker's comic evolutionary narrative than does *Land of the Dead*. Meeker's description of the comic way argues that participants are successful because "they live and reproduce even when times are hard or dangerous" rather than proving themselves "best able to destroy enemies or competitors" (1997, 20). Although some critics take issue with how well, as Kevin Jagernauth states in a *Playlist* review, the film "create[s] new rules" (2013) for zombie/human interaction, we assert that in *Warm Bodies*, both humans and zombies choose cooperation, accommodation, and adaptation instead of destruction. The film may, as Chris Packham of the *Village Voice* (2013) suggests, fail as an adaptation of *Romeo and Juliet*, but for us it succeeds as an alternative narrative in which both humans and zombies survive. Beginning with an opening that highlights one of the elements that separates the film from other zombie movies (R's zombie point of view), the film emphasizes R's cognitive abilities and desire to be human, a desire that ultimately contributes to the "new story" R and Julie begin.

By using a voice-over to reveal R's thoughts, *Warm Bodies* most effectively demonstrates how a comic evolutionary narrative potentially can sustain both humanity and zombies. R's voice-over seems to speak both to himself and the audience, explaining his story and, as Stephanie Zacharek of Film.com declares, "exploring what makes us human by contrasting it with a character who has lost all the basics and is desperate to get them back" (2013). We see him shuffle through an airport with other zombies, but his voice-over tells himself, "Stand up straight" and asks why he's unable to "connect with you." The question seems to point to a tragic tale, but his answers illustrate a comic tone and the potential for a comic evolutionary narrative: "Oh, I'm dead," R decides, and then declares that he "shouldn't be so hard on [himself]" before humorously explaining, "I wish I could introduce myself, but I can't remember my name. I think it started with an R. That's all I have left. It's kind of a bummer."

R's narration also serves as exposition for the film and explains roles that zombies formerly played. Upbeat music parallels the humor demonstrated by this opening, and a montage of images establishes that he and the other zombies used to be human before the "apocalypse." R suggests one zombie was once a CEO, and another a personal trainer, but "now [he's] a corpse." He provides background information that helps us "get a handle on how the apocalypse happened," suggesting it could have been a nuclear holocaust or an airborne virus. For R "it doesn't really matter. This is what we are now." As his voice-over explains, a typical day for R and his fellow corpses includes "shuffle[ing] around, occasionally bumping into one another, unable to apologize or say much of anything." Yet when R thinks, "It must have been so much better when everyone could express themselves and communicate … just enjoying each other's company," a flashback shows human airport travelers on cell phones without interaction.

Connecting himself more fully with humanity, R distinguishes himself from the "bonies," zombies who "give up," "lose all hope," and shed their human qualities, including their skin. Zombies like R, on the other hand, "don't want to be this way." As R declares, "I'm lonely. I'm lost. I mean, I'm really lost. I've never been in this part of the airport." Despite his amusing aside, R sees two child zombies wearing name tags and muses, "I wonder if these guys are lost too"; he asks, "Do they feel trapped? Do they want more than this?" And as the sun sets, he reveals how he may be different from even other zombies. "Am I the only one?" he asks as he climbs into an airplane he calls home. He touches a bobble-head dog and turns on a turntable that plays John Waite's "Missing You." R's love of music and human artifacts like the dog seems to set him apart from both the bonies and (to a certain extent) other still humanlike zombies, even though we perceive this zombie world only through R's thoughts. Other zombies maintain some of their human elements as well, however. A former airport worker scans zombies each day as they walk through a metal detector, for example. R's best friend, M (Rob Corddry), even communicates with R. He sits at an airport bar when R approaches him and after grunts and awkward stares states, "Hungry."

M replies, "City," and because they "share similar taste in foods," they and other zombies "travel in packs" and stumble slowly toward a human meal. Even when walking toward such violence, however, R maintains his sense of humor thinking, "God, we move slow."

Their move to the city introduces the human perspective in the film and suggests that they have chosen to follow a tragic evolutionary narrative that seeks to destroy rather than accommodate other species. An overhead shot establishes the city as a walled military outpost. Here human volunteers watch a video that thanks them for their "service today." According to Grigio (John Malkovich), the leader on the screen, the "plague destroyed our world" eight years before. Grigio introduces the expected human response to the zombie plague as well, explaining, "Corpses look human. They are not. They do not think. They do not breath. Whether they are your mother or your best friend, they are beyond your help. They are uncaring, unfeeling, incapable of remorse." For Grigio and most humans, zombies are inhuman enemies. Juxtaposing this statement after our introduction to R, however, highlights its unreliability. We have heard R's thoughts, which suggest that at least one zombie cares. Although Grigio's daughter, Julie (Teresa Palmer), suggests that her father is as unfeeling as the zombies he describes, Grigio asserts that she and the other volunteers "are a critical part of what stands between [humans] and extinction."

These volunteers' search for supplies outside the city's walls connects *Warm Bodies* to other zombie movies in which supply runs connect humans and zombies, including Romero's *Dawn of the Dead* and *Land of the Dead*. In *Warm Bodies*, however, the connection transforms from a stage for violent human deaths in the face of voracious zombie hunger to a comic narrative based on interdependent bonds. The encounter between zombies and humans begins with the usual violence. R and the other zombies hear and smell Julie and her comrades and attack them. Humans "aim for their heads." But when R looks up and sees Julie crying under a desk, the soundtrack brings up the song "Missing You," and R stops, perhaps remembering the record he plays in his airplane home. When Julie's boyfriend, Perry (Dave Franco), shoots him in the chest, R attacks him, but his thoughts tell us his own ambivalence about his destruction of humans:

Now I'm not proud of this. In fact, I might appreciate it if you look away for a minute here . . . . But this is the world now. The new hunger is a very powerful thing. If I don't eat all of him. If I spare his brain, he'll rise up and become a corpse like me. But if I do, I get his memories, his thoughts, his feelings. I'm sorry. I just can't help it. The brain's the best part. The part that makes me feel human again.

Instead of focusing on R's ingestion of Perry's brain, however, the film shows us the pleasant memories R internalizes. We see fireworks and hear R's internal thoughts telling Perry, "I don't want to hurt you. I just want to feel what you felt. To feel a little better . . . and less dead." A montage of images reveals those feelings. In one memory, Perry rides a bike down a country road before the plague. Memories of Perry's connection with Julie, however, serve as a catalyst for R's change. "I miss airplanes," Julie says in Perry's thoughts. And when R looks up, Julie is there, yelling for Perry. She throws a knife at R, but when he comes up to her, he says her name and wipes his blood on her face to hide her scent. "Safe," he says, and she leaves with him while her best friend, Nora (Analeigh Tipton), watches from under a desk.

R's reaction illustrates the beginning of a comic evolution of accommodation, but the change is too new yet for R to understand. Instead, he questions his behavior:

I don't know what I'm doing. What's wrong with me? These others would never bring a living person home. You know why? Because that's crazy. Right now they just think she's another one of us. A new edition to the family. They would think I'm insane, if they could think. Why do I have to be so weird? What am I doing?

Yet his promise to keep her safe continues. He stows her in his airplane home, shows her a snow globe he collected from the pharmacy and tells her, "Not eat." To more fully understand Julie and her situation, he ingests more of Perry's brain, however, discovering more about her father, her mother's death, and a secret passage past the city's concrete wall. He also sees Perry's zombie father attacking them, and Julie shooting him down.

The images cause R pain and draw him closer to Julie, broaching evolutionary changes of both accommodation and adaptation. The connection between these two species may align with structural principles of ecology that highlight how actions of one species affect others. As Meeker asserts, "Energy and nutrients flow through an ecosystem, causing a constant rearrangement of the major elements, revising and recombining parts of the system in never-ending variety" (1997, 21). As if illustrating this flow, R tells her he saved her because he saw her "cry." But he reinforces their interconnected relationship when he finds food for her and protects her from the other zombies. In turn she begins to call him by a name instead of labeling him a corpse. Together they drive a car on the tarmac and share music on a turntable. He explains that the records provide "better sound" and tells her he "collect[s] things." When R eats the last of Perry's brain, he spits it out to avoid seeing his own attack on Julie's boyfriend. Most importantly, he prevents his best friend, M, from harming Julie. M says, "Eat," but R says, "No" and pulls Julie away, even when the bonies chase them.

R's choice sparks a change in M as well, extending the evolutionary adaptations to other zombies. When R and Julie reach the tarmac to escape the bonies, M is waiting for him there in a luggage cart and tells them, "Want to help?" He even asks R if he's okay. When R takes Julie's hand, the transformation become more powerful. M and other zombies stand back instead of giving in to the hunger. Instead of returning to their routine shuffling through the airport, they stop in front of a poster of a couple holding hands. M asks others, "Feel it?" and they sigh and smile. We see their hearts begin to light up in red. The change is so substantial that the bonies smell M and roar. He is no longer one of them.

R has changed so much that when he and Julie reach an empty suburban home, he apologizes for killing Perry. More importantly, after saying, "I'm so sorry," he falls asleep and dreams. In his dream the sun is shining brightly, and he walks across a green field toward Perry, Julie, and Nora. They are talking about their dream jobs. Nora wants to find a cure. Julie wants "someone [to] figure out this whole thing and exhume the whole world." Julie believes exhuming will revive them, but when Perry tells her it means to "dig up, as in digging up a corpse," he points to what may be the real source of their salvation—interdependent relationships with the very zombies who have destroyed them. As if on cue, R arrives in the dream, and Perry asks him why he's there. Because she now views R as a friend, however, Julie tells Perry, "He can dream if he wants to" and assures R, "You can be whatever you want."

Although Julie is gone when R awakens, the change is cemented. While walking in the rain, for example, R feels cold, even though, as he thinks, "corpses don't get cold." His friend M, too, has changed and leads a group of zombies away from the bonies. M has even had a dream and tells R, "I saw pictures last night. Memories. My mom. Summertime. Cream of Wheat. A girl." R makes their evolution explicit when he tells M and the others, "We are changing," and their now-blue eyes seem to reflect the inner transformation. Their evolution prompts R and the others to reconcile with humanity. They help R enter the city to tell Julie about the change and ally with the humans to battle the bonies who now wish to destroy R and Julie to offset a change that they see as dangerous because it means their own species' end.

Julie and Nora help resolve the human-zombie conflict and begin moving humans and zombies off a tragic evolutionary path. Julie and Nora at first fail to convince Julie's father that R and the others are becoming more human, but the returning zombies change his mind: M and the now hundreds of changing zombies attack bonies to protect human soldiers, and R jumps hundreds of feet into a pool of water using his body to protect Julie. R awakens after the fall with a beating heart, and Grigio orders his soldiers to stand down because "the situation has changed." R's sacrifice has made both zombies and humans more humane. As he explains, "On the one hand, getting shot in the chest hurt, like a lot, but on the other, it felt good to bleed. To feel pain. To feel love. I wish I could say we killed the bonies with love, but really we just straight up killed them all. . . . That sounds kind of messed up, but they were too far gone to change. It was a good bonding experience for us and the humans. After we joined forces, they didn't have a chance." A new day dawns after the battles end, and a montage of scenes show zombies becoming more human, and humans becoming more accepting, more accommodating.

As Richard Roeper states, the ending of *Warm Bodies* is "unabashedly romantic and unapologetically optimistic" (2013). For us this resolution also underlines one of the principles of ecology and a comic evolutionary narrative: "Each species in an ecosystem is affected by the actions and events of other species, so that the whole is an ever-changing process that never ends or holds still" (Meeker 1997, 21). The changes these interactions broach develop a new "niche in the ecosystem" (21), but they also help write a new story, which, as Meeker explains, creates "new opportunities and possibilities ... for other niches, assuring that novelty and surprise are present" (21). R sums up the change well when Julie asks him, "You don't want your old life back?" R answers, no, "I want this one." And the wall comes down, opening up possibilities for new stories in which humans and zombies learn from one another.

Like science fiction the horror genre offers a space in which to explore current social issues and, sometimes, condemn ineffective or destructive practices of humanity. For us the zombie film provides a stage for addressing some of the negative effects humans have had on their environment. Environmental themes permeate zombie movies both before and after Romero's *Night of the Living Dead*. Early zombie films such as *White Zombie*, of course, highlight issues related to class and colonialism, but they also illustrate human consequences of exploiting natural resources like sugarcane. As late as 1966, *The Plague of the Zombies* was still offering the same plot, manufacturing its voodoo with witch doctors from the colonized island of Haiti and moving its class and environmental exploitation to 1860s England. These early films also explore the negative repercussions of disturbing the natural order to control human labor.

The environmental causes for the zombie plague in later films explicitly underscore such themes and may also serve as a warning to humanity about warfare and biological and chemical experimentation that puts Earth and its inhabitants at risk. Romero's *Dawn of the Dead* effectively critiques consumerism and suggests that overconsumption turns humans into zombies. But it also includes an explicitly environmental cause for the change, a zombie virus, and broaches biological questions about what makes us human. In Wilson Yi's *Biozombie* (1998) and D. Kerry Prior's *The Revenant* (2009), on the other hand, zombies are created by military forces, perhaps as a way to critique biological and chemical warfare.

In most zombie films after *Night of the Living Dead*, because many people act less human than the zombies they battle, their "humanity" is called into

Warm Bodies: R and Julie demonstrate the power of evolutionary love.

question. In an ultimate instance of anthropomorphism, the zombie monster not only used to be human but also sometimes preserves more of its humanity than its human opponents. Such a questioning of our humanity is explicitly addressed in *28 Days Later*, when our destruction is an inevitable product of a constructed rage virus. Here Sergeant Farrell (Stuart McQuarrie), one of the soldiers in a military encampment, asks if it is our presence or our absence that is a natural part of Earth's evolution. Because humans have "only been around for a few blinks of an eye," he asserts, "if the infection wipes us all out, that is a return to normality." In *28 Days Later*, Earth's evolution may or may not include humans.

Although most of these later zombie movies tell stories that present a pessimistic picture of humanity's future, they all provide a site in which we can try out new, sometimes destructive, evolutionary narratives. These stories seem to ask what might happen if we continue down a dangerous path that includes nuclear warfare, ineffective toxic waste disposal, or unchecked chemical and biological experimentation. They also ask evolutionary questions about who we are, where we're going, and which story of ourselves we choose to construct: a tragic or comic evolutionary narrative. As Thiele asserts, "An individual becomes a self . . . by abstracting a persona from its narrative passage through space-time" (2006, 203). Who we are is "distilled from the multiple, variegated, spatio-temporal sequences of events that are formatted into the story of an individual life" (203).

In order for humans to develop, however, their stories must not be closed. Instead, as Thiele asserts, such development "occurs through the hermeneutic engagement with narratives that, at times, are radically different from those that have shaped one's being" (2006, 276). *Land of the Dead* and *Warm Bodies* illustrate new stories in which humans and zombies develop because they choose open stories, comic evolutionary narratives built on accommodation and adaptation. In both films walls must come down for humanity to develop. In *Warm Bodies* especially, destroying those walls opens up stories in which humans and zombies grow in relation to one another. Although these are horror films, they serve as metaphors for new stories we might choose, as well. They highlight how interdependent relationships can build a comic evolutionary path built on ecosystem survival. As Thiele suggests, this comic evolutionary narrative proves more successful than a tragic narrative of extermination: "Awareness of the web of relationships that we act within but cannot control might well heighten our sense of responsibility. Minimally it should prompt us to refrain from seeking mastery in all things. Such a chastening is in order lest the human race as a whole suffer the fate of Oedipus" (2011, 203).

6

Laughter and the Eco-horror Film

The Troma Solution

The success of the hit romantic horror comedy *Warm Bodies* demonstrates how much audiences like to laugh. With its comic evolutionary narrative, *Warm Bodies* ends on a high note, favoring love over the gore and violence necessary to destroy the bonies and reconnect zombies and humans. Despite its emphasis on interdependence, however, *Warm Bodies* is a "safe and unthreatening" comedy (King 2002, 2) that most viewers see as light entertainment. But what happens when comedy is more disruptive than entertaining? The independent Troma Studios provides an answer.

Beginning in the 1980s Troma Studios has turned monstrous nature on its head, playing campy yet subversive eco-themes for laughs by showcasing comic eco-heroes instead of the tragic hero of most horror films. Troma's *Toxic Avenger* series (1984, 1989, and 2000) and *Class of Nuke 'Em High* and its sequels (1986–2013) look at toxic waste dumping, energy overconsumption, and radiation poisoning from a more comic perspective. As in *Warm*

The Toxic Avenger: Toxie and Sara seal their comic evolutionary narrative.

Bodies and *Land of the Dead*, rugged individualism is replaced with more communal approaches to solving ecological problems. But Troma films move beyond these traditional comic horror films by exploiting, satirizing, and sometimes parodying historical and current events with help from the laugh-inducing antics of a bumbling comic eco-hero. In *The Toxic Avenger* and *Class of Nuke 'Em High* films, toxic waste and radiation contamination disasters are played for both laughs and results.

As comic eco-horror *The Toxic Avenger* (1984) uses the negative repercussions of toxic waste to comic effect. To accentuate both its comedy and eco-message, the film's hero, Melvin (Mark Torgi), mutates into the Toxic Avenger (Mitch Cohen) after being humiliated by a clique of vicious jocks at the health club where he works as a custodian. The jocks not only terrorize Melvin, the "mopboy"; they also gleefully seek out victims with their souped-up car. They repeatedly run their car over a child on a bike and point a shotgun at a baby. They even chase Melvin through a health club window into the vat of toxic waste, so the Toxic Avenger's gory revenge seems just. To heighten his moral standing, the Toxic Avenger saves those in distress, destroys corrupt politicians, and is rewarded with a beautiful blind girlfriend. The message here supports a community free of those who exploit the weak. The film's take on nature may seem less clear cut because toxic waste—an environmental pollutant—causes Melvin's transformation into the Toxic Avenger and a moral readjustment of Tromaville. Yet Nature seems to fight back in the Toxic Avenger films, since exploited-figure-turned-comic-hero Melvin destroys the power hungry.

The Class of Nuke 'Em High (1986) argues directly against leaving nuclear power plants unchecked by the EPA (Environmental Protection Association) and the NRC (Nuclear Regulatory Commission) in relation to the same Tromaville, New Jersey, setting found in *The Toxic Avenger*. As in *The Toxic Avenger*, the opening establishes the toxic environment both condemned and ridiculed by these Troma films, but this time the film seems to respond to contemporaneous nuclear disasters such as the 1979 Three Mile Island reactor meltdown in nearby Middletown, Pennsylvania. The film also brings to mind the 1986 Chernobyl explosion and the successful protests against the Shoreham Nuclear Power Plant from 1979 until a plan to decommission the plant was approved in 1989. Instead of taking a serious look at the dangers of nuclear power, as does *The China Syndrome* (1979) and *Silkwood* (1983), *The Class of Nuke 'Em High* plays eco-horror for laughs. School jock Warren (Gil Brenton) and his cheerleader girlfriend, Chrissy (Janelle Brady), are transformed by toxic "atomic" marijuana into comic eco-heroes who are perhaps less bumbling than Toxie.

Both *The Toxic Avenger* and *Class of Nuke 'Em High* films beg the question, what's so funny about environmental disasters? But they also point out a change of strategy—laughing about the environment and its degradation may not only stimulate awareness; that laughter might also point out a path toward change. In spite of their sometimes overpowering campy humor and horrifying violence, these Troma films show the consequences of disturbing a pristine ecosystem and offer a viable solution to greedy humans' exploitation of the natural world. They may clearly be what Derek Armstrong calls "horror comedies" (2002), but they may also serve as viable alternatives to the serious ecocinema of the 1970s and today.

This shift to eco-horror comedy occurs for at least three reasons. First of all the genre has come of age and can now be satirized through comic versions like *The Toxic Avenger* and *Class of Nuke 'Em High*. These films also exploit their cultural and historical contexts, making us laugh for different reasons and with differing results. These Troma films also reflect a movement from rugged individualism to a more communal approach to solving ecological problems, a change in the evolutionary narrative that reflects a movement from a tragic to a comic eco-hero. This evolutionary change also aligns with anthropological theories of laughter's origin. Examining *The Toxic Avenger* and *Class of Nuke 'Em High* movies in relation to theories gleaned from cultural studies, anthropology, and examinations of the comic eco-hero may also demonstrate the positive results possible when a genre comes of age: a raised awareness of the disastrous consequences of environmental degradation.

A Brief History of the Genre

The work of film critic Stephen Keane builds on Maurice Yacowar's historical and structural analysis of the disaster genre, providing both an overview of the history of the genre and an analysis of the social and cultural influences behind the genre's changes and fluctuating popularity. According to Keane, "disaster films are born out of times of impending crises" (2001, 7–8). Keane also foregrounds technological innovations as key to the spectacular events driving most disaster films from the 1890s forward. He argues, for example, that these technologies can also be drawn through the 1930s historical disaster cycle, again with the qualification that what might be so much engineering was fundamental to the resulting spectacle and subsequent commercial draw of these films. From Georges Melies's trick shots and stock footage of Vesuvius blowing its top to the full-size sets built and destroyed by D. W. Griffith and Cecil B. DeMille, the 1930s would see the full scope of earth, fire, wind, and water effects (11). John Ford's *The Hurricane* (1937) is representative of this period. Keane's work most closely examines what he calls "disaster dramas" (121) from the 1970s through 2000.

For Keane disaster films are serious. Yacowar, however, ends his list of disaster genre types with an extensive discussion of comic disaster films in which he delineates three subcategories of disaster comedies: films with "happy endings," films in which "the destruction can be extended into exuberant absurdity," and "parody" (1977, 282). This shift from serious disaster films to parody aligns with the shift we see in monstrous eco-disaster films from the 1950s to the present, a shift that moves these films into the comic realm and away from a "nature attacks" vision to one in which humans attack the natural world.

The Toxic Avenger and *Class of Nuke 'Em High* movies serve as monstrous eco-horror comedy films that illustrate both of these shifts. Ecological disaster melds well with comic plots and characters in the films. Together they serve as a call to eco-action and an indictment of unsafe disposal of toxic and radioactive waste. Geoff King explains how satire is comedy with a "political edge" (2002, 18). Parody, on the other hand, shifts comic motivation from "the social-political arena to that of film forms and conventions, although this distinction is far from always entirely clear" (2002, 18). As comedies these Troma films include elements grounded in both satire and parody, since they couch a political message in comedy, while also responding to particular film forms and conventions. Both of these Troma series interrogate extreme political corruption and end in communal revolts against state power and ritual destruction of Tromaville's leaders.

From another perspective, the films provide a space in which ecological problems that audience members are now aware of can be examined and scrutinized through campy humor that intensifies an environmental message while minimizing didactic and pedantic proselytizing that a more serious approach might foster. Keane argues that "camp involves the ironic appreciation of low, failed culture, and the parody of taste codes that rank cultural works as 'high' or 'low'" (2001, xiv). He suggests that "disaster movies are especially prone to unintentional camp for the way they juxtapose low, trivial pop culture sensationalism with the high and important fight for group survival and, in many cases, the endurance of the United States" (xiv). Because that camp is intentional in the Troma films, it becomes part of the comic view of the environment that both characters and audience members share.

Comic Eco-horror and the Comic Hero

These Troma films also respond to the heroic motifs of tragedy by comically constructing the characters of drama to serve both a comic purpose and a satirical premise and plot. In an eco-comedy, heroes with more than one tragic flaw replace the traditional tragic hero, according to Joseph W. Meeker's *The Comedy of Survival* (1997). Heroes in comedies tend to bumble and require a community of allies to succeed, as they do in *The Toxic Avenger* and its sequels, demonstrating the move from tragedy to comedy in eco-disaster films.

Meeting a disaster as a community separates eco-comedies from eco-tragedies. Only in 1950s science fiction classics like *Them!* do we see a matching of communal elements in both the human and the "ant" worlds—as is reflected by the Troma films. But *Them!* highlights no single hero, even a bumbling one. Instead, the community of scientists, politicians, police, and a well-prepared military work together to eliminate the foe their radiation has created. In serious dramatic and/or tragic eco-disaster films where a hero stands at the center, that hero takes on the characteristics of Meeker's tragic hero. *Land of the Dead* (2005), *Godzilla* (2014), and *Noah* (2014) include tragic heroes who adopt such roles.

As a way to define differences between the serious and the comic, Meeker begins with the premise that "literature is essentially an imitation of the actions of men" (1997, 155) but distinguishes between tragic and comic perspectives on these actions, concluding that the comic is "universal" because it "grows from the biological circumstances of life" (158). Tragedies like *Oedipus the King*, on the other hand, depend "upon particular ideologies or metaphysical circumstances" where the hero "takes his conflict [with nature, the gods, moral law, passionate love] seriously, and feels compelled to affirm his mastery and his greatness in the face of his own destruction" (157). See, for example, this section's *Land of the Dead* and the more recent *Noah*. In contrast a comic hero may be "weak, stupid, and undignified," but he "survives without [ideals]" (158).

Meeker claims that comedy reflects mature nature and its actors and "depicts the loss of equilibrium and its recovery" (1997, 159), demonstrating that humans "muddle through" without concern for "progress or perfection" (160). Once ecosystems mature, heroic solitary pioneers, the tragic heroes represented by *Land of the Dead*, *Godzilla*, and *Noah* become not only unnecessary but also subordinate to the group. In a mature or climax ecosystem, "it is the community itself that really matters, and it is likely to be an extremely durable community so long as balance is maintained among its many elements" (163).

Literary and film comedies offer a space in which to explore how humans might survive in a mature, climax ecosystem where the goal is survival of the community rather than "survival through the destruction of all our competitors and ... achieving effective dominance over other forms of life" (Meeker 1997, 162). Meeker states, "Civilization, at least in the West, has developed as a tragedy does, through the actions of pioneering leaders who break new ground and surmount huge obstacles" (162–63)—overcoming and/or subjugating other humans on the basis of religious and/or philosophical differences and destroying or exploiting other species for the good of their own.

Not only classic literature such as *Oedipus the King* but also nineteenth-century and contemporary fiction highlight this tragic view. Realist and Naturalist fiction by authors such as Jack London, Joseph Conrad, and Stephen Crane takes a serious look at nature, sometimes with natural elements serving as characters more powerful than their human contenders. Contemporary authors such as Carl Hiaasen and Sheri Tepper explore environmental issues from a tragic perspective in which heroes resist their destructive enemy no matter how horrific the results. Hiaasen's *Sick Puppy* and Tepper's *The Gate to Women's Country* illustrate this turn. Edward Abbey's *The Monkey Wrench Gang* asserts an outlaw approach to overcoming environmental issues—ecoterrorism.

Comedy, on the other hand, pokes fun at heroic intentions, demonstrating our heroes' flaws. Meeker mentions a revisionist look at *Oedipus*, but few literary and/or filmic works take a comic view of nature and environmentalism, except perhaps in fantasy and science fiction films so campy they become humorous, like *The Time Machine* (1960) or *The Day of the Triffids* (1963). Eco-film comedies, however, burgeoned from the late 1980s till the present, perhaps because they poke fun at extremists and provide a space where heroes like Melvin of *The Toxic Avenger* are so flawed they become nearly ineffective. These films have the potential to show us the positive consequences of placing the good of community above the individual—a climax ecosystem.

Anthropological Approaches to Humor and Laughter

A comic approach works because audiences both in and outside the film are aware of this communal need. This shared knowledge helps build community. For example, the Cretins of *Class of Nuke 'Em High*—former honor students mutating because of exposure to radioactive waste—become ridiculous as well as frightening because they are outside the human group. The communal, sometimes comic, attack reflects both an anthropological view of evolution like that Mahadev Apte describes in *Humor and Laughter: An Anthropological Approach* (1985), and the more literary view focusing on climax ecosystems and flawed heroes like those Meeker asserts emulate mature communities in the natural world. But more than anything, these Troma films provide a space in which we can laugh at monstrous nature, even those built on the technological innovations of the modern film industry, look at environmental catastrophe with a sense of humor and, perhaps, make changes that will serve both humans and the natural world best.

Apte's anthropological perspective specifically applies to our reading of these Troma films. As he argues, the reasons why humans laugh at comedy depend on biology, sociocultural perspectives, and, of most interest for our reading of these films, evolutionary change. According to Apte, "facial expressions acquired communicative functions during the evolutionary process" (1985, 242). Since laughter is chiefly a human expression of joy, it is said to come later in infants than smiling (248). Humans smile innately, but "the question of whether laughter is innate has not been satisfactorily answered" (249).

Multiple anthropological studies of the evolution of laughter inform our reading of *The Toxic Avenger* and *Class of Nuke 'Em High* movies. Humans gained the ability to laugh through evolutionary changes, according to Apte and more-recent anthropologists. As Apte explains, "The innate, involuntary smiling that occurs in infants right from birth becomes social smiling as a result of interaction with adults .... Laughter is generally more susceptible than smiling to restraint in accordance with socio-cultural norms of propriety because laughter has more apparent derogatory and aggressive connotations" (1985, 259–60). Smiling and laughter in humans, then, have become social acts performed in conjunction with acceptable stimuli and sociocultural contexts. Marina Devila Ross and her colleagues' 2009 study, "Reconstructing the Evolution of Laughter in Great Apes and Humans," advances Apte's assertions, demonstrating explicitly that "the evolutionary origins of human laughter can be traced back at least 10–16 million years to the last common ancestor of humans and modern great apes" (Ross, Owren, and Zimmermann 2009, 1109).

Other recent studies support and expand Apte's arguments. Matthew Gervais and David Sloan Wilson's 2005 article in the *Quarterly Review of Biology* declares, for example, that "laughter and humor were accorded high evolutionary significance by Darwin (1872) and have received increasing attention from biologists and psychologists during the last 30 years" (2005, 396). Gervais and Wilson argue for an interdisciplinary approach to the study of laughter's evolution in humans and hypothesize that different types of laughter should be distinguished "in terms of antecedent stimuli, emotional relevance, or physical characteristics" (2005, 400).

Gervais and Wilson define two types of laughter, non-Duchenne and Duchenne. Non-Duchenne laughter is defined as "spontaneous conversational laughter that occurs in the absence of attempts at humor" (2005, 401). It tends to serve conversational purposes such as appeasement, aggression, and derision, rather than resulting from emotional experience. Duchenne laughter, on the other hand, is humor-driven and emerged "during the fleeting periods of safety and satiation that characterized early bipedal life." Duchenne laughter responds to humorous emotional experiences possible during these times of safety. As Gervais and Wilson assert, "a generalized class of non-serious social incongruity would have been a reliable indicator of such safe times and thereby come to be a potent distal elicitor of laughter and playful emotion." Gervais and Wilson's arguments align well with Yacowar's claims that "a genre comes of age when its conventions are well known to be played for laughs in parody" (1977, 283).

Cultural Context and Comic Eco-Horror

The power of comedy to do more than induce laughter and look at issues with a sense of humor is clear, especially within the context of *The Toxic Avenger* and *Class of Nuke 'Em High* movies, where an environmental message is heightened by the film's absurd camp. Comedic films are a complex form of cultural expression, which have a history of both perpetuating the social order and attempting to subvert it. Comedies are a way to demonstrate the absurdity of society's problems and hypocrisies.

Even though President Ronald Reagan was in office for much of the 1980s, from the 80s through the early years of the twenty-first century, eco-disasters served as fodder for comedy because audiences knew enough about the issue to laugh about it. Comic films make fun of issues that audiences understand, and those issues change as times and audiences change. By the 1980s problems associated with environmental disasters seemed old hat. The 1979 Three Mile Island accident and the 1986 Chernobyl disaster awakened people to the horrors of nuclear catastrophes. Gas was unleaded, catalytic converters on cars were mandatory, recycling was on the rise around the country, ozone depletion was being addressed, and new EPA controls were firmly in place. Film audiences no longer needed to be warned or taught about environmental problems, and they already had institutions in place that took the issue seriously, so some films highlighting environmental problems took a comic turn. *The Toxic Avenger* and *Class of Nuke 'Em High* films respond to these environmental crises, as well as the unique context of industrial New Jersey, with comedy rather than serious and perhaps didactic appraisals of modernism.

What these eco-comedies show us is a change in cultural context, a change in audience expectations, and a change in genre focus for presenting significant ecological problems and possible solutions to them. An overview of previously broached psychoanalytic readings of humor and laughter provides another context for our reading of these films. The power of laughter as a coping and teaching tool increases as awareness, and the apathy it sometimes causes, intensifies. John Cleese suggests, in a conversation with psychoanalyst Jennifer Johns, that comedy "frees people up to have new thoughts" (1994). At the same time, however, Freud argues that jokes are part of a "social process" (1963, 171), in which audience members must comprehend the joke's context. According to Freud, "jokes are the most social of mental functions with a requisite condition of intelligibility" (179). Jokes are meant for an audience that understands the punch line, so they build community (and are built on it) and don't work without awareness—understanding.

Comedy can easily be seen as a cultural force. Film comedies can also be an effective way of commenting on aspects of society, examining hypocrisies and how absurd they are. Some may seek to deal with the painful aspects of life in such a way that the humor not readily apparent in such things as Nazism or racism is used to diffuse the horror surrounding it. Kaminsky notes that in the remake of Ernst Lubitsch's *To Be or Not to Be* (1983), for example, Mel Brooks "has attempted to retain the comic persona against the serious background of a social issue, fascism" (168) because "the vision of struggle might not be accepted by audiences without the performer's comic persona" (168).

These Troma films provide a space in which ecological problems that audience members now know about (as part of their own current sociocultural contexts) can be examined and scrutinized. They can be laughed at—as a community—when illustrated through campy humor that intensifies an environmental message while minimizing didactic and pedantic proselytizing that a more serious approach might foster. A comic approach works because of this awareness, and the shared knowledge helps build community, even as the films' monsters become ridiculous rather than frightening. When the audience sees these attacks as comic, and the film's community fights back as a collective, two theories are on display: both an anthropological view of evolution like that Apte describes and a more literary view focusing on climax ecosystems and flawed heroes like those Meeker asserts emulate mature communities in the natural world.

In these comic eco-horror films, comic heroes start out as underdogs and then, through something like a toxic waste accident, become superheroes who fight injustice with no way back into a distrustful community. Michael Herz and Lloyd Kaufman's *The Toxic Avenger* 1–4 and *Class of Nuke 'Em High* 1–3 highlight blatant environmental messages—against toxic waste dumping and uncontrolled nuclear energy—with comic results. Both series of films foreground nerds that are transformed by toxic waste—one becomes a superhero (*The Toxic Avenger*) but the others, in *Class of Nuke 'Em High*, serve only as comic relief. Both film series draw from the historical and cultural events of the late 1980s and beyond and hyperbolize an industrialized (New Jersey) setting.

The Toxic Avenger: An Unlikely Comic Hero

The first of these Troma Studio films, *The Toxic Avenger,* came out in 1984, at a time when the Rust Belt was growing even rustier, and industrial values were being questioned. Instead of intensifying such a negative mood, the Troma films took a comic approach to toxic waste dumping and nuclear radiation spilling that seemed inevitable in urban industrial centers, especially, perhaps, in New Jersey. Appearing just a few years after the Carter administration relocated seven hundred families from the Love Canal area of Niagara Falls because of exposure to toxic waste, *The Toxic Avenger* is a product of its period. According to the 2012 New Jersey Office of Science's Environmental Trends Report *Solid Waste and Recycling,* during the 1970s and 1980s, "New Jersey received large amounts of waste from other states; it is estimated that more than 12 million tons of waste per year, much of it from New York and Pennsylvania, were deposited in New Jersey." Many of these toxic waste dumps were designated as Superfund sites beginning in 1980, but as of 2014, there were approximately 230 New Jersey Superfund sites listed on the EPA Superfund website. *The Toxic Avenger* setting illustrates the possible consequences of unregulated and uncontrolled dumping.

The opening of *The Toxic Avenger* illustrates the horrors of the film's New Jersey setting both visually and in its narration. The narrator explains that industrial advancement has "a price to pay—pollution," and scenes of garbage-strewn streets and toxic waste dumps reinforce the claim. Tromaville proudly announces itself as the Toxic Chemical Capital of the World on its city sign. The opening is juxtaposed with scenes of the Tromaville Health Club, where our comic hero is introduced. Melvin is a mop boy who is harassed daily by a small group of cruel male and female bullies. Melvin's transformation into the Toxic Avenger first establishes him as a tragic hero working as an individual "pioneer," as Meeker explains. But when the blind Sarah befriends him, accepting him despite his mutated face and body, Melvin and the Toxic Avenger he has become transform into a comic hero who places the good of the community (and a climax ecosystem) above the individual.

Early in the film, the Toxic Avenger acts more like a tragic than a comic hero. He secretly attacks Tromaville's criminals, including the jocks who terrorized him in the health club. He first saves the life of an honest police officer O'Clancy (Dick Martinson) by fighting off Cigar Face (Dan Snow) and his gang. At a Mexican restaurant he fights off Frank (Larry Sultan) and his gang. Although he connects with Sarah after the fight, taking her back to her apartment because the gang has shot her guide dog, the Toxic Avenger continues his lonely quest until he and Sarah leave their toxic-dump home for a vacation at Miller's Farm, a "wilderness" haven outside Tromaville where they live in a tent rather than a dump. Ultimately he attacks his four perpetrators one by one, revealing the corrupt political machine supporting them, including Mayor Peter Belgoody (Pat Ryan), who leads a group of corrupt neo-Nazi police officers in a drug ring centered at the health club.

The Toxic Avenger transforms into a comic hero when he believes he has killed an innocent woman and leaves Tromaville in shame. He and Sarah retreat to Miller's Farm, but Toxie's heroic acts have fostered community support that ultimately brings him back. When Mayor Belgoody calls in the National Guard to destroy the Toxic Avenger, the townspeople revolt, surrounding Toxie's tent and shouting for justice. Some wear their "I heart the monster" T-shirts. Even the National Guard captain (uncredited) and his men refuse to fire, stopping their tanks and trucks. When the mayor shoots the Toxic Avenger multiple times without injuring him, Toxie kills the mayor. But the town supports Toxie now, so much so that when he tells Officer O'Clancy to "take care of this toxic waste," turning the mayor's body over to him, O'Clancy complies and the crowd applauds. In *The Toxic Avenger* the comic hero builds a community that might also clean up the literal toxic waste that created the monster.

The focus on comic evolution in *The Toxic Avenger* also highlights how the eco-horror genre has "come of age," perhaps also suggesting the shared knowledge of ecological issues provides the kind of safety Gervais and Wilson describe. American film comedies highlighting environmental problems have been around since at least 1952, when Robert Wise directed *Something for the Birds*, a satire targeting lobbyists—one working on behalf of preservation of the California condor (Patricia Neal), and the other for oil interests threatening the birds' sanctuary (Victor Mature). But until *The Toxic Avenger*, few films took a comic look at eco-horror with a human cause. Stephen Holden of the *New York Times* suggests that the film has "a maniacally farcical sense of humor" and points to the ingenious (and ridiculous) ways Toxie destroys the criminals of Tromaville: "One is dry-cleaned to death, another made into a pizza, a third partly French-fried." Holden also asserts that the film "ridicules all movies that sentimentalize the love between the ugly and the blind" and illustrates this claim with a scene in which Sarah "hands her true love an overstuffed sandwich fizzing with Easy-Off and sprinkled with Drano" (1986).

These scenes foreground both the Toxic Avenger's role as comic eco-hero and the toxic community from which he sprang. Although Toxie's toxic origin somewhat dilutes its environmental message, the film's campy humor also intensifies its environmental message. When we cheer for the Toxic Avenger along with the community at the film's end, we also applaud his efforts to clean up a corrupt society that has turned Tromaville into a dump.

The Toxic Avenger Part II (1989) and *The Toxic Avenger Part III: The Last Temptation of Toxie* (1989) more blatantly address environmental consequences of corporate corruption while still drawing on the elements of the comic eco-hero Meeker describes. In *Part II* Toxie (Ron Fazio) thwarts an evil corporation appropriately named Apocalypse Inc. In *Part III* Toxie (Ron Fazio) joins the corporation to finance eye surgery for his blind girlfriend, Claire (Phoebe Legere). In both films Toxie defeats the Apocalypse Inc. chairman (Rick Collins) and the toxic chemical industries that the chairman and his company bring into Tromaville.

In *The Toxic Avenger Part II*, the environmental conflicts arise because Toxie must cope with the sense of loss he feels after cleaning up Tromaville. In his opening narration Toxie explains how Tromaville has become a nice place to live without criminals and oppressive politicians. Instead, citizens dance in the street, manufacture orange juice, exterminate vermin, and watch excellent movies. Out of work as a superhero and cleaning toilets at Claire's Center for the Blind, however, Toxie becomes depressed. The only cure seems to be fighting off Apocalypse Inc. henchmen attempting to kill Toxie and bring their toxic chemical storage facilities to Tromaville. And the only way Apocalypse will succeed is if Toxie is destroyed. As the company's chairman declares, "Without Tromaville, we'll never take New York." The only way to destroy Toxie is to turn him back into Melvin (Toxie's pre–toxic waste persona) with an "antitromatron" weapon. Then he'll be easy to kill. To connect Toxie with the weapon, Apocalypse bribes his psychiatrist (Erika Schickel), so she convinces Toxie that the only cure for his depression is reconnecting with a father (Rikiya Yasuoka) who she says now lives in Tokyo.

The environmental messages in the film become more blatant after Toxie leaves for Japan. While Toxie looks for his father in Tokyo, Apocalypse Inc. takes over Tromaville, spreading chemical pollution by changing an orange juice plant to an Agent Orange factory and building chemical plants producing fluorocarbons in a bird sanctuary and DDT in the city park. Ultimately Toxie discovers his father is actually a drug smuggler and annihilates him despite being hit by the "antitromatron weapon." After some quick rehabilitation at a sumo wrestling center, Toxie returns to Tromaville and saves it from Apocalypse Inc. As in *The Toxic Avenger*, Toxie serves as a comic eco-hero who succeeds only with help from a community that includes blind girlfriend Claire and two senior citizens (Bill Ferris and Irene Scase Summerville).

The Toxic Avenger Part III: The Last Temptation of Toxie continues the story begun in *Part II*. In fact directors Michael Herz and Lloyd Kaufman cut *Part II* in half because it was more than four hours long. In *Part III* Toxie becomes a spokesperson for a company he only learns later is Apocalypse Inc., so he can earn money for a surgical procedure to restore Claire's eyesight, even though she tells him, "I look at it this way. I'll never have to see ugliness or poverty or war or the Chevrolet Nova." In this third installment Toxie uses his sumo wrestling moves to defeat the Apocalypse Inc. chairman once it is revealed that he is actually the devil. With a nod toward Faust, the film examines levels of hell, but it maintains its comic bent by integrating outrageous sumo moves and ending with an unlikely marriage between a now-sighted Claire and her toxic fiancé.

In the most recent *Citizen Toxie: The Toxic Avenger IV* (2000), however, the environmental message is broached only during a scene recalling Melvin's fall into the vat of toxic waste. In part 4 an explosion in a school for the "very special" sends the Toxic Avenger (David Mattey) over to an alternate Troma universe, Amortville, and replaces him with his doppelganger, Noxie (also David Mattey). For most of the film, Toxie fights off the evil versions of Troma's superheroes, so he can return home to Tromaville and his beloved Sarah (Heidi Sjursen). Toxie successfully defeats Noxie and saves Tromaville from the corrupt "Nazi" police "captain" and the diaper gang he leads. The film concludes with a long duke-out between Noxie and Toxie and their soon-to-be born offspring. The most relevant eco-comic scene, however, comes after this when evil Melvin (Mark Torgi) emerges from Noxie's now-annihilated body and, as in the original *Toxic Avenger*, runs through a window into a vat of toxic waste. The scene is literally spliced from the first film and reminds viewers of the series' comic eco-horror origins.

The Class of Nuke 'Em High and Radioactive Laughter

To reinforce its radioactive Tromaville setting, *The Class of Nuke 'Em High* opens with a pan from the New York City skyline to the New Jersey side of the Hudson with chemical plants replacing skyscrapers. This opening shot dissolves to a nuclear power plant, "Tromaville Nuclear Utility," where, according to Vincent Canby of the *New York Times*, "drain pipes . . . look as if they'd been stolen from the House of the Seven Gables" (1986). Signs announce dangers everywhere in and outside the plant—"Radioactive waste," "Toxic Waste," "SPILL!" And then an alarm announces real danger right before a shot of another sign, emphasized with a smiley face—"We're part of the Nuclear Generation!" These signs seem like hyperbole until plant manager Mr. Finley (Pat Ryan) corroborates the alarm siren, exclaiming, "This plant will be here long after most of you are gone" to his workers and refusing to shut down because then the EPA, the NRC, and the PTA would investigate, especially since the plant sits right next door to Tromaville's high school.

These opening scenes recall the successful protests citizens led to decommission Long Island's Shoreham Nuclear Power Plant. They also set the stage for a comedy that points out the dangers of radiation and toxic-waste leakage through a campy spoof of both nuclear plant mismanagement and high school cliques of the 1980s. Green toxic waste oozes into the Tromaville High School and out of its drinking fountains. A nerd drinks green ooze and mutates instantaneously to his death. Former honor society students have already transformed into "Cretins" after they smoke "atomic pot" infected with nuclear waste. The movie's heroes, Chrissy (a cheerleader) and Warren (the star athlete), mutate after smoking the same laced pot—Warren goes in and out of a macho man persona, but Chrissy somehow becomes impregnated with a mutant monster salamander she births into a toilet.

Campy and over-the-top humor overpowers the plot, but the film still carries a community-minded environmental message.

In *Class of Nuke 'Em High*, the exploitive villains are the Cretins and nuclear plant manager Mr. Finley, who sets all the conflict into motion. Warren (and perhaps Chrissy's salamander monster) serves as the comic eco-hero necessary for a balanced community. The Cretins are a gang of anarchic mutants who try and fail to take over the school and the town of Tromaville. Because Warren protects the "nerds" in the school and fights back, the gang sees him as its enemy and captures Chrissy to lure him in for an attack. But Warren and Chrissy's offspring, now a huge toxic monster, saves the town and the rest of the students. The monster kills gang members and their leader while the rest of the students wait outside during a false radiation drill initiated by the Cretins. Warren too fights the Cretins, while fleeing from the toxic monster.

Ultimately, when the monster ensnares Chrissy, Warren shoots it with a laser in the science lab, blowing it up and cleansing the school. Chrissy and Warren escape, but the Cretins and Mr. Finley die in the explosion. We see one more sign after the explosion—"Tromaville High School will be temporarily closed for remodeling"—but Warren and Chrissy's kisses in the midst of cheering students and blaring fire trucks end the film, while a 1980s new wave song about nuclear waste plays in the background. All seems well, but the monster fish baby miraculously survives, and the nuclear power plant is still there, so this comedy, because of its sequels, does not provide community equilibrium. Still the high school seems to be back to normal, with the mutants destroyed and only the usual gangs and cliques remaining. This comic eco-horror film provides a temporary sense of balance with help from its comic eco-hero team.

Class of Nuke 'Em High Part 2: Sub-Humanoid Meltdown (1991) takes the first film's premise into a community college setting. Again set in Tromaville, New Jersey, the second installment in the series begins with a recap of the first film and a reference to the 1986 Chernobyl nuclear power plant disaster. According to the film's narrator, the experience in Chernobyl parallels that in Tromaville, where "students mutated and transmortified and worse. It caused them to dance badly when the Smithereens showed up." As the narrator explains, "Tromaville High became Nuke 'Em High and had to be destroyed." In the sequel the owners of the Nukamamma corporation's Tromaville Nuclear Power Facility built a junior college, Tromaville Institute of Technology (TIT), between its cooling towers to atone for the 1986 meltdown.

The film's plot at first seems less critical of nuclear power than the original film with its focus on the college's ace reporter Roger Smith (Brick Bronsky) and his search for love. When he becomes romantically involved with a so-called subhumanoid named Victoria (Leesa Rowland), however, at least two nuclear-powered subplots emerge: the creation of subhumanoids like Victoria from radioactive injections and the accidental creation of giant squirrels from nuclear waste. Roger's love for Victoria also transforms him into a bumbling comic eco-hero who, unlike Warren and Chrissy, successfully establishes a more balanced community in Tromaville.

The subhumanoids are the brainchild of resident genetic scientist Professor Holt (Lisa Gaye). These subhumanoids are genetically created humanoids who fully mature within nine months to perform the manual labor real humans reject. Initially the subhumanoids assimilate into the college's student population, usually as bully members of the "Squirrel" gang, but the new life forms are unstable and go into meltdown quickly, secreting green slime and transforming into furry green football-sized creatures. Roger and Holt also become aware of Dean Okra's (Scott Resnick) plan to turn all the subhumanoids into slaves.

The actual squirrels first serve as a way to break up the odd scenes in TIT. Shots of a red squirrel scurrying in a grassy field offset sexist images of female students in bikinis and leather. But these shots also connect the "Squirrel" gang with the real rodents when the actual squirrels find and eat radioactive waste from a discarded cooler and transform into giant monsters. Only Holt's antidote and Roger's love for Victoria can save the subhumanoids from inevitable meltdown syndrome.

The green creatures the subhumanoids become join Roger and help destroy the dean as well. A giant nut serves as a decoy to lead the squirrels away from the nuclear reactor. The antidote for meltdown syndrome brings humans and subhumanoids together, "with liberty and charge cards for all." Although its critique of the dangers of nuclear waste is diluted by blatant exploitation of women's bodies and a confusing ending, *Class of Nuke 'Em*

High 2 maintains its focus on the horrific (and sometimes comic) repercussions of environmental degradation with help from Roger's bumbling attempts at eco-heroism. In *Class of Nuke 'Em High Part 3: The Good, the Bad, and the Subhumanoid*, Roger's story continues from the perspective of his twin sons, Adlai and Dick (Brick Bronsky). Dick is raised as a thug by the evil Dr. Slag (John Tallman), so it is up to Adlai to save Tromaville from Dr. Slag's plan to turn the town into a toxic wasteland.

The most recent installment of this franchise, *Return to Nuke 'Em High Volume I* (2013) reboots the first *Nuke 'Em High* film to celebrate the Troma Studios' fortieth anniversary. Rather than adding a sequel to the series, *Return to Nuke 'Em High* amplifies the exploitation elements found in the earlier version. As *New York Post* reviewer Lou Luminick explains, "The nuclear plant from the earlier films, including 1991's *Class of Nuke 'Em High Part 2*, has been turned into an organic food factory whose products cause eruptions of lots of green slime from the orifices of its customers. But mostly, *Return to Nuke 'Em High* is an occasionally hilarious series of parodies: *Carrie, Soylent Green, Glee, Cat Ballou*, you name it" (2014).

Return to Class of Nuke 'Em High and *Citizen Toxie: The Toxic Avenger IV* point to a change in historical and cultural context and, perhaps, in the evolutionary narrative informing comic horror film. From the 1984 *Toxic Avenger* until at least 2003, eco-comedy films gained popularity not only in animated films but also in live-action adult comedies such as *Arachnophobia* (1990), *The Freshman* (1990), *Men at Work.* (1990), *Naked Gun 2½* (1991), *Eight Legged Freaks* (2002), and *Crocodile Hunter* (2003). Except in animated features such as WALL-E and the occasional spoof such as *Tucker and Dale vs. Evil* (2010), since *The Day after Tomorrow* (2004) ecocinema has again taken a serious turn. Responding to new horrors associated with climate change, recent eco-horror takes viewers back to the 1970s, perhaps because this new environmental threat seems unbeatable. Whether humanity or the natural world will survive seems unclear in tragic eco-horror films such as *The Bay* or *Land of the Dead*.

Comic eco-horror films, on the other hand, show us compromises, with the human community prospering (not just its pioneers) and the natural world surviving (or at least saved from certain death from toxic chemicals).

In *The Toxic Avenger*, for example, Tromaville gains some relief from vicious sociopathic jocks and corrupt politicians and police officers, and Toxic and Sarah find happiness in a tent outside their waste-dump home. In *The Class of Nuke 'Em High*, the relief from toxic waste and radiation poisoning is more obvious when a noxious monster explodes when hit with a laser and destroys the toxic school.

Eco-comedy films of the 1980s, 1990s, and early years of the twenty-first century grew out of the environmental movements that came before them. The year 1970 served as a turning point for environmental programs and services and agencies like the EPA. In the 1970s, however, filmic representations of environmental problems were much more earnest and intense, since the environment and its exploitation were taken seriously at local, state, and federal levels of government. Even science fiction films of the period such as *Silent Running* (1972) and *Soylent Green* (1973) were serious fare.

Environmentalism seemed more like an "ivory tower" issue, taken seriously only by left-leaning actors like Robert Redford and conservatives like Clint Eastwood, who had no financial or survival concerns to challenge their belief in environmental protections. Redford's *Milagro Beanfield War* (1988) and *A River Runs through It* (1992) and Eastwood's *The Outlaw Josey Wales* (1976) and *Pale Rider* (1985) highlight these actor-directors' shared environmental concerns. Environmentalists seemed laughable to people in the mainstream who could not afford to luxuriate in the ideals of the Sierra Club. Working-class people of the 1980s were more concerned with loss of jobs and lack of support for themselves and their families than with protecting and/or nurturing nature.

By the late 1980s, however, film audiences no longer needed to be warned about environmental problems, it seemed, since the United States already had institutions in place to tackle the issue. After the fall of the USSR in 1989, Americans also felt no threat of a nuclear holocaust. It may be that American film audiences grew complacent about eco-disasters and bored with serious discussions about environmental issues. Media representations of environmentalists as "granola eaters" and "Birkenstock Bourgeoisie" may have made it easier to laugh at environmental problems—the context for environmentally conscious films changed in the 1980s and so did audience reactions to environmental issues. Perhaps, as Gervais and Wilson explain,

Class of Nuke 'Em High: Honors students transform into toxic Cretins.

this laughter emerged "during the fleeting periods of safety and satiation" in the United States after the end of the Cold War.

The cultural and historical context of the period seems to have made it possible to laugh at the environment—to find a way to represent environmental concerns in comic ways. But the translation of that comedy into a different view of the hero—a more communal and interdependent one—may be how these eco-comedies actually communicate important messages about the environment. Environmental exploitation served as fodder for comedy because audiences know enough about it to find it funny. Comic films make fun of issues that audiences understand, and those issues change as times and audiences change. With Earth Day far behind us, and eco-solutions under debate, comic eco-horror and the comic eco-hero thrived. In the early years of the twenty-first century, comic eco-narratives will return when we feel safe enough to laugh.

Poisoned Waters: Industrial farming sometimes has monstrous results.

7

Parasite Evolution in the Eco-horror Film

When the Host Becomes the Monster

Comic eco-narratives are not the only evolutionary paths present in contemporary films. Tragic eco-narratives are the driving force in most monstrous-nature films. This evolutionary view is most evident in films highlighting humanity's creation of deadly natural monsters like the parasite. While biologists would agree that parasites are a necessary part of our biosphere, the general public tends to view parasites as complicated, dangerous, and deadly. Animal Planet's *Monsters inside Me* presents parasites not only as monstrous but also as deadly invaders. Here parasites do not merely obtain nourishment and shelter from another organism. These living predators destroy their hosts surreptitiously like shadowy monsters eating their way out of their human hosts.

In the first episode, for example, three disparate cases of parasite infestation are examined: a baby boy gets infected with a species of roundworms that causes him to sleep excessively, lose his balance and vision, and, ultimately, lose his cognitive ability. Forty years after being infected and returning from the

Vietnam War, a veteran must cope with another type of roundworm spread by mosquitos that causes potentially fatal swelling and leaking from his legs. And a young man gets the long, slim *schistosoma mansoni* flukes in his brain, causing violent dizziness and nausea. Each segment of the episode turns the illness and diagnosis into documentary horror with extreme close-ups of each patient's infection and of the parasite infecting them (sometimes magnified thousands of times), as well as a frightening voice-over and soundtrack to heighten the spectacle.

Despite the monstrous images on display, however, the parasites high-lighted in the series are based on authentic biology. They survive sometimes for decades in their hosts, obtaining nourishment from them over the long run rather than destroying them immediately. Likewise, most of the patients showcased in the series recover from their infections, despite what may be years of suffering and years in which their respective parasites lie dormant, waiting for the appropriate time to reproduce and spread. Although para-sites harm their hosts, it is in the parasite's best interest not to kill the host because it relies on the host's body and body functions, such as digestion or blood circulation, to live. In fact, *The Monsters inside Me* demonstrates that typically a parasite and its host evolve together. In a biotic community like that depicted in this series, parasites adapt to their environment by living in and using hosts in ways that harm without killing them, at least immediately. And hosts develop ways of getting rid of or protecting themselves from the parasites infecting them.

But what if that biotic community were disrupted by the activity of the human hosts to which various parasites cling? *The Monsters inside Me* turns parasites into monsters using conventions of the horror film. But eco-horror documentaries such as *Frontline*'s *Poisoned Waters* (2009) and feature films such as *The Thaw* (2009), *The Bay* (2012), and *Upstream Color* (2013) explore how parasites transform into deadly beasts not because the camera or soundtrack amplifies their horror but because their environment has become toxic. The films seem to respond to parasitologists Daniel R. Brooks and Eric P. Hoberg's assertion: "More recent human activities associated with the evo-lution of agriculture, domesticated livestock, urbanization, and now global climate change have served to broaden the arena and disseminated the risk for Emerging Infectious Diseases (EID) on a global scale" (2007, 572). Representations of parasites in eco-horror films explore this broadening arena.

With the same investment in authentic science found in *The Monsters inside Me, Poisoned Waters* and *The Bay* especially show us the real horror behind parasite evolution: the environmentally destructive behaviors of the human host. *Poisoned Waters* establishes the narrative for *The Bay*, the docudrama that utilizes similar information revealed in the former film. Although *Poisoned Waters* examines how toxic both Chesapeake Bay and Puget Sound have become, *The Bay* responds explicitly to the first segment of the documentary and its Chesapeake Bay focus. According to the documentary's narrator, the Chesapeake Bay is the canary in the coal mine reacting negatively to toxins entering its waters. *Poisoned Waters* also draws on current scientific research and blames agricultural runoff and industrial waste for the polluted bay waters and mutated parasites threatening animals and humans. *Poisoned Waters* also draws on nostalgia as a reason to solve the eco-problem that the Chesapeake Bay has become, strategies also applied to the documentary's exploration of the perilous conditions new sources of contamination have brought to estuaries on the East and West Coasts of the United States.

As an eco-horror thriller film shot in the "found footage" documentary style, Barry Levinson's *The Bay* explores similar scientific evidence documented in *Poisoned Waters* by telling the story of a small Chesapeake Bay town suffering a catastrophic onslaught of water-borne parasites. The parasites turn enormous and deadly when chemical runoff from area chicken farms and radiation released from a nuclear power plant cause them to mutate. The rapidly evolving parasites infest both sea life and human hosts and, within the course of one Fourth of July, kill hundreds of townspeople.

The Bay transforms the research documented in *Frontline*'s *Poisoned Waters* into an audience-friendly genre film. Using a "found footage" approach like that in *The Blair Witch Project* (1999) and *Paranormal Activity* (2007), Levinson provides an intimate portrait of eco-horror based on current technology and the science of parasite evolution. In order to preserve the Chesapeake Bay as a source of recreation and sustenance, both *The Bay* and *Poisoned Waters* argue that we must address the environmental disasters and infectious monsters that our own destructive behaviors have created.

Parasites and Evolution: A Brief Overview

Without the exposure to toxins like those spilled into the Chesapeake Bay, parasites and their hosts primarily evolve together as part of an interdependent biotic community. To illustrate the interdependent relationships that hosts and parasites may share, Claude Combes's *The Art of Being a Parasite* (2005) defines and illustrates the multiple levels of parasitism. Combes differentiates those parasites that feed off a host without benefiting it from two other types: commensals and mutualists. Commensals live on or within another organism without harming or benefiting the host. Mutualists, on the other hand, help their hosts. According to Combes, "Mutualism differs from parasitism in only one way: instead of one partner in the association exploiting the other without reciprocity, in mutualism each partner exploits the other" (145). Orchids are an apt example because to extract pollen from orchids, moths must have a long proboscis. As Combes explains, "The long spur has a selective advantage in the orchid population, and the trait long proboscis has a selective advantage in the moth population" (145). As with some parasites and their hosts, orchids and moths have evolved mutually, deriving benefits interdependently.

Although he emphasizes the interdependent relationships shared by parasites and their partner hosts, Combes debunks notions of mutualism that romanticize nature. Instead, parasites are part of a biotic community in which producers and consumers interact interdependently, surviving in relation to a food web that includes both life and death. Combes declares that "some examples of mutualism ... can lead one to believe in the evolution of [the] sort of harmony" found in films such as *Snow White* (1937) and *Bambi* (1942).... However, one can also "defend the diametrically opposite viewpoint, that harmony is nothing but an illusion: everyone knows perfectly well that spiders chase innocent insects in the understory and on the ground, that snakes smother little rodents, and that foxes eat birds" (2005, 147). Despite this skepticism, Combes notes that mutualism may have led to three important advances: "the colonization of certain inhospitable environments, an increase in biodiversity, and the tremendous proliferation of certain groups in the course of evolution" (148).

Rather than nurturing every other living thing, parasites serve a role in a food web that includes both producers and consumers. They sometimes share a symbiotic relationship with a partner host as a mutualist; they sometimes exploit it without causing harm as a commensal, and they sometimes cause harm and even death as a parasite. Parasites also primarily evolve from free-living ancestors in three stages, according to Combes. They first live "near the surface of the host" but feed not on the host but on part of its food. In a second stage the parasite may "take its food directly from the surface or innards of the host." And last, in "a more pronounced step in the evolution of parasitism," the parasite may "bury itself in the host, or at least anchor itself very firmly in the host's body" (2005, 25).

In turn hosts evolve various ways to combat parasites. They may avoid them, but they may also either expel or build immunity toward them. Combes illustrates this second line of defense in a study of blue tit parents and their chicks that reveals, "in response to parasitism by fleas" the parents "do not merely give more food to their chicks . . . . It seems they can also transmit 'immunological weapons' to them" (2005, 114). Human hosts fight parasitic and infectious diseases not only through the evolution of their immune systems but also through scientific progress made possible with the evolution of the human brain.

Shane Carruth's independent science fiction film *Upstream Color* (2013) explores such notions of parasitism in a world in which parasites that feed off orchids are used to control human behavior. Once ingested by humans the parasite multiplies and achieves two functions: absorbing their hosts' consciousness and making them highly susceptible to hypnotic suggestion. In the unsettling opening act of the film, Kris (Amy Seimetz) is attacked in a parking lot and forced to ingest this parasitic bug that makes its way into her bloodstream. Once the bug starts to take effect on Kris's consciousness, her assailant, The Thief (Thiago Martins), lures Kris into a deep hypnotic trance and forces her to withdraw all her money. After The Thief has finished stealing Kris's money, another ominous man, The Sampler (Andrew Sensenig), removes the parasite from her body and implants it into a piglet. According to Carruth, the idea was partly inspired by real-life parasites that have been documented for their ability to control the behavior of other entities. "There are these parasites that burrow into the heads of wasps and ants and make them fly erratically or climb to the top of trees and throw themselves off in order to benefit from something else, maybe a fungus on the forest floor," he told *Indiewire* (quoted in Kohn 2013). In the film, however, the parasites are removed from their human victims and implanted in nonhuman pig hosts who cannot be manipulated by the slugs, signifying how scientific progress (at least in this science fiction setting) may conquer infectious parasites.

Parasites in the Science Fiction Horror Film:
Weapons for and against Humanity

Unlike films such as *Upstream Color*, most parasite movies take a Big Bug approach to their subject. Although films as early as Winsor McCay's animated short *How a Mosquito Operates* (1912) address parasites, the vast majority of these films merge science fiction with horror, highlighting parasite attacks from (or in) outer space. The remakes of *The Thing* (1982, 2011), for example, center on an alien parasite that causes its canine and human hosts to mutate once they are infected. The original *Thing from Another World* (1951) cements the remakes' connection to the Big Bug movie phenomenon of the 1950s and 1960s, since it serves as a response to the Cold War Red Scare and a warning against the horrors of possible alien invaders from the USSR and beyond. Don Siegel's *Invasion of the Body Snatchers* (1956) even more explicitly addresses the Red scare, and its remakes (1978 and 1993) highlight our continuing fear of alien invasions. Although invading from the center of the Earth rather than outer space, the parasites in *The Brain Eaters* (1958) parallel these same fears.

Other parasite films from the 1980s and 1990s offer a comic approach to such alien invasions, as do *Star Trek 2: The Wrath of Khan* (1982), *Night of the Creeps* (1986), and *Men in Black* (1997) (and its sequels). This comic turn continues with *Slither* (2006). Fear of aliens invading our bodies and worlds is renewed in the 1990s and early years of the twenty-first century with films such as *The Puppet Masters* (1994), *The Faculty* (1998), *Dreamcatcher* (2003), *Splinter* (2008), and *Cloverfield* (2008). But parasite science fiction horror reached its apex with *Alien* (1979) and most of its sequels (*Aliens* [1986], *Alien 3* [1992], and *Alien: Resurrection* [1997]). The recent prequel *Prometheus* (2012) explores the source of this alien parasite even more extensively.

Despite these *Alien* films' focus on transforming an extraterrestrial parasite into a powerful weapon, research on the films chiefly responds to the so-called feminist message of the films and their protagonist, Ripley (Sigourney Weaver). James H. Kavanagh asserts, for example, that the "death of the alien, as *Alien* has it, is the triumphant rebirth of humanism, disguised as a powerful, progressive, and justifying feminism" (1980, 91). According to Linda K. Bundtzen, on the other hand, "*Aliens* ... is a profoundly disturbing allegory about contemporary feminism, and it is far from resolving the issues it explores about woman's nature vs. her culture-making aspirations" (1987, 11).

A few parasites seem to be supernatural, as in *The Puppet Master* (1989), *Slither* (2006), and *The Ruins* (2008), but more science fiction horror films illustrate the multiple ways humans may create parasites, deliberately or through various types of eco-disasters. The futuristic camp horror film *Parasite* (1981) centers on lab parasites created by researcher Dr. Paul Dean (Robert Glaudini) as weapons so deadly they must be destroyed. As a William Castle thriller, *The Tingler* (1959) is most famous for its theater scare tactics than its plot. Its suggestion that our fears can create lobster-like parasites that cause death unless destroyed by our screams may respond at least peripherally to the Cold War and the Red scare. But the film also may illustrate reactions to psychoanalysis in late 1950s culture. Film scholar Mikita Brottman suggests, for example, that the film "is about what Philip Rieff has described as 'the triumph of the therapeutic,' a trait of which is the widely held belief—almost a commonplace by 1959 . . .—that emotions we fail to get 'out' somehow remain repressed 'within' us until they find their way 'out,' possibly of their own accord, and possibly in a rather frightening and dangerous way" (2005, 9). David Cronenberg's *Shivers* (1975) explores human psychology as well, with an emphasis on a sexuality unleashed by parasites created by a mad scientist, Dr. Hobbes (Fred Doederlein), to reduce inhibitions.

Climate Change and Parasite Evolution:
The Case of *The Thaw* (2009)

For us, however, parasites created by climate change and toxic waste most accurately align with the possibilities for their own evolution. Recent studies of parasites take into account the impact of human-induced climate change and pollution on their evolution. According to zoologist Robert Poulin, for example, "Human activities have resulted in substantial, large-scale modifications to the natural environment, especially in the past century" (2007, 263). Many scientists note the multiple negative effects that global climate change will have on parasite evolution. When Brooks and Hoberg argue that human-caused climate changes "should be associated with the origins of new parasite-host associations and bursts of EID" (2007, 572), they point out that global climate change will lead to increases in both parasites and EID, leading to "the planet [as] an evolutionary and ecological minefield of EID through which millions of people wander daily" (573). Many scientists concur, noting, as does Camille Parmesan, that climate change is causing parasites, so-called pest species, to move "poleward and upward" (2006, 650). Mark A. Lewis's *The Thaw* explores these possible effects in the context of eco-horror.

The Thaw connects the horror genre with possible consequences of climate change and human exploitation of the environment in the Anthropocene Age. Like *The Bay*, *The Thaw* includes documentary-like elements to legitimize its assertions about the negative externalities associated with anthropogenic global warming. The film's protagonist, Dr. Kruipen (Val Kilmer), maintains a video diary, for example, in which he reveals, bit by bit, an ecoterrorist plan to attack climate change cynics. A montage of images highlights the misplaced fervor of these skeptics, even in the face of flooding, hurricanes, and overpopulation. The montage slows with the question, what happens "when nature is the terrorist?" The first hint of the source for Dr. Kruipen's plan comes early in the film, when a shot shows a woman with what looks like a tick climbing in and then back out of her forehead.

Our introduction to Kruipen comes in a flashback and further explains the source of the ecoterrorism broached in the video diary. The setting is late spring on Barley Island in the Canadian Arctic, but rocks and steppe are bare of snow, and a polar bear searches anxiously for food. Kruipen and Jane (Anne Marie DeLuise) photograph the bear while the rest of the team tranquilizes it for study. At four hundred pounds, the bear is underweight and has traveled far to find food because the ice has melted. More important to the film's premise, the bear has been feasting on a parasite-ridden woolly mammoth carcass once buried beneath the melting ice. Kruipen's interspersed video diary entries heighten the horror associated with an anthropogenic change in climate that exposes prehistoric mammals and revives dormant deadly parasites. In a move reminiscent of Terry Gilliam's *Twelve Monkeys* (1995), Kruipen connects these parasites with what he sees as monstrous hosts, claiming that "sacrifices" must be made to change humanity's dangerous behavior. Because these parasites have reawakened only because human activity has warmed the earth and melted the ice, Kruipen decides to unleash them on populations in the United States, infecting enough humans to "make a real difference." Through biological ecoterrorism, he hopes to change the minds of climate-change cynics, even if it means he and many others may die.

The Thaw begins to illustrate the magnitude of those sacrifices by personalizing them. For example the entrance of Kruipen's daughter, Evelyn (Martha MacIsaac), as one of three student interns chosen to work with the team amplifies the force of his ecoterrorist inclinations. We learn that Kruipen and his daughter have conflicts associated with work and divorce that Evelyn hopes to resolve. The film takes the time to explore how her father's work and absence result in both anger with and connection to him. Before her arrival at the Arctic camp, for example, Evelyn declares to the other student interns, "Honestly, I think that people are incapable of change, and their days are numbered." Despite his poor parenting skills, Kruipen attempts to stop Evelyn from joining the team and being exposed to the parasites, suggesting that personal connections could influence humans' actions toward both human and nonhuman nature.

The film also draws on the suspense of the horror genre to slowly expose the biological effects caused by parasites unleashed from the prehistoric mammoth, displaying the monstrous results of their infestation in both animals and humans. As Noel Murray of the *A.V. Club* declares, "*The Thaw* sports some genuinely scary bug effects" (2009). First, the polar bear dies after ingesting parasites from the woolly mammoth. Team members exposed to the parasites start exhibiting symptoms of infection, and when Jane discovers Kruipen's plan, she shoots and wounds him and kills the other researchers to stop the spread of the parasite, returns to camp, and sabotages their helicopter. When the student interns arrive at the base camp and find the rotting polar bear carcass, they and their pilot, Bart (Viv Leacock), also become infected, with horrific results.

In one scene, for example, student researcher Ling Chen (Steph Song) is bitten after making love in a sleeping bag. She declares, "It's just a bug," but the next day she is covered with bites. Jane is now quarantined in a base-camp bed, but her symptoms have worsened. Black bile comes out of her mouth as she tells everyone to leave. When they examine Jane's body, they find bug bites and eggs, and parasites begin to climb out of her eye. Jing and the others suffer similar fates. Even when Bart chops off his infected arm, the parasites linger. Seemingly immune, Evelyn wonders "how long they stay in the larval state" and explains that they are prehistoric infectious parasites that thawed with the ice.

Instead of the climate change that unearthed deadly parasites, however, the film seems to suggest that the real horror of the film is Kruipen's eco-terrorist plan. As evidence for this connection between ecoterrorism and horror, Evelyn is appalled when she discovers his scheme while watching her father's video diary, hearing him explain that he will expose others to the parasite, one of the horrors that will come from global warming, because "no one cares." She watches him cut himself, providing an entry site for a parasite to bury itself quickly. Because Evelyn has seen the ramifications of exposure to this deadly parasite, she leaves her father to die in the base camp and returns home to warn scientists and the American public about the horrific ramifications of Anthropogenic Era climate change. "I used to believe that people couldn't change; that all we could do is have as much fun as we could before it all came to an end. And now, now I don't want it to end," she explains, perhaps providing some hope until, in the film's last scene, a hunting dog finds a parasite-ridden bird near an urban area.

Documenting Eco-horror: *Poisoned Waters*, Humans, and the Monsters They Create

Anthropocene Era climate change and air, water, and terrain pollutants are already negatively impacting adaptation and evolution. As C. Harvel Drew and his colleagues declare, "If shifts in host or parasite ranges lead to disease emergence, the rate of pathogen evolution and host evolutionary response could be critical to predicting disease spread and subsequent effects on biological diversity" (2013, 2162). These changes have already impacted the oyster populations in and along the Atlantic Coast of the United States. The range of the oyster parasite *Perkinsus marinus* extended all the way to Maine from its original stopping point of the Chesapeake Bay, according to Camille Parmesan. Climate change has not only increased the range of these parasites but also accelerated their evolution.

Although human-caused climate change is one of the most destructive forces affecting the natural world, Robert Poulin asserts that "chemical pollution is perhaps the most pernicious, immediate, and widespread environmental change resulting from human activities" (2007, 264). As Poulin declares, "Fresh and marine habitats are particularly susceptible, receiving industrial effluents, agricultural and domestic waste as well as many accidental spills, all containing toxic chemicals of many types" (264). These pollutants also increase parasites and accelerate their evolution. Both *Poisoned Waters* and *The Bay* explore the horrific impact of pollutants like these on the ecosystem of the Chesapeake Bay, the breeding ground for dangerous parasites that evolve and kill wildlife, creating dead zones that may be impossible to heal.

Poisoned Waters sets up the narrative for *The Bay*, providing the facts on which Levinson's eco-horror was constructed. According to the documentary's narrator, the horrific state of the Chesapeake Bay should serve as a warning. The death of this bay points to the contamination of other bodies of water, including Puget Sound, discussed later in the film. Like *The Bay*, the bulk of *Poisoned Waters* blames agricultural runoff, as well as industrial waste, for polluted waters that threaten animals and humans in and around the toxic Chesapeake Bay. And like *The Bay*, *Poisoned Waters* draws on nostalgia as a reason to solve the eco-problem the Chesapeake has become. In order to preserve the bay as a source of recreation and sustenance, the documentary asserts, we must address the environmental disasters that our own behaviors have created. Scenes of boaters enjoying what look like pristine waters in the Chesapeake illustrate the goal, but the voice-over reveals its deceptive view. As the narrator explains, the "good times of bountiful harvest are slipping away." Although populations of rockfish and straight bass seem to be okay, oysters and crabs are almost gone.

The documentary explores whether humans and nature can coexist in the wake of overfishing, man-made pollution, and dead zones caused by overuse of fertilizer. According to the narrator, agricultural runoff accounts for overgrowth of algae, which kills off all the fish by eliminating oxygen. The documentary also confirms claims made by the fictional film *The Bay* that "as much as 40 percent" of the bay is a dead zone in the summer. Contaminants in the bay also infect humans if they come in contact with water, damaging the tourist, recreation, and seafood industries. The narrator calls this "the public's failure," claiming we know what is necessary but need the political will to act. Collectively, we don't care enough" now, he explains, but offers a nostalgic view of a time when we did through the personal and collective memories conveyed by Robert F. Kennedy Jr.

The nostalgic view illustrated by Kennedy's voice-over offers reactions to environmental catastrophes in the late 1960s: Earth Day and the passage of the EPA and Clean Water Act because twenty million Americans protested against the big polluters. According to Kennedy the Chesapeake became fishable and swimmable by 1983 due to the changes these new legal actions required. The massive protests provided legislators with the political will to act, according to Kennedy, even overriding Richard Nixon's veto of these environmental laws. They banned DDT, reduced automobile emissions, and sued cities polluting the air. They also cleaned up a bay that smelled so bad no one would go near it. The laws led to an end to the poorly treated sewage running into the Chesapeake and the modernization of sewage treatment plants across the United States.

The narration also provides a historical view of the demise of these changes. During the Reagan era, the film explains, the political climate changed, emphasizing deregulation and gutting of the EPA. Instead of political will, the EPA now relied on voluntary compliance. Factory farms began dumping unregulated waste into the Chesapeake just as in the fictional film *The Bay*. Instead of the eco-horror of Levinson's film, *Poisoned Waters* offers the perspective of Rick Dove, an investigator for a citizen's lawsuit against agricultural polluters. As in *The Bay*, Dove objects to poultry waste loaded with nitrogen and phosphorus being dumped into ditches running directly into streams and rivers that feed the Chesapeake Bay. These are the ingredients creating the bay's algae-infested dead zones. Like Levinson's eco-spy, Dove photographs huge piles of poultry waste and maps out their routes to the Chesapeake. Tests reveal that the excrement-infested water contains ten thousand times the *E. coli* and nine times the arsenic allowed by the EPA.

Poisoned Waters explicitly documents the impact that runoff from chicken farms is having on the Chesapeake, a point Levinson takes up in *The Bay*. *Poisoned Waters* explains and illustrates the Perdue Chicken Corporation's changing farming practices referred to in passing in *The Bay*. The move from independent farms to a vertically integrated conglomerate increased profits and efficiency but also drastically elevated pollution, which is now under limited control. The film shows piles of poultry waste so high that earthmovers are needed to contain it. The 570 million chickens on the farms produce 1.5 billion pounds of manure, more than three big cities, the film explains. Local crop farmers can't absorb the manure either. Agriculture has become the Chesapeake's biggest polluter because there are too many animals in one place. The runoff from chickens, hogs, and cattle is destroying ecosystems. In order to save the bay, the narrator declares, animal manure must be controlled.

To illustrate the massive mess these farms produce, the documentary shows one chicken farm that lost its Perdue license because the owner refused to comply with the company's rules. According to the owner, Perdue owns everything but the waste and bears no responsibility for its disposal because manure is considered a resource. American agriculture has successfully fought off pollution controls and water pollution regulations, so waste from these farms is not treated. Taking a cue from Reagan-era policies, Perdue and other big chicken corporations fought any move to regulate and encouraged self-regulation instead.

As in *The Bay*, *Poisoned Waters* shows us that the poultry waste has resulted in massive fish kills in the region. The poultry waste contains chemicals that mimic hormones called endocrine disruptors. The documentary also links these hormones with fish-killing parasites. According to the documentary, these endocrine disruptors are unregulated by the EPA and unaffected by sewage-treatment plants. Although the rest of the documentary explores the ecological disasters faced by human and nonhuman nature in and around Puget Sound, the parallels between the first part of *Poisoned Waters* and *The Bay* suggest a deliberate connection.

Parasite Evolution and Toxic Waste: *The Bay* and Eco-horror

Barry Levinson's *The Bay* fictionalizes the catastrophe documented in *Poisoned Waters*. In an interview with *Mother Jones*, Levinson explains that he was approached to do a documentary about the Chesapeake but "started doing research and found there was already a great *Frontline* doc, but nobody cares—people say, 'It's polluted, so what?' I said no. But a few months later, I thought, 'we've gathered all this research; why don't we tweak it for a theatrical release? We can scare an audience with a story that is 80 to 85 percent science and facts'" (2012). To emphasize this basis in science, *The Bay* approaches the Chesapeake's "poisoned water" by merging horror with docudrama. The film begins with a montage of what looks like documentary footage of huge dead fish along the bay and huge die-offs of starlings in a suburban community. A voice-over explains that their deaths are an environmental mystery, with massive fish kills in Sebastian Inlet, and deaths of up to two million black birds all over the region. When the scene shifts to ex-reporter Donna (Kether Donohue) speaking in 2012 on a webcam as a single witness to the July 4, 2009, eco-disaster, her testimony provides details of catastrophic events around the Chesapeake Bay and changes the genre from documentary to something more like a docudrama horror film.

This approach authenticates the environmental horrors on display in the film. According to Donna's report, human deaths in and around the bay began during Fourth of July festivities three years before in Claridge, Maryland, a town on the Chesapeake Bay. The footage we see is the first public revelation of that disastrous day. Claims are made that the government might be suppressing the evidence Donna reveals. Using Donna's news reports of devastation at the festivities and what looks like found footage from various survivors and victims, the film hems together the events of the day to begin explaining the cause of the multiple human and nonhuman deaths in the town.

The Bay works in flashback throughout most of the film, moving from one source of found footage to another to provide differing perspectives on the eco-catastrophe and offer a nostalgic view of a carefree life in Claridge before the monstrous parasite infestation. The approach replicates a compilation documentary style, but it also heightens suspense by revealing the mystery and its solution only gradually. As revealed in *Poisoned Waters*, toxic runoff from area chicken farms and other sources has entered the bay and begun accelerating the growth and evolution of deadly parasites.

Donna's interview with the town's mayor (Frank Deal) provides some of the first evidence for the cause of the deaths shown in the opening montage. As a summer intern in 2009, Donna recorded the events of the day, nostalgic small-town entertainment that begins with a crab-eating contest. The town and its economy are introduced in a voice-over explaining that the chicken industry grew during the mayor's tenure due to the water desalination plant he developed. The chicken industry requires massive amounts of water, we learn, and competes with the restaurants and summer tourism industry that have sustained the community. According to Donna, during this interview, she had "no idea how culpable he was for what was about to happen."

Found footage then takes us back six weeks earlier, when the bodies of two scientists were found in the bay, and their cause of death was labeled as unknown. The two oceanographers were measuring pollution levels in the bay, especially in conjunction with the chicken runoff spilling into the water from the now-massive farms. When their deaths are investigated, however, shark attacks are blamed. Video from the oceanographers maintains the documentary feel of the film and reveals high levels of PCBs, Viagra, and estrogen in the water, primary products of the chicken farms and other waste runoff.

Other footage reveals conflicting perspectives on the farms. At a political luncheon the EPA is blamed. But video from an eco-spy who infiltrated and filmed one of the farms exposes how chicken excrement drains into ditches that empty into the Chesapeake Bay. Donna's voice-over highlights one ramification of building factory chicken farms in a recreation area: a desalination plant that provided water for more chicken farms and for a growing tourist industry. It also provided the ingredients for a deadly outcome. As Donna explains, "Everything seemed really pretty good" until film footage from the July 4 festivities shows the first evidence that the bay has become so contaminated, it has become toxic to humans. In one shot, for example, a woman rushes through the crowd screaming in pain from sores covering her body. Dead fish float to the top of the water. Crab-eating contestants begin vomiting, and welts appear on children.

Found footage from other witnesses augments Donna's report. Video from the hospital fill in more gaps as Dr. Abrams (Stephen Kunken) documents the strange ailment patients bring to the emergency room. Soon he is treating hundreds of patients, many of whom die quickly. He films the blisters covering one woman's back and shares his evidence with the Center for Disease Control (CDC) through video connections available to scientists who suspect a bacterial outbreak. Other footage comes from police officers documenting crime scenes. They report the first death when they find a body and, without bullet wounds, cannot determine the cause of death. The officers also document a 911 call from a woman "who saw something bad." Outside a house we learn that victims' tongues and guts seem to have been torn out of their bodies.

Later video evidence from the oceanographers reveals the most devastating consequence of the chicken farms: parasites growing rapidly and destroying the bay's sea life. The town's mayor is informed of the larvae hatching inside fish but fails to act, choosing instead to maintain the deadly juxtaposition of chicken farming alongside a tourist industry that relies on bay waters for recreation. Even when the cause of the eco-disaster is clear, the mayor claims deaths are either rumors or due to domestic disputes rather than parasites. The rise in bacteria levels is seasonal, he claims, his explanation for the rashes and digestive problems.

The oceanographers' later reports concur with those disclosed in *Poisoned Waters*, however, asserting that 40 percent of the bay is a dead zone, and its oysters are dying. They also discover that the parasites latching onto fish gills are isopods, one of the world's oldest creatures. They eat through the tongues of animals they infect, the oceanographers explain, as a "mutated version of the isopods … eating the fish alive." Although the footage is sent to both the mayor and the Chesapeake Environmental Organization, the scientists receive no response.

Instead, the mayor and the organization ignore the finding, leaving it to Donna and the various witnesses to substantiate the oceanographers' claims. Donna provides voice-over for this private footage from a family traveling by boat to Claridge, and a teenage couple killed by huge parasites in the bay. According to Donna, they had "no idea something dark and sinister [was] about to happen." Video from Stephanie (Kristin Connolly) and Alex (Will Rogers), a family taking their boat to Claridge to celebrate Independence Day, provides more evidence of the outbreak and its cause, especially after we see Stephanie pushing Alex into the bay. In video retrieved from a soaked camera, a teenage boy attempts to help his girlfriend when she jumps into the parasite-infested Chesapeake and begins to scream in pain.

Video of parasite-infested humans heightens the suspense, leaving us wondering if Alex will acquire the parasite because he too swam in the contaminated waters. When phone calls from Stephanie's parents don't reach them on the boat, found video reveals that Stephanie and Alex reach Claridge that night, where they discover hundreds of dead tourists, victims whose faces have been eaten away. The voice-over explains that chicken excrement in the bay contained steroids that accelerated the growth of parasites by fifty to sixty times, and a montage of images illustrates the isopod's evolution. The results of this accelerated evolution becomes more personalized when Alex too begins to exhibit boils on his face. The parasite is infecting just about everyone in the town: police officers, Alex, Dr. Abrams, and most of the town's inhabitants. The mayor avoids a parasite infestation only because he dies in a car wreck.

In *The Bay*, despite all the evidence that the found footage from the oceanographers and private citizens provides, none of the environmental organizations or political entities respond. In the context of Donna and the film's rhetoric, they are all culpable in the deaths of much wildlife and many people. According to the report, they had sixteen days after the death of the oceanographers to warn the townspeople. Ultimately the federal government seals off the town, kills off the parasites with chlorine, and hides the cause of the multiple human deaths during the incident. Even Donna's testimony must be surreptitious to protect her from retribution. The film ends by declaring that the Chesapeake remains 40 percent lifeless. In *The Bay* the emphasis is on revealing the causes for these massive dead zones rather than their solution. What makes this eco-horror film most effective, however, is its basis in truth, not only because of its docudrama approach but also because it draws on the real environmental disasters contributing to parasites' rapid evolution explored with more complexity in *Frontline*'s *Poisoned Waters* (2009).

Although *Poisoned Waters* and *The Bay* approach their subject differently, they both address the horrific aquatic conditions humans produce when they pollute their environments. Restoring the health of the Chesapeake Bay will recuperate the recreation, tourism, and food industries, the films assert. They also blame humanity for the eco-disaster the Chesapeake Bay has become. The evidence on which these films build their arguments, however, is what makes their message more powerful: Our monstrous behaviors have caused dead zones in the bay, killing off fish and endangering our own health with toxic waste from poultry farms and other industries.

The Bay: Villagers flee monstrous parasites.

Multiple reports substantiate this claim. For example, David E. Hess reports in an April 2013 *PA Environment Daily* that pollution contributed greatly to fish kills in the Chesapeake Bay and its watershed. As Hess asserts, "Scientists believe that nitrogen and phosphorus pollution may be contributing to fish deaths and diseases in two ways. The first is by spurring the growth of parasites (myxozoans and trematoads) and their hosts (worms and snails). The second is by feeding algal blooms that raise pH levels and lower oxygen concentrations, stressing young smallmouth bass" (2013). Hess advises a similar solution to the massive fish kills he documents: regulate poultry farms and their massive toxic runoffs to "reduce nitrogen and phosphorus pollution." Parasitologist Robert Poulin substantiates this need, declaring, "There is mounting laboratory and field evidence that these pollutants affect both parasites and their hosts" (2007, 264). For Poulin and other parasitologists, "parasites are seen as potentially very useful indicators of not only of the presence of certain pollutants in a locality, but also of general environmental quality and ecosystem health" (264). As Poulin explains, "These are the sorts of environmental pressures likely to lead to evolutionary changes in the biology of parasites" (264). They also demonstrate well how a human host can become more monstrous than the parasites it sustains.

4

Gendered Landscapes
and Monstrous Bodies

American Psycho: Yuppie cannibal Patrick takes on Wall Street.

8

Gendering the Cannibal

Bodies and Landscapes in Feminist Cannibal Movies

> All these years I think you are wendigo, but no, you are just another white man.
> —Tonto (Johnny Depp) to Cavendish (William Fichtner) in *The Lone Ranger* (2013)

Humans may also become like parasites when their hunger for flesh and resources grows voracious. In a pivotal scene in Antonia Bird's cannibal Western, *Ravenous* (1999), F. W. Colqhoun (Robert Carlyle), a stranger suffering from frostbite and seeking solace in the California fort at the center of the film admits he survived a lost wagon train journey from Virginia by feeding on the travelers who "expired from malnourishment." Instead of offering sympathy, however, the fort's American Indian guide, George (Joseph Runningfox), grows anxious and calls him wendigo, showing the fort's commander, Colonel Hart (Jeffrey Jones) a wendigo Ojibwa myth illustrated on a blanket. According to the myth, when a man eats another's flesh, usually an enemy, he steals his strength, his essence, his spirit, so that his hunger becomes craven and insatiable. The more he eats, the more he wants, and the stronger he becomes. For George, when men become cannibals, they become wendigo, superhuman monsters with insatiable appetites. In the context of the westward movement Colqhoun embodies, wendigo may also coincide with the white man's voracious hunger for land.

Yet the explicit connection between cannibalism and Manifest Destiny moves beyond the wendigo myth when gender is added to the equation. After revealing his own cannibalism, Colqhoun convinces Colonel Hart to return with him only by suggesting that the one woman in the group might still be alive. As he exclaims, "I'm ashamed to say that I acted in the most cowardly manner. It would have been nobler, I know, to have stayed and protected Mrs. MacCready ..., but I was weak. I fled. It was nothing less than pure providence that I arrived here." *Ravenous* argues vehemently against the cannibal-like exploitation sometimes associated with Manifest Destiny through the image of the wendigo. But the insertion of the feminine decoy amplifies the relationship between consuming the body and consuming the land by drawing on what Annette Kolodny calls "America's oldest and most cherished fantasy." According to Kolodny, this pastoral fantasy is grounded in "a daily reality of harmony between man and nature based on an experience of the land as feminine—that is, not simply the land as mother, but the land as woman, the total female principle of gratification—enclosing the individual in an environment of receptivity, repose, and painless integral satisfaction" (1975, 4).

Such a fantasy has negative consequences, however, constructing men, especially white men, as dominant figures who, like the wendigo, are stronger than their passive prey, whether it be women or the nature they represent. As Kolodny asserts in *The Land before Her*, "With promising regularity, the promise and its disappointment were succeeded by guilt and anger as, again and again, Americans found themselves bearing witness to the mutilation and despoliation of their newfound Earthly Paradises" (1984, 4–5). To counter this fantasy, Kolodny offers the perspective of women pioneers seeking a garden in the wilderness of the American West. For Kolodny "men sought sexual and filial gratification from the land, while women sought there the gratifications of home and family relations" (1984, 12). Yet even Kolodny admits, "Each in their own way, however, enacted sanctioned cultural scripts" (12).

That same enacting of cultural scripts occurs in cannibal horror films from *Texas Chainsaw Massacre* (1974), *The Hills Have Eyes* (1977), *Motel Hell* (1980), and *The Lone Ranger* (2013) to *Blood Diner* (1987), *Ravenous*, *American*

Psycho (2000), *Trouble Every Day* (2001), and *Jennifer's Body* (2009). Separated by decades these films make similar statements about our desecration of the natural world. What separates *Blood Diner*, *Ravenous*, *American Psycho*, *Trouble Every Day*, and *Jennifer's Body* from their counterparts, however, is their treatment of gender. Perhaps because these films were directed by women, these cannibal films take a different approach from what Carter Soles calls "urbanoia films," which he contends provide " the most productively ambivalent and ideologically challenging depictions of the murderous, anti-heroic hillbilly who, as those films contend, are really a horrifying reflection of our own 'civilized' cultural anxieties about our own rape of the natural world" (2013, 248). Instead, these later cannibal films explore multiple manifestations of cannibalism within a gendered framework that complicates colonial fantasies of land, women, and wendigo.

With at least some emphasis on the connection between various frontiers and the human body, these gendered cannibal films explore cannibal horror in two distinctive ways. *Ravenous*, *Trouble Every Day*, and *American Psycho* most closely connect with films such as *Texas Chainsaw Massacre* and *The Hills Have Eyes*, critiquing consumerism and exploitation of frontiers in different contexts, but their emphasis on gendered bodies separates them from more traditional cannibal horror. *Blood Diner* and *Jennifer's Body* connect cannibalism to the supernatural, but because the transformed bodies are those of women who feed primarily on men, they turn cannibal horror on its head, exploring bodies and landscapes from an explicitly ecofeminist perspective that condemns exploitation of women's bodies as frontiers. As Serpil Oppermann asserts, ecofeminism, or what she calls feminist ecocriticism, "considers gendered bodies, not as purely cultural or discursive constructs, but as differentially constituted material-discursive subjects, enmeshed in the material world of powerful volatile agents" (2013, 1). In the cannibal horror film, gendered bodies and the volatile agents of the material world they inhabit may become violently intertwined.

Constructing the Cannibal

The May 2013 unearthing of what Nicholas Wade of the *New York Times* calls "the first physical evidence of cannibalism among the desperate population" (2013) at the Jamestown colony site in Virginia demonstrates how pervasive cannibalism becomes when survival depends on it. According to Wade, archeologists found "cut marks on the skull and skeleton of a 14-year-old girl [that] show that her flesh and brain were removed, presumably to be eaten by the starving colonists during the harsh winter of 1609." This evidence corroborates written reports from the period and builds on a history of cannibalism among humans and other species.[1] As paleoanthropologist Carole Travis-Henikoff declares, "Few people believe their ancestors practiced cannibalism, and some scholars deny its existence altogether, but the truth is ... we all have cannibals in our closets" (23). According to Travis-Henikoff, "Cannibalism is the ingestion of other of one's own species and is practiced throughout the animal kingdom, from one-celled organisms to humans. The reason for cannibalism's ubiquitous nature lies in its antiquity. Recent finds of species-specific tooth marks on dinosaur bones prove occurrences of cannibalism dating back to the Mesozoic era" (2008, 23). In her *Dinner with a Cannibal: The Complete History of Mankind's Oldest Taboo* (2008), Travis-Henikoff offers evidence for multiple types of cannibalism, from the survival cannibalism noted in Jamestown to the medicinal cannibalism of the Inquisition.[2] As she and others note, cannibalism is celebrated in at least one book and film, *Alive* (1993), despite the R rating for cannibalism and ulcerative sores. Her work builds on the research of scientists and scholars from multiple fields, substantiating the existence of cannibalism without condemning its practice.

Many scientists agree with Travis-Henikoff's premise. In a *Science News* article, for example, Bruce Bower highlights the work of geneticist John Collinge of University College London. Collinge and his colleagues' studies have concluded, "Cannibalism among prehistoric humans may have left lasting genetic marks, a team of scientists contends. Their controversial argument hinges on a link between specific DNA mutations and a disease that afflicted South Pacific villagers who practiced cannibalism as late as 1950" (Bower 2013, 229). Biologists Volker H. W. Rudolf and Janis Antonovic assert, "In the animal kingdom, cannibalism is generally a one-on-one interaction in which a larger and stronger individual kills and consumes a smaller and weaker conspecific (Polis 1981). Under these conditions, cannibalism is likely to be an ineffective mode of disease transmission" (2007, 1207). And Scott A. Wissinger and his colleagues' *Ecology* article "suggests that recruitment regulation by cannibalism is most likely when young-of-the year are vulnerable to cannibalism but have low dietary overlap with cannibals" (2010, 549).

Most anthropologists also acknowledge the existence of cannibalism in human history, exploring the phenomenon in particular contexts and for specific purposes. Ilka Thiessen analyzes "cannibalism's recounted past, present, or mythical existence in relation to female imagery," in Papua, New Guinea, and concludes that cannibalism, real or mythic, "becomes a defining characteristic of what it means to be female or male in these societies" (2001, 142). Shirley Lindenbaum asserts, "Even among sceptics, cannibalism is acknowledged in several forms. Survival cannibalism and cannibalism as psychopathology are most frequently noted" (2004, 477). According to Lindenbaum, constructions of "cannibalism as a sign of strength, self-reliance, and possibly a threat to outsiders" may have "transformed a taboo into a totem and redefined anthropophagie primitivism as a positive value" (493). And Marshall Sahlins declares, "The deconstructive strategy is not to deny the existence of cannibalism altogether. That would invite consideration of the substantial historical record of the practice, whereas the objective rather is to establish doubt about it. Not that there was no cannibalism, then, only that the European reports of it are fabrications (Obeyesekere 1998). Even so, not all such reports need be questioned" (2003, 3).

Scholars in the humanities also concur with arguments from the sciences. According to linguist Ellen B. Basso's study of South American oral history, "The warriors in these stories stand out most vividly as men who tried to reconfigure certain basic values central to their particular designated roles. Their actions thus transcend the time of cannibalism and blood feuding, of desperate migrations in search of a place to live peacefully" (1995, 304). Historian Phillip P. Boucher complicates constructions of cannibalism when he asserts that "the Island Caribs' refusal to accept religious and political— but not economic—hegemonization certainly prolonged their existence as an autonomous people" (1992, 8). Boucher leaves the question regarding whether Caribs were cannibalistic unanswered. He first suggests that "their cannibalistic practices were limited to occasional consumption of prisoners of war and were thus a minor aspect of their culture" (6). But according to Boucher's research, they also may have "killed male captives in elaborate rituals, that they burned their captives' flesh and carried the ashes in small calabashes around their necks, ate the fat on certain occasions, and finally, used human bones to make flutes" (7). Boucher concludes, however, that these stories, or those told by Caribs themselves, are irrelevant. Instead, "what is clear about the issue of cannibalism is that, starting with Columbus and the Spaniards, Europeans leveled grossly distorted charges of man-eating against potentially enslavable peoples who ferociously resisted incursions into their island homelands" (7).

Boucher's conclusion regarding representations of Caribs and other indigenous people as cannibals broaches another strong area of research among anthropologists and scholars in the Western humanities: how the trope of cannibalism has been developed and used to exploit colonized people and their land. W. Arens broaches this trope in his 1979 work, *The Man-Eating Myth: Anthropology and Anthropophagy*. Visual culture scholars Barbara Creed and Jeannette Hoorn's edited volume *Body Trade: Captivity Cannibalism and Colonialism in the Pacific* (2001) highlights cannibal narratives of the fantastic, asserting that anthropophagy, or ritual uses of cannibalism, typically was constructed to vilify indigenous people, dehumanizing them by associating them with cannibalism. As Creed and Hoorn assert, "This book uses the concept of 'body trade' as a means of re-reading traditionally racist, sexist and Eurocentric views about race relations in the Pacific from the time of early European contact to the present" (xiv). Creed and Hoorn's study "bring[s] together the inter-related ways in which the indigenous body has been marked and exploited by colonial practices" (xiv).

Comparative literature scholar Zita Nunes concurs in *Cannibal Democracy: Race and Representation in the Literature of America*, exploring "the metaphor of cannibalism as a mobile metaphor that inheres in attempts to conceptualize the relationship between race and democracy extending far beyond Brazil and that the original national focus was insufficient" (2008, xvi). Told from the perspective of indigenous people, Jack D. Forbes's *Columbus and Other Cannibals* connects the metaphor of cannibalism to the wetiko disease, "the disease of exploitation" (1992, xix) illuminated in *Ravenous*. Forbes asserts, "It is my hope that enlarging upon the concept of the wetiko disease and discussing its origin, epidemiology, and characteristics that I can be of some help to [people] concerned about violence, about the environment, about decency, and about human authenticity" (xxi). After outlining a history of exploitation, of "cannibalism" of cultures and their people, Forbes proposes a good, "sane" path that embraces interdependence. Catalin Avramescu's *An Intellectual History of Cannibalism* (2003) examines this construction of cannibals in philosophical accounts.

Historians take a variety of approaches to the issue and history of cannibalism. Francis Barker and her colleagues declare in their edited volume, "Where in the past the figure of the cannibal has been used to construct differences that uphold racism, it now appears in projects that deconstruct them" (1998, 242). Other historians examine specific instances of colonizers' use of the trope to subjugate and/or dehumanize indigenous people.[3] In his review of four late 1990s studies of cannibalism and genocide, ethnohistorian Dan Beaver updates these arguments, concluding, "Historically, the term cannibal often has expressed the unreflective hatred and distrust of one culture for another, leading some scholars to approach the term as a metaphor for the 'primitive' or 'savage'. . . . The cannibal metaphor has extended in contemporary fiction to the 'savage' excesses of the American financial elite of the 1990s" (2002, 672). As Jennifer Brown asserts, cannibal representations in literature and film demonstrate that Westerners "are rapacious, cannibalistic aggressors" (2013, 14). These manifestations of the cannibal metaphor are broached both explicitly and implicitly in *Ravenous*, *American Psycho*, and *Trouble Every Day*.

Resisting Wendigo in *Ravenous*

Set in 1847, immediately after the Mexican-American War and right before the California gold rush, *Ravenous* explicitly addresses the wendigo cannibal myth. In *Ravenous* wendigo is both reality and metaphor for Manifest Destiny and the environmental and human exploitation that accompanies it. Inspired by the Donner party incident of the same year and the trial of 1870s cannibal prospector Alfred G. Packer, the film follows Capt. John Boyd (Guy Pearce) to Fort Spencer, a desolate military outpost in the Sierra Nevada. He has been banished because he is viewed as a coward; yet he is also honored as a hero because he bravely defeated a Mexican fort after ingesting the blood of his peers. His commander, General Slauson (John Spencer), belittles this bravery, however. After watching Boyd's inability to consume a large steak at a victory dinner, he declares, "You're no hero. I want you as far from my company as possible."

At Fort Spencer, Boyd joins a group of misfits with little to do on this empty range: Hart, the commanding officer; Toffler (Jeremy Davies), the company chaplain; Knox (Stephen Spinella), the drunken doctor; Reich (Neal McDonough), the only real soldier of the group; Cleaves (David Arquette), the heavily medicated camp cook; and George and his sister, Martha (Sheila Tousey), the troop's Indian guides. The dull life they maintain in this wilderness fort is shattered, however, when Colqhoun/Colonel Ives arrives and introduces cannibalism and the wendigo myth into the plot. Colqhoun also gives a name to the cravings Boyd so wishes to end and amplifies the impact of gender on its manifestation. Although an emasculated Boyd resists wendigo, and Martha escapes its effects, Colqhoun embraces it.

Frostbitten and famished, Colqhoun provides the narrative that transforms *Ravenous* from Western to horror. Colquhoun's westward movement story first connects him with the Manifest Destiny of both the Mexican-American War and the westward movement. According to Colqhoun,

> We left in April. Six of us in all. Mr. MacCready and his wife, from Ireland. Mr. Janus, from Virginia, I believe … with his servant, Jones. Myself—I'm from Scotland. And our guide … a military man, coincidently. Colonel Ives. A detestable man … and a most disastrous guide. He professed to know a new, shorter route through the Nevadas. Quite a route that was. Longer than the known one … and impossible to travel. We worked … very, very hard. By the time of the first snowfall we were still a hundred miles from this place. That was November.

When the journey from Virginia to California is disrupted by the horrific winter conditions of the Sierra Madres, however, their pioneering spirit transforms into the wendigo to which it is compared:

> Preceding in the snow was futile. We took shelter in a cave. Decided to wait until the storm had passed. But the storm did not pass. The trails soon became impassable, and we had run out of food. … We remained famished. The day that Jones died I was out collecting wood. He had expired from malnourishment. And when I returned, the others were cooking his legs for dinner. Would I have stopped it had I been there? I don't know. But I must say, when I stepped inside that cave … the smell

of meat cooking . . . I thanked the Lord. I thanked the Lord. And then things got out of hand. I ate sparingly. Others did not. The meat did not last us a week and we were soon hungry again only, this time our hunger was different. More severe, savage.

Colqhoun's story prompts George to recount the wendigo myth, highlighting Colqhoun's literal cannibalism as well as the imperial repercussions his journey westward represents. As Danette DiMarco articulates so well in her "Going Wendigo: The Emergence of the Iconic Monster in Margaret Atwood's *Oryx and Crake* and Antonia Bird's *Ravenous*," the film "is an appropriative text that invokes the Wendigo myth and evaluates cannibalistic discourse more broadly in order to critique Western cultural crisis" (2011, 134). Through the figure of the wendigo, the film elucidates a direct relationship between literal cannibalism and figurative consumption of the American frontier; Jack D. Forbes calls this figure the wetiko disease, "the disease of exploitation" (1992, xix). According to Forbes "wetiko is a Cree term (windigo in Ojibway, wintiko in Powhatan) that refers to a cannibal or, more specifically, an evil person or spirit who terrorizes other creatures by means of terrible evil acts, including cannibalism" (24). For Forbes "imperialism and exploitation are forms of cannibalism and, in fact, are precisely those forms of cannibalism which are most diabolical or evil" (24). Jennifer Brown reinforces this connection between imperialism and cannibalism in *Ravenous*, asserting, "Rather than the colonial use of cannibalism as tag of the savage, it is the white man who is barbaric and the Native American who is calm, intelligent, and reminds us that 'whites eat the body of Christ.'" (2013, 226).

Although some anthropologists and historians associate the cannibal metaphor with negative constructions of indigenous people colonized by oppressors, Forbes takes an opposite stance. According to Forbes, "traditional ritualistic 'cannibalism' (so-called) found among many folk peoples was essentially an act of eating a small portion of a dead enemy's flesh in order to gain part of the strength or power of that person or to show respect (in a spiritual way) for that person" (1992, 24). For Forbes this ritual is not wetiko. Instead, "cannibalism . . . is the consuming of another's life for one's own private purpose or profit. . . . Thus, the wealthy exploiter 'eats the flesh of oppressed workers, the wealthy matron 'eats' the lives of her servants, the imperialist 'eats' the flesh of the conquered, and so on" (25). Colqhoun's/ Colonel Ives's speech near the end of *Ravenous* highlights this definition well: "Manifest destiny. Westward expansion. You know, come April, it'll all start again. Thousands of gold-hungry Americans will travel over those mountains on their way to new lives, passing right through here. We won't kill indiscriminately. No, selectively. Good God! We don't want to break up families. Of course, we've no wish to recruit everyone. We've enough mouths to feed as it is. We just need a home. And this country is seeking to be whole. Stretching out its arms and consuming all it can. And we merely follow."

DiMarco connects wetiko to *Ravenous*, relying primarily on definitions of wendigo espoused by Atwood, but she also notes the multiple times the film's characters invoke the myth. For example, she cites Colonel Hart's translation of George's explanation of wendigo after Colqhoun's speech as both an introduction to its power and a warning against its dangerous repercussions. Hart calls it "an old Indian myth from the North. A man eats another's flesh. It's usually an enemy, and he takes . . . steals . . . his strength . . . his essence . . . his spirit, and his hunger becomes craven . . . insatiable. And the more he eats, the more he wants, too, and the more he eats the stronger he becomes." Ultimately, that craven hunger causes Colqhoun to cannibalize almost the entire rescue party and, when he returns as Colonel Ives, the remaining men in the fort, so only Boyd and Hart survive. Ives spares Hart, transforming him into a cannibal, perhaps because, as Hart explains, "It's lonely being a cannibal."

With such a demonstration, it comes as no surprise that Ives's references to wendigo reinforce those that George broaches earlier in the film. He sings the praises of wendigo when he confronts Boyd:

[takes a big breath of smoke] You know, not too long ago I couldn't do that. Could barely take a breath without coughing up a pint of blood. Tuberculosis. That along with fierce headaches . . . depression . . . suicidal ambition. I was in pretty horrible shape. In fact I was on my way to a sanatorium to convalesce when a native scout told me a curious story. Man eats the flesh of another, he takes the other man's strength, absorbs his spirit. Well. Naturally I just had to try. Consequently I ate the scout first and you know he was absolutely right. I grew stronger. Tuberculosis?

Vanished. As did the headaches and the black thoughts. I returned that spring happy. And healthy. And virile.

According to Ives cannibalism has made him stronger and perhaps more masculine. At the end of his speech, however, Ives broaches Boyd's resistance to wendigo: "And that's what surprises me about you, Boyd. You've tasted it . . . felt its power. Yet, you're resisting. Why?" Boyd's answer underlines the gendered frameworks on which Wendigo is constructed and can be, at least individually, opposed. When Boyd explains that he avoids cannibalism "because it's wrong," Ives connects this "morality" with Boyd's cowardice. For Ives "morality [is] the last bastion of a coward." Ives argues, "It's courage to accept me." For Ives resisting cannibalism proves Boyd's cowardice.

But Boyd began as a coward unwilling to embody a masculinist agenda, too scared to act while the rest of his unit died during the war. He could fight back and take a command post after an inadvertent act of cannibalism: "I was buried, with my commanding officer's half shot off head in my face, his blood running down my throat." Instead of embracing cannibalism and the strength it provides him, Boyd resists its pull almost immediately, refusing to eat the steak offered to him as a reward and nearly vomiting over the visions of death he sees in the meat.

This "emasculated" Boyd also seeks advice not from Ives but from Martha, George's sister, the only woman, and the only remaining American Indian in the fort. After assuring her that he did not kill George, he exclaims, "I need to know how to stop it! How do you stop?" Instead of offering reassurance, Martha explains, "You don't. Wendigo takes. It never gives. You must die." Martha's answer could have swayed him toward Ives, in order to survive. Instead, it seems to empower him even more to destroy Ives and attempt to drive out the wendigo within him. In the end Boyd continues to resist Ives's attempt to turn him into a wendigo, choosing to combat the craving within him with his own and Ives's death.

The cycle of exploitation will continue, the film confirms, showing us General Slauson ladling up and enjoying a stew of cannibalized soldiers. But in the last scene, Martha escapes, leaving the fort behind to start a new life beyond the wendigo. In *Ravenous*, then, the emasculated male, Colonel Boyd, and the autonomous Indian female, Martha, resist a masculinist wendigo, illustrating the "sanity" that Jack D. Forbes suggests is necessary to move beyond the cannibalism of exploitation. For Forbes, however, we must move beyond Paulo Friere's humanism and "take 'critical awareness' beyond the limits of purely human situations" (1992, 172). To escape Wendigo we must embrace what Forbes calls "'lifeism', more respect for life, more respect for the living, more respect for all forms of life. That is a tree that has borne good fruit. That is a tree that still bears good fruit" (178). Leaving wendigo behind and choosing life, Martha resists a literal exploitation of human flesh, but she also resists the degradation of a land and people trampled under the boots of Manifest Destiny and a destructive frontier myth.

American Psycho and Trouble Every Day: Expanding the Frontier, Expanding Wendigo

Ravenous explicitly connects with traditional views of Manifest Destiny and wetiko or wendigo based on definitions of the American frontier that primarily examine movement westward from the 1600s until approximately 1890, when Frederick Jackson Turner (1893) hypothesized that the frontier had closed. *American Psycho* and *Trouble Every Day*, however, illuminate expanded definitions of frontier constructed on similar dichotomies: colonizer/colonized, masculine/feminine, nature/culture, and wendigo or wetiko/sustainability.

According to Annette Kolodny, a frontier, and the literature and film that embody it, "may be identified by its encoding of some specifiable first moment in the evolving dialogue between different cultures and languages and their engagement with one another and with the physical terrain" (1975, 13). Kolodny's definition of frontier expands it beyond traditional views of the American West to include multiple collisions between "a currently indigenous population and at least one group of newcomers or 'intruders'" (13). Despite their contemporary contexts, *American Psycho* and *Trouble Every Day* highlight similar collisions from a gendered perspective.

Scholars examining Mary Harron's film adaptation of Bret Easton Ellis's *American Psycho* (1991) primarily explore how the film plays with and responds to genre expectations, with a nod to Patrick Bateman's (Christian Bale) identity construction and status as an unreliable narrator. David Eldridge's "The Generic American Psycho," for example, asserts that "the power of genre classifications was a constant concern" in both novel and film (2008, 19). David Robinson's "The Unattainable Narrative: Identity, Consumerism and the Slasher Film in Mary Harron's *American Psycho*" also highlights the film's genre responses, asserting that the film "borrows the horror genre's trademark self-consciousness and takes it to a new level, marrying the genre to a larger body of cultural narratives, including those of television, pop musing, news media, and advertising" (2006, 26). These multiple cultural narratives also provide fodder for Bateman's identity construction as both venture capitalist and real or imagined cannibal serial killer.

We assert, however, that in *American Psycho* Patrick Bateman, a wealthy New York investment banking executive, negotiates a postcolonial frontier in which women become landscapes to exploit, annihilate, and cannibalize, just as he and his colleagues consume material culture and collide with those who provide it. Although Bateman hides what could be psychopathology from his coworkers and friends and dives deeper into a deviant world like that described in wendigo mythology, his aberrant responses to the 1990s yuppie world of excess merely amplify theirs. According to Jennifer Brown, in *American Psycho* "the cannibal has become the reviled image of overindulgence, overspending, and overexploitation of resources" (2013, 214), more "us" than "them." As a contemporary wendigo, Bateman bumps up against the feminine underclass on Wall Street, negotiating a modern frontier without the sanity that Forbes prescribes. Only Jean (Chloë Sevigny), Bateman's secretary, survives the crash.

Although the female body primarily bears the brunt of masculine exploitation in *American Psycho*, Bateman also misuses more traditional frontiers where cultures clash and both a land and its people are threatened. As David Eldridge reiterates, Bateman's "main victims are [according to Faye Weldon] 'the powerless, the poor, the wretched,' those who 'don't rate' in Reaganite America" (2008, 23). The same could be said of those exploited at a distance. In a conversation with friends in one of the many restaurants cited in the film, for example, Bateman challenges his colleague Timothy Bryce (Justin Theroux) about the extent of the massacres in Sri Lanka. Bateman exclaims, "There are a lot more important problems than Sri Lanka to worry about. Sure our foreign policy is important, but there are more pressing problems at hand." He then delineates several more potentially exploitative clashes:

"Well, we have to end apartheid for one. . . . We have to provide food and shelter for the homeless and oppose racial discrimination and promote civil rights while also promoting equal rights for women."

When Donald Kimball (Willem Dafoe), a private investigator, interviews Bateman about the last time he saw Paul Owen, one of Bateman's victims, Bateman again invokes frontiers, claiming, "We had . . . gone to a new musical called . . . *Oh Africa, Brave Africa*. It was . . . a laugh riot . . . and that's about it. I think we had dinner at Orso's. No, Petaluma. No, Orso's." Both these examples connect the consumption of food with the figurative consumption of cultures, updating the American frontier in a late twentieth century upper-class economy. They also introduce an indictment of wendigo/wetiko that Bateman reifies on the bodies of his victims.

Women's bodies also become landscapes captured by Bateman and his video camera in several scenes in *American Psycho*, as upper-class sex objects or disenfranchised female prey. Batemans's fiancée, Evelyn (Reese Witherspoon), is the most prominent of the upper-class women whom Bateman exploits in the film. Evelyn seems powerless in voice-overs Bateman provides, declaring with annoyance, "I'm trying to listen to the new George Michael tape, but Evelyn—my supposed fiancée—keeps buzzing in my ear." Although Evelyn rejects Bateman's sexual advances, choosing to watch the Home Shopping Network instead, in the end he tells her, "You're just not terribly important to me" and leaves her alone to "return videotapes." As a rich daughter of a prominent family, Evelyn could provide the status symbol Bateman at least initially craves, but ultimately he chooses a more literal form of wendigo/wetiko, not only consuming resources and identities but bodies as well.

Although women's bodies become territories for Bateman in the film, as Stephen Holden of the *New York Times* asserts, "compared with . . . robotic cobras [such as Bateman], the women are almost poignantly human" (2000). Christie (Cara Seymour), a streetwalker Bateman hires, and Jean, Bateman's secretary, most explicitly highlight this connection between women's bodies and landscapes. Bateman hires Christie to participate in videotaped sessions. She survives the first, leaving badly bruised and bleeding after an offscreen offensive that includes a coat hanger stored in an armoire drawer. She initially refuses a second encounter, but when he waves a huge wad of bills out the car window, she relents in desperation. Back at his apartment, Bates videotapes himself with Christie and a second woman, a model socialite, Elizabeth (Guinevere Turner). Christie shuts her eyes and grimly concentrates on her performance, turning her head every so often to check the progress of her partners, promoting David Eldridge's suggestion that the "camera . . . delivers a 'moral gaze'" (2008, 24). Although Eldridge asserts that "the only object in the film that could be described as pornographic is Bateman himself, fetishized in the display of Christian Bale's buff body" (24), the rest of the scene responds explicitly to Bateman's viewing of *The Texas Chainsaw Massacre*.

In *American Psycho*, however, women's bodies have been transformed into landscape-like obstacles blocking Christie's escape. Elizabeth becomes a landscape painted in blood after Bateman begins devouring her flesh. When Christie runs from the room, slamming the mirrored door behind her, we see Elizabeth writhing in pain on the bed. Christie meets other human obstacles as she runs down a darkened hallway, frantically opening doors, looking for an escape from a chainsaw's roar coming from the bedroom. She opens a closet where she finds two dead women hanging inside. In another dark room, she sees a head on the top of a television. As she runs, Christie trips over Elizabeth's body, now halfway in the bathtub. Still screaming, Christie makes it out the front door and runs down the hall, banging on doors and pushing elevator buttons until she sees the stairwell and races for it. Bateman follows, revving the chainsaw. When he leans over the railing, aims the chainsaw at her and drops it, the stairwell looks like a canyon, and after the chainsaw stabs her, Christie's sprawled body seems to melt into the floor.

Jean, on the other hand, survives despite the woman's head visible in the freezer when Bateman offers her some sorbet. Although it is Evelyn's phone call that disrupts Bateman's attempt to shoot her with a nail gun, Jean's desire for self-preservation saves her. When Bateman asks her if she wants to get hurt, Jean says no, "I don't want to get bruised" and leaves, the only possible escape from gendered exploitation and a yuppie wendigo in *American Psycho*.

Claire Denis's Paris-centered anticolonial horror film *Trouble Every Day* even more explicitly transforms bodies into landscapes. The wendigo disease has been imported from postcolonial South America after a research expedition led by Dr. Leo Seneneau (Alex Descas). And the disease infects both

Leo's wife, Coré (Béatrice Dalle), and an American male colleague, Shane Brown (Vincent Gallo). But the responses to cannibalism are even more gendered in *Trouble Every Day* than in *American Psycho*. Whereas Coré must be sacrificed after preying on and devouring several men, Shane remains unpunished, even though he too cannibalizes at least one victim, Christelle (Florence Loiret Caille), a hotel maid. Her interactions with both Shane and his wife, June (Tricia Vessey), humanize Christelle, heightening the horror when Shane tortures and murders her and feeds on her flesh; yet because Shane is a respected male doctor, he is free to return home washed clean of guilt. As both victim and perpetrator, Coré must die, perhaps reifying her pleas to Leo: "I can't wait any longer. . . . I want to die."

Although scholarship exploring *Trouble Every Day* primarily highlights how the film plays with genre and/or style, we see the film as a comment on intruders violating interconnected frontiers.[4] As in *American Psycho* the literal cannibalism that both Coré and Shane perform in Paris parallels the consumption of resources. This time the exploitation is in Guyana and also serves as the source of their disease. According to a website explanation of Dr. Leo's bioprospection mission in Guyana, "These samples and analyses should in the near future help us to focus our pharmacological research into nervous diseases, pain, mental diseases, and problems of libido." The following year a bulletin article published in *Revue of the Association of Neuroscientists* explains, "Leo Seneneau has released several studies about botany applied to neuroscience." And in flashback we see Leo working in the jungle with a variety of plants. Other flashbacks show Coré and Shane with Leo in his rainforest camp.

The connection between Western intruders and postcolonial indigenous populations is complicated only by June's interaction with a French African porter (Bakary Sangare) outside her Paris hotel where she desperately looks for Shane in the pouring rain. In a more positive connection between colonized and colonizer, he offers her an umbrella while she stands drenched and frozen in doubt in the darkness asking her, "Wouldn't you prefer to wait inside? It is warm." According to Andrew Asibong, "these moments constitute a radically post-colonial break from the status quo" (2011, 158–59). Shane's interaction with Christelle, however, perpetuates this status quo, reaffirming the exploitation of natives and their resources that he and Leo began in

Guyana. He seems to render Christelle invisible when she and June make their hotel bed, literally stepping out of the frame. But he gazes at her neck as she walks down a hall, metaphorically colonizing her by fragmenting her body into parts.

The most exploitative consumption in *Trouble Every Day*, however, is the literal ingestion of human flesh that results from Shane and Leo's misuse of Guyana's resources. In visual compositions, the film "gender[s] the land as feminine" (Kolodny 1975, 8), a gendering that reveals the two sides to a mythology that constructs women and the nature with which they are compared as both nurturing mothers and whores. Both cases, however, suggest that women and nature are meant to be exploited, with or without their consent. An opening close-up of a heterosexual couple kissing reinforces the latter construct, for example, especially when it cuts to a setting sun over water and an extreme close-up of Coré's face that reveals fecund lips and piercing eyes. She retains her role as sexual temptress even after devouring a truck driver. When her husband, Leo, finds her, he merely hugs her, kisses her forehead, and buries the driver.

In Denis's film, however, the metaphor of the land as woman is complicated in two ways: Coré becomes both cannibal and cannibalized because her wendigo disease was forced upon her by Leo and Shane's experiments with exploited South American resources. And even though he leaves Paris unscathed, Shane too contracts the infection from their postcolonial research. Defying the frontier myth, both male and female bodies become landscapes in *Trouble Every Day*, especially in the film's two key horrific cannibal scenes. In the first Coré seduces a neighbor, who breaks into her house and pulls down the boards that Leo has hammered across her bedroom door. She teases him first, climbing on top and kissing him. But then her kisses turn into bites, continuing even when he yelps for her to stop. The extreme close-ups suggest the intruder's body is a landscape, with a camera hovering over body parts while she bites and pulls off his flesh. She kisses him as he struggles to breath but pokes his wounds with her fingers and laughs. The approach, as Ian Murphy states, is "anthropological," with "copulating human bodies registered in an unusual manner: not as clear figurations or distinct forms, but as dislocated swatches that took several moments for a viewer to recognize and identify as muscle, hair, or skin" (2012). The result is a transformation of body into a landscape on which, as Laura U. Marks puts it, Coré "grazes" (2000, 162).

In the second brutal cannibal scene, Shane confronts Christelle in the hotel employee locker room to (the film suggests) avoid having sex with his wife and devouring her. After the multiple images of Christelle as both maid and human, however, the camera pulls away instead of veering in on her body as landscape. What begins as a stolen sexual moment shown in a medium long shot, however, becomes a violent rape scene amplified by Christelle's unanswered screams. Unlike the vivid cannibal sequence with Coré, however, the horror is revealed visually primarily after the attack, with shots of Christelle's now-motionless body and Shane's bloodied face. Tears run through his blood, as well, matching the lines of blood on the curtain during his post-murder shower.

He and June are reunited with a puppy to provide the warmth he cannot. But the suggestion that Shane's one attack might have satiated him becomes less reliable when juxtaposed with June's frightened and distrustful eyes when he hugs her and asks her to take him home. Although *Trouble Every Day* complicates a frontier myth that constructs a land as female to justify the exploitation of its resources, its conclusion offers no solution to the destructive results of the metaphor. Instead, Shane's seeming ability to contain his desires by satisfying them through the literal cannibalizing of the native "other" continues the wetiko/wendigo cycle Forbes describes.

Blood Diner and *Jennifer's Body*: When Women's Bodies Fight Back

Although director Jackie Kong's *Blood Diner* and director Karyn Kusama and writer Diablo Cody's *Jennifer's Body* differ in their approaches to the horror genre, they both integrate the supernatural into at least partial ecofeminist approaches to cannibalism. *Blood Diner* plays homage to Herschell Gordon Lewis's B-horror film *Blood Feast* (1963), transferring its tale of an Egyptian caterer combining body parts to resurrect a dormant Egyptian goddess to a late 1980s vegetarian restaurant. As an exploitation movie, the film is described by Caryn James of the *New York Times* as "celluloid swill" (1987). *Blood Diner* at its best is "bloody good fun" (2005), according to Clint Morris of *Film Threat*, but at its worst, as Ken Hanke of the newspaper *Mountain*

Xpress, suggests, the film is an "intentionally funny thriller [that] isn't as funny as the straight films it mocks" (2004).

More satiric teen thriller than horror, *Jennifer's Body* may be lampooned as "a premeditated cult classic" (2009) by Nick Pinkerton of the *Village Voice*, but it also received high marks from the *New York Time*'s A. O. Scott (2009), Roger Ebert (2009), and Dana Stevens of *Slate.com* (2009). Scott declares, for example, that "Ms. Cody and Ms. Kusama take up a theme shared by slasher films and teenage comedies—that queasy, panicky fascination with female sexuality that we all know and sublimate—and turn it inside out." According to Scott, *Jennifer's Body* "tak[es] the complication and confusion of being a young woman as its central problem and operating principle." Dana Stevens asserts, "Jennifer's body is luscious and powerful, sexy and scary, maddening at times, but impossible to stop watching. So is *Jennifer's Body.*" And Roger Ebert declares, "This isn't your assembly-line teen horror thriller. The portraits of Jennifer and Needy are a little too knowing, the dialogue is a little too off-center, the developments are a little too quirky.... I'd rather see *Jennifer's Body* again than *Twilight.*" Despite their glaring genre differences, however, *Blood Diner* and *Jennifer's Body* both reverse representations of wendigo/wetiko, exploring female bodies and the landscapes they are said to represent from an ecofeminist perspective. In *Blood Diner* and *Jennifer's Body*, women successfully defeat their oppressors, at least in the context of their respective films.

In *Blood Diner* Michael (Rick Burks) and George (Carl Crew) follow their Uncle Anwar's (Drew Godderis) direction and construct what they call a perfect female body out of women's body parts to host the spirit of a decadent ancient Egyptian goddess, Shitar. Their murdered victims become fodder for customers in their so-called vegetarian restaurant, providing humorous scenes of vegetarians inadvertently ingesting human flesh. Eventually, two inept but persistent detectives, Sheba Jackson (LaNette La France) and Mark Shepherd (Roger Dauer), discover the boys' plan to resurrect Shitar. They learn more about Shitar's Lumerian Cult from an archaeologist who explains how the gruesome goddess entices followers to participate in a literal blood feast. Michael and George plan to re-create this feast.

Although Michael and George successfully construct their goddess and bring her back to life with a ritual Uncle Anwar provides, their plan fails when a newly arisen Shitar feeds on George instead of the female virgin, Connie (Lisa Elaina), they have provided her. Detective Shepherd shoots Michael, freeing Connie and angering George, who yells, "You killed my brother!" But Detective Jackson kicks George into a hungry Shitar's fanged stomach, and she eats his head. With shots of electric low-budget effects, Shitar seems to explode in a blast, seemingly destroying her and the brothers who created her. The remains of the drugged revelers line the floor and stage in the club. When one wakes up, a police officer shoots her. But in a final scene, a woman in red walks away. It is Shitar transformed. A young man picks her up in his convertible and tells her, "You look hot, bothered, and horny." Shitar smiles, revealing her fanged teeth. In this campy B cannibal horror film, Shitar may be the product of male exploitation. But she also destroys the colonizers who create her.

Jennifer's Body takes an approach to cannibalism that builds on the supernatural elements of *Blood Diner* and the constructions of masculinity explored in *Ravenous* and *American Psycho*. Unlike *Blood Diner* the focus of the film is not on the ritual that creates the cannibal but on her hunger: Its satiation makes a statement about the multiple masculine representations in small towns like the Devil's Kettle of the film, as well as the limitations of female power within its context. In *Jennifer's Body* Jennifer (Megan Fox) is transformed into a cannibalistic succubus by a satanic ritual performed by indie band Low Shoulder to ensure their success. When she and best friend, Anita "Needy" (Amanda Seyfried), hear them play at a local bar that suddenly catches fire, Nikolai (Adam Brody), the band's lead singer, recruits her for their ritual, thinking she's a virgin. Because Jennifer has had multiple sexual experiences, however, the ceremony backfires, turning Jennifer into a demon-possessed monster who feeds on men.

Jennifer recounts the tale for Needy in a scene later in the film, and we see her experience with Low Shoulder in flashback. Jennifer calls them "agents of Satan with really cool haircuts." From Jennifer's point of view, we see the inside of their van on her drive away from the bar. There are occult books on the floor, and Nikolai declares, "God, I hate girls," when she begins to cry. To stop them Jennifer claims she is a virgin, not knowing they need a virgin sacrifice for their ritual. She tries to escape, but they're determined because they believe it's the only way they can succeed as musicians. As

Nikolai explains: "Do you know how hard it is to make it as an indie band these days? There are so many of us, and we're all so cute and it's like if you don't get on Letterman or some retarded soundtrack, you're screwed, okay? Satan is our only hope. We're working with the beast now. And we've got to make a really big impression on him. And to do that, we're going to have to butcher you. And bleed you. And then Dirk [Juan Riedinger] here is gonna wear your face." After repeating some words from an Internet download, Nikolai begins stabbing her with a knife and then throws it into a bubbling whirlpool under the town's waterfall. When Jennifer wakes up, she has been transformed into a demonic cannibal who feeds on men to maintain her beauty and strength. When her tongue lights up in flames after a kill, for example, she tells Needy that she "feels like a god."

By including sympathetic male victims, however, the film takes a more subtle approach to its ecofeminist message. Jennifer's prey are not the typical villains found in revenge films but stock character types found in teen films: the class jock and the sensitive Goth poet. In both of the murder and cannibal scenes, the natural world responds to Jennifer's violence, watching her raptly as she devours each of her frightened victims and providing a macabre interpretation of the woman/nature connection perpetuated by dualistic thought. The first victim we see is Jonas (Josh Emerson), a football player upset about losing his best friend in the bar fire. She lures him into the woods and claims his friend told her they would make a great couple: "Feel my heart, Jonas. I think it's broken," she exclaims and begins taking off his clothes. The atmosphere grows eerie when animals begin surrounding them in a weird Disney's *Snow White* moment. When Jonas looks at the animals nervously, Jennifer tells him they're waiting and opens his shirt and pants. "You're going to see your buddy really soon," she tells him and attacks. When she lures the Goth poet Colin (Kyle Gallner) to a deserted house, rats and roaches appear right before she kills and eats him. Each of these masculine character types, the film suggests, both satisfy and strengthen the supernatural wendigo. By choosing males so willing to ravish her perfect body, however, Jennifer serves as both cannibal and cannibalized, perhaps ineffectively avenging the damage done to frontiers of nature and women's bodies.

Jennifer's role changes, however, when she shifts her attention to Chip (Johnny Simmons), Needy's boyfriend. Unlike Josh and Colin, Chip rejects

Jennifer's advances after she lures him to a pool house on the way to the school dance. Needy hears his calls, but when she reaches him, Jennifer has already bitten him. He's dying but hands Needy pepper spray to protect her. Jennifer vomits black blood and rises above the pool: "Do you have to undermine everything I do? You're such a player hater," she tells Needy. Needy confronts her about Chip, and before Jennifer can kill her, Chip spears Jennifer with a pool tool. "You gotta tampon?" she asks Needy and jumps out a window. "I should have believed you. I'm sorry," Chip says and tells Needy he loves her.

By murdering Chip Jennifer has also transformed Needy, sparking her to return for revenge with a box cutter. Jennifer bites her, but Needy cuts a cross into Jennifer's body and takes her BFF necklace. Jennifer falls back on the bed, and Needy stabs her in the heart. Jennifer's breathing stops, and her color returns. Jennifer's mom finds Needy, and in the next scene, Needy is in solitary at the mental hospital that opened the film. She tells the audience, "I'm a different person now." She has absorbed some of Jennifer's powers because she survived the bite and floats up to a high window in her cell and escapes in her bunny slippers. The knife that turned Jennifer into a cannibal appears, along with the red balls from science experiments. Needy picks up the knife and hitchhikes toward Low Shoulder's next concert, telling a driver that "tonight will be their last concert." The film ends with a photomontage of the band after its concert, first with groupies partying in their hotel suite. Then images change to blood and their bodies covered in plastic. The photographs look like forensic evidence now. A last shot shows us Needy in a surveillance camera walking away and pulling up her hood. Needy defeats both cannibals in *Jennifer's Body*, destroying an indie band whose success was built on Jennifer's violated body and the succubus they perhaps inadvertently created. By rejecting the construction of woman as victim, *Jennifer's Body* may also disrupt a pastoral fantasy and frontier myth that feminize nature in order to exploit it.

Blood Diner, *Jennifer's Body*, and to a certain extent *Trouble Every Day* may construct women as monsters rather than victims, especially, as Barbara Creed argues in *The Monstrous-Feminine: Film, Feminism, Psychoanalysis*, "in relation to her mothering and reproductive functions" (1993, 7), but the monstrous

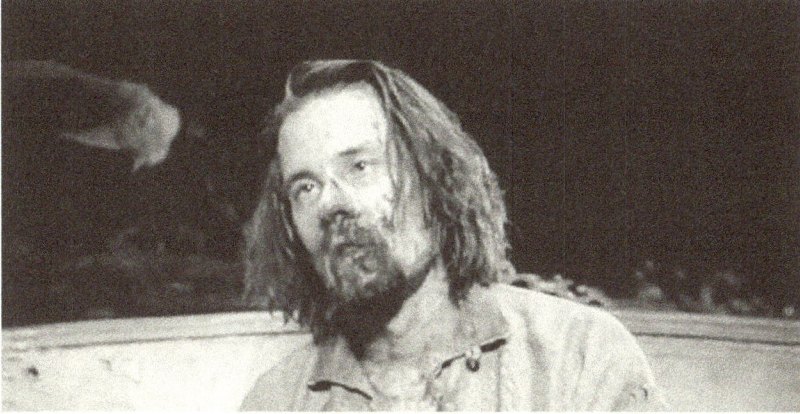

Ravenous: Captain John Boyd resists cannibalism.

actions of Shitar, Jennifer, and Coré are produced by male "intruders" who may, as Jack D. Forbes suggests, be the real cannibals in these films. As ecofeminist Jytte Nhanenge argues, "there is an interconnection between the domination of women and poor people, and the domination of nature" (2011, xxvii). Creed asserts that what she calls the monstrous-feminine can "provide us with a means of understanding the dark side of the patriarchal unconscious" (1993, 166). Perhaps it can also blur boundaries between male and female, and between culture and nature, offering a saner approach to the frontiers of land and body that reject the wetiko disease. Forbes observes, "The wetiko psychosis is a sickness of the spirit that takes people down an ugly path with no heart. They may kill, but they are not warriors. . . . Above all, the wetiko disease turns such into werewolves and vampires, creatures of the European's nightmare world, and creatures of the wetiko's reality" (1992, 188). Instead, Forbes argues, we can choose to follow "a good path, a path of beauty" (189) that encourages love for the earth, "more respect for life, more respect for the living, more respect for all forms of life," (178), including the nonhuman.

Ravenous, American Psycho, and *Trouble Every Day* illustrate some of the horrific consequences of choosing the cannibal path, either literally or figuratively. In their fictional contexts, the films critique Manifest Destiny, yuppie excessive consumerism, and postcolonial resource exploitation as figurative forms of cannibalism or, as Forbes declares, the wetiko psychosis. Although their narratives are less didactic, *Blood Diner* and *Jennifer's Body* illustrate the negative consequences of a pastoral myth that constructs frontiers of both the natural world and women's bodies as nurturing mothers or seductive and promiscuous whores. They may also demonstrate the need for "a partnership ethic" like that historian Carolyn Merchant describes, in which "the needs of both humans and nonhumans would be dynamically balanced" (2013, 206). All these films leave viewers with more complex visions of cannibalism, a gendered disease with multiple sources but only one cure.

9

American Mary and Body Modification

Nature and the Art of Change

At a turning point in the contemporary feminist "Frankenstein" film *American Mary*, Ruby (Paula Lindberg)—one of Mary's future body-modification clients—explains why she wants to change her appearance: "I don't think it's really fair that God gets to choose what we look like on the outside," she proclaims. Ruby's declaration at first seems to align well with scholars' assertions that humans decorate and modify their bodies to separate themselves from the animals and nature, for, as genetic researcher Gillian M. Morriss-Kay argues, "Creating visual art is one of the defining characteristics of the human species" (2010, 158). Morriss-Kay agrees, suggesting, "The earliest known evidence of 'artistic behaviour' is of human body decoration, including skin colouring with ochre and the use of beads, although both may have had functional origins" (158). Ruby's desire to determine what her body looks like on the outside seems to take this characteristic just a little further, since, as anthropologist Enid Schildkrout (2010) of the *Smithsonian*

Young Frankenstein: "It's alive!"

states, "there is no logical reason to separate permanent forms of body art, like tattoos, scarification, piercing, or plastic surgery, from temporary forms, such as makeup, clothing, or hairstyles." More extreme forms of body modification convey information about a person's identity in ways similar to the more traditional and temporary choices people make to color their hair and shave their faces.

For Ruby, a fashion designer and owner of Ruby Real Girl designs, surgically changing her body provides some of the same results as fashion and makeup, except that those changes are more permanent. It seems to separate her from her natural "God-given" form and from the natural world it represents and inhabits. The claim is that animals change their appearance only because evolution has determined those changes ensure survival, both physical and sexual. And those changes rely on internal biological responses rather than deliberate additions from the external environment. A cuttlefish may change the color and shape of its skin and body to hide from predators, hypnotize prey, and seduce potential sex partners, but these survival adaptations are evolutionary rather than learned behaviors and draw on biology rather than the incorporation of external objects. Yet we argue that this separation between humans and animals rests on a limited perspective of the natural world. Although the body modification illustrated in *American Mary* may amplify the drive for individuality found in makeup and hair changes, it does not necessarily separate humans from animals. Instead, it replicates the behaviors of animals from the bowerbird to particular species of spiders and caterpillars. When characters in *American Mary* modify their bodies to express their individuality and survive, they don't separate themselves from nature; instead they align themselves with the animal world. When either animals or humans change their appearance, they gain an evolutionary advantage that assures their reproductive and biological persistence.

What Is Body Modification?

Anthropologists explore body modification in relation to a variety of cultural practices. In "Enhancement Technologies and the Body," Linda Hogle asserts, "Humans have always modified their bodies. What distinguishes these techniques is that bodies and selves become the objects of improvement work, unlike previous efforts in modernity to achieve progress through social and political institutions" (2005, 695). Steven W. Gangestad and Glenn J. Scheyd's "The Evolution of Human Physical Attraction" explores the question, "can human standards of physical attractiveness be understood through the lens of evolutionary biology?" (2005, 523). And Rosemary A. Joyce examines the body as a "site of embodied agency" (2005, 139) that changes in response to individual and cultural experiences rather than remaining static. Anthropologist and museum curator Enid Schildkrout suggests that body art and the body modification it involves is universal. In fact, "there is no culture in which people do not, or did not, paint, pierce, tattoo, reshape, or simply adorn their bodies." According to Schildkrout (2010), "Body art communicates a person's status in society; displays accomplishments; and encodes memories, desires, and life histories."

Body modification may be ephemeral, as with body painting, makeup, and hairstyles. But it may also include more permanent changes, such as body shaping, scarification, tattooing, and piercing. Directed by Jason Gary and Greg Jacobson, the 2005 documentary *Modify* reinforces Schildkrout's definition with images of the varied forms of modification and testimony from those who personally modify their own bodies and the artists and surgeons who modify the bodies of others. The documentary asserts that there are four reasons for body modification: aesthetics, sexual augmentation, shock value, and spirituality. For most of the experts documented in *Modify*, body modification is body art and includes hair color, ear piercing, and body building, as well as tattooing, body piercing, and plastic surgery.[1]

The documentary highlights the wide range of body modification techniques available "to make you look like you want." A female impersonator and Las Vegas entertainer discusses the artistic challenge his career offers while we watch him prepare his stage persona. Plastic surgeon Dr. Julio Garcia discusses the multiple procedures available while a montage of images shows us his work: liposuction, breast augmentation, and facelift surgeries. According to Garcia, "we modify our bodies every day," again noting how many choose to color their hair or shave their beards. Plastic surgery too is seen as an everyday occurrence, with 300,000 liposuctions, 250,000 breast augmentation surgeries, and over two million Botox treatments a year in the United States alone. Plastic surgeon and urologist Dr. Gary Alter amplifies Dr. Garcia's testimony, adding and showing viewers the surgeries needed for a sex-change operation. Other experts discuss the multiple types of piercings and the reasons behind them. The documentary stresses how they serve as a sign of individuality that varies by culture. Piercings can serve as a rite of passage or a way to enhance sexual experiences. Tattoo and piercing artist Allen Faulkner introduces viewers to suspensions, an extension of piercings that includes the insertion of metal rings from which the body is suspended by a series of wires.

Modify expands definitions of body modification to include the more everyday bodybuilder who expands his muscles with steroids, growth hormones, and ardent weight lifting. Bodybuilders highlighted in the documentary discuss their exercise and diet regimen, as well as their need to tan and shave their bodies to compete in tournaments, but they also mention the hormones they ingest to amplify results. Their body modification differs from those seen as more extreme only because of social stigmas. *Modify* shows us images of scarification, tattooing, and body shaping for beautification and ritualistic purposes. Body implants are also discussed as sculptures to help those who are unsatisfied with their bodies. Body-implant specialist Jessie Jarrell asserts that as long as the modifications are safe, sane, and consensual, they are an art form and a means of exhibiting an identity rather than a form of mutilation.

But Jarrell also makes a claim that is meant to separate humans from the natural world. He claims that the changes his engineered parts and sculpted implants create allow humans to view such body modification as a sign of our superiority. It is "just the idea that we're the first species capable of altering our physical form with our own free will." For Jarrell and the other experts documented in *Modify*, body art is a human endeavor unseen in other species. Cognitive researcher Nancy Etcoff argues similar points in her "Born to Adorn: Why We Desire, Display, and Design," stating, "Getting dressed is a uniquely human activity" (2010, 3). Instead, evolutionary changes that Darwin called "sexual selection" provided males with "frills, colors, and beauty" to charm females of their species and "canines, antlers, or massive size" to deter their competitors (3). Etcoff suggests that the adornments humans choose draw on Darwin's notion of sexual selection, arguing that our "evolutionary impulses for protection, attention, love, beauty, and status remain" (17). For Etcoff as for Jarrell, however, our impulses differ from those of animals because "we acquire clothes and jewelry" as "part of our extended phenotype ... part of the 'self' we create, and use to protect and define who we are" (7). Our evolutionary narratives, unlike those of nonhuman nature, extend beyond biology, according to Etcoff and Jarrell.

Animal and Insect Body Modification

Although focusing primarily on separating humans from nonhuman nature, Etcoff also notes that at least one animal "exhibits a form of dressing" (2010, 6): the bowerbird, which builds and decorates a bower to attract a mate. Etcoff's admission in some ways contradicts her assertion that the adornments of dress are uniquely human. It also broaches questions that may connect our evolutionary paths more explicitly to those of the animal world: Are there other species of animals that use ornaments outside their bodies for decoration or disguise? And do these examples begin to redefine our own connections to the natural world and evolution? Do they also reshape the purpose behind the changes we make to our bodies and selves? For us the body modifications explored in *American Mary* do not separate humans from nature. Rather, they demonstrate all too well our connections to it.

The male of the multiple subspecies of bowerbirds, for example, builds bowers consisting "of a thatched twig tunnel forming an avenue" decorated with bones, shells, berries, nuts, and stones, which the male displays to potential mates. They arrange the objects in regular patterns, creating an illusion that seems to increase their size, according to biologists Laura Kelley and John Endler (2012). The bowers are works of art meant only for seducing female bowerbirds, not for nesting, and clearly require objects external to the birds to build them. David Attenborough's documentary *Bowerbirds: The Art of Seduction* (2012) highlights the behaviors of multiple species of bowerbirds and demonstrates how deliberately the birds place their artifacts. In one scene, for example, Attenborough moves objects, and a male bowerbird immediately replaces them.

Other animals decorate their bodies rather than create external bowers. Sandhill cranes preen their feathers with mud, turning their gray bodies red or brown during spring and summer. The purpose behind the preening may be related to breeding because it ends when the feathers molt in the fall. And the looper caterpillar ornaments its body with plant parts from the flowers on which it is feeding. According to Miklos Treiber (1979), the loopers change the flower parts when they move to another flower as well. Here the plant pieces act as camouflage. Treiber hypothesizes that the looper's ability to change disguises allows it to have a much more varied diet than some other caterpillars because it isn't restricted to eating only those flowers or plant parts that it resembles in appearance. Multiple videos document the looper's amazing camouflage.

Bringing to mind the action movie *RoboCop* (1987) and its 2014 remake, Neill Blomkamp's *Elysium* (2013) shows some of the positive outcomes of body modification that line up with those used by the looper caterpillar: self-defense.[2] Max (Matt Damon) is fused with a robotic exoskeleton to defend himself rather than disguise his body, but the purpose behind his choice is similar. Using one character's plight in a postapocalyptic future, the film condemns huge disparities between rich and poor and the environmental and social problems they promote. As in Blomkamp's *District 9* (2009), Earth has become an environmental disaster plagued by overpopulation and the crime and starvation it produces. Only the rich can escape the polluted planet by purchasing access to an orbiting space station with forests, green lawns, golf courses, and oversized homes—shown in glorious CGI. And only a human machine can bridge the gap between rich and poor that it enforces.

Despite the film's failure to address environmental racism and justice issues on Earth, *Elysium* provides an optimistic view of technology and the cyborg as a solution to at least some of the externalities human overconsumption has created. Although *Elysium* does not address the environmental degradation on Earth's surface, we assume the robots that once controlled humans will now clean up their waste. Despite the film's confusing plotline, it demonstrates how humans (especially men) may benefit from merging with technology. By donning a mechanical exoskeleton, Max saves those he loves, freeing Earth's poor in the process. Like the looper caterpillar's added flowers, an external body modification helps Max thwart a despotic government. He may not survive, but his friends will.

Body Modification, Feminism, and the Cyborg

Research in the area of body modification connects with multiple disciplines that focus most explicitly on gender and sexuality, a focus that also connects with the bowerbirds and their sexual selection practices. A few articles examine the body in relation to feminist disability studies. Rosemarie Garland-Thomas's "Feminist Disability Studies," for example, explains how such studies uncover "communities and identities that the bodies we consider disabled have produced" (2005, 1557). Feminist disability studies research seeks to illuminate how our culture constructs definitions of disability and "questions our assumptions that disability is a flaw, lack, or excess" (1557). Instead, the disability may help build communities that may be disrupted when the so-called flaw is addressed by the medical community. For example, a recent study by Sujata Gupta (2014) in *Matter* suggests that cochlear implants are destroying a subculture and devaluing the identities of persons who are hearing impaired.

Perhaps because of this connection between bodies, identities, and communities, much of the research focused on bodies and body modification examines a gendered body through a variety of feminist lenses. Several articles examine cosmetic surgery as body modification. For example, Ann J. Cahill's "Feminist Pleasure and Feminine Beautification" distinguishes between the "process of beautification and its product" (2003, 61) and suggests that beautification may be "a positive experience for women," but "being viewed as a beautiful object is almost always opposed to women's equality and autonomy" (42). Alexander Edmonds views beautification as only a positive experience in his exploration of cosmetic surgery and class in Brazil. According to Edmonds such cosmetic body modification offers "a means to compete in a neoliberal libidinal economy where anxieties surrounding new markets of work and sex mingle with fantasies of social mobility, glamour, and modernity" (2007, 363). In "Bodies of Change: A Comparative Analysis of Media Representations of Body Modification Practices," Josh Adams explores cosmetic surgery in relation to tattooing and piercing and asserts that "piercing is often negatively framed as an unhealthy and problematic practice" (2009, 103). As an aside Adams suggests that gender may serve as "a method of reinforcing normative expectations" (103).

Other feminist readings of body modification highlight how sexual politics and cultural context intersect with the altered body. Victoria Pitts's "Visibly Queer: Body Technologies and Sexual Politics" argues that body modification may not oppose a "(hetero) dominant culture" because agency is "limited by and constituted within regulatory regimes of power, such as heteronormativity, pathologization, and colonialism" (2000, 443). Pippa Brush also explores agency in relation to body modification in her "Metaphors of Inscription: Discipline, Plasticity and the Rhetoric of Choice." Drawing on Foucault's disciplinary regime, Brush examines both the existence of a material body and the "cultural and social contexts within which the body is always placed" (1998, 22). Brenda R. Weber's "Masculinity, American Modernity, and Body Modification: A Feminist Reading of *American Eunuchs*" (2013), on the other hand, focuses specifically on *American Eunuchs* and how the documentary perpetuates the mind/body bifurcation (dualism) and reinforces masculine associations with the rational. Women become invisible in this hypermasculinized (if desexualized) world.

Still other feminist readings of body modification focus on the cyborg, cyberpunk, and cyberculture in science fiction film and literature. Celan Ertung's "Bodies That [Don't] Matter: Feminist Cyberpunk and Transgressions of Bodily Boundaries" asserts that despite "its revolutionary promise as a gender free space, cyberculture, in its actual manifestation and literary representations, duplicates the power dynamics of sexist and racist practices perpetuating inequality" (2011, 77). In "Bodies That Matter: Science Fiction, Technoculture, and the Gendered Body," Kaye Mitchell explores questions such as the following: "Will technology render us posthuman in its blurring of the boundaries of human and machine? Will the practical and theoretical 'fluidity' of sex and gender (from gender reassignment surgery to drag performance to theories of a 'last sex') bring about a world that is properly or positively post-gender?" (2006, 109). According to Mitchell's study of a variety of science fiction narratives, "bodies really do (and are) matter—but the meaning(s) of 'matter' may be endlessly deferred and re-negotiated" (126).

A few Japanese body-modification films draw on this feminist cyborg myth either explicitly or implicitly, providing a speculative connection between humans and animals that biologically modify their bodies. Three of these films connect the cyborg myth with the natural world and produce hybrid beings with capabilities more like cuttlefish than a decorated human: *Machine Girl* (2009), *RoboGeisha* (2009), and *Tokyo Gore Police* (2008).[3] According to the documentary *Kings of Camouflage* (2007), "the cuttlefish [is] a flesh-eating predator who's a master of illusion, changing its shape and color at will. It can hypnotize its prey or even become invisible." In the film scientist Mark Norman explains their amazing modification abilities: "They've developed this skin that can do the amazing changes in color and changes in shape. And what fascinates me the most is how different cuttlefish species have taken that basic tool that probably evolved for camouflage, and they've taken it a step further and said, 'All right, how can we use this in other ways?'"

Noboru Iguchi's *Machine Girl* and *RoboGeisha* and Yoshihiro Nishimura's *Tokyo Gore Police* highlight how women take "basic tools" and gain power when they are transformed into cyborgs. What changes in these Japanese films, however, is the interconnection between nature and machine embodied by each character's bodily changes. These films amplify the connection between animal and human body modification by including biological and evolutionary changes missing from films such as *Elysium* (2013). In these Japanese cyborg films, body modification immerses women in both nature and culture. The modification explored here blurs nature-culture boundaries and aligns human change with cuttlefish evolution.

As Donna Haraway explains in her "Cyborg Manifesto," "a cyborg is a cybernetic organism, a hybrid of machine and organism, a creature of social reality as well as a creature of fiction" (1991, 149). For Haraway cyborg fiction offers a space in which women can deconstruct binaries that construct nature and the feminine as inferior to their binary opposites, the masculine and culture. Haraway suggests the "cyborg myth is about transgressed boundaries, potent fusions and dangerous possibilities which progressive people might explore as one part of needed political work" (154). Because Western culture is grounded in such binaries, alternative perspectives are needed to blur exploitative boundaries. As Haraway contends, "Most American socialists and feminists see deepened dualisms of mind and body, animal and machine, idealism and materialism in social practices, symbolic formulations and physical artifacts associated with 'high technology' and scientific culture" (154).

The American socialists and feminists Haraway describes might agree with the view that "a cyborg world is about the final imposition of a grid of control on the planet, about the final abstraction embodied in a Star Wars apocalypse waged in the name of defense, about the final appropriation of women's bodies in a masculinist orgy of war (Sofia 1984)" (1991, 154). But contemporary Japanese body modification horror supports a second perspective, one in which "a cyborg world might be about lived social and bodily realities in which people are not afraid of their joint kinship with animals and machines, not afraid of permanently partial identities and contradictory standpoints" (154). In *Machine Girl*, *RoboGeisha*, and *Tokyo Gore Police*, women, nature, and the machine merge, creating new organisms with the ability to modify themselves from within.

Directed by Noboru Iguchi, *Machine Girl* most clearly aligns with the traditional view of the cyborg as a hybrid of machine and organism when the film's protagonist Ami (Minase Yashiro) loses a hand and replaces it with a gun. The opening scene introduces her alteration and highlights the schoolgirl Ami's quest to avenge her brother Yu's (Ryôsuke Kawamura) murder. "You're the ones who made it my business," she says, as she kills a group of young men taunting a schoolboy. She has lost a hand, and when gang members throw knives at her, she attaches an automatic weapon and shoots off their heads. Blood spurts everywhere, so much so that the schoolboy calls her a murderer despite her having saved his life.

The film then flashes back to situate the opening scene: six months before "she could hold her little brother with her left arm." She excelled at basketball and cared for her brother, Yu, after their parents committed suicide. They seem like a contented nontraditional family until Yu borrows money from a gang to buy a videogame. When he cannot repay the debt, Yu is thrown from the top of a parking garage and dies. Despite discovering the gang is run by the son of a Yakuza boss, Ryûji Kimura (Kentarô Shimazu), Ami wishes to avenge her brother's death and infiltrates their hideout, where she is captured and tortured. She manages to escape, but loses her hand in doing so. A machinist and his wife, Miki (Asami), replace her hand with a custom-made automatic weapon. Because she lost her son to the Yakuza, Miki helps Ami defeat Kimura and his family while Yu's ghost applauds, connecting machine with a supernatural element that complicates the cyborg myth.

Iguchi's *RoboGeisha* provides a more explicit connection with biology, since the cyborgs created in the film mingle machines with bodies and minds. The film's opening introduces the Goblin Squadron, a group of female cyborgs who attack a prime minister's security guards. Yoshie (Aya Kiguchi)—the RoboGeisha of the title—intervenes, saving the prime minister. The RoboGeisha explains her situation, telling the audience, "I am not a monster. I am a robot." Another cyborg shows her spinning-saw mouth, but the RoboGeisha protects the prime minister and declares, "Violence has no place in the world of the geisha." From here the film flashes back to the RoboGeisha cyborg's origin as Yoshie, the younger of two sisters working in a geisha house. Although her older sister, Kikue (Hitomi Hasebe), is considered the superior geisha, Yoshie proves the most powerful. A customer and owner of a steelwork company, Kageno (Takumi Saitô), discovers Yoshie's natural strength and fighting ability and recruits her into an army of geisha assassins, including her sister, as part of the Goblin Squadron. During training parts of each woman recruit's body are altered into weaponry directly linked to their brains, turning them into cyborgs with ties to the natural world.

When Yoshie refuses to destroy members of a family rescue organization attempting to find their lost daughters, Kageno nearly destroys her, but she survives and discovers that Kageno's real plan is to have his robotic castle throw a new and very powerful nuclear bomb into the center of Mount Fuji, effectively destroying Japan. With the help of the family rescue organization members who find and repair her, Yoshie sets out to stop him and his robotic warriors. Ultimately Yoshie destroys Kageno and his robot castle only by reconnecting with her elder sister. Together their cyborg strength knocks the robot castle into space, where it explodes into harmless fireworks. In *RoboGeisha* bodies and machines merge both individually and through sibling connections.

Yoshihiro Nishimura's *Tokyo Gore Police* even more blatantly alters the cyborg myth by merging science and technology with genetics. The film is set in a future-world vision of Tokyo where the police have been privatized and destroy lawbreakers with unfettered violence. The samurai-sword-wielding Ruka (Eihi Shiina) leads the police squad with a mission to destroy homicidal mutant humans known as "engineers" who possess the ability to transform any injury into a weapon in and of itself. Ultimately Ruka becomes an engineer when a genetic key is inserted in her wounded body, which gives her access to the power needed to avenge her father's death. As Grady Hendrix explains, she "can't accomplish her goals until she disposes of her bogus old body and accepts a gnarly new mutated one" (2010, 57). Once she discovers the police whom she works for assassinated her father, Ruka joins forces with the keyman (Itsuji Itao) who created the engineers. As a powerful biological cyborg, Ruka overthrows the police, halting their violent assault on the citizens of Tokyo.

Although these three films approach the cyborg in varying ways, they all reinforce Haraway's claims: "The cyborg is a matter of fiction and lived experience that changes what counts as women's experience. . . . This is a struggle between life and death, but the boundary between science fiction and social reality is an optical illusion" (1991, 149). They also highlight, if in fictional form, our connection with the natural world. According to the narrator of *Kings of Camouflage*, "Evolution means change, so maybe in a few million years, the flamboyant will march on eight legs right onto the beaches. Or the broadclub will hypnotize its predators as well as its prey. Perhaps the Australian giants will invent even more daring strategies to outwit their rivals." *Machine Girl*, *RoboGeisha*, and *Tokyo Gore Police* offer a space in which to explore how evolution may also change us.

Frankenstein, Body Modification, and the Natural World

Perhaps the most iconic work addressing the horrors of modifying and reanimating bodies is Mary Shelley's *Frankenstein*. Not surprisingly, much of the scholarship exploring the novel considers the role of nature in the human world. In "Home Is Where Mamma Is: Reframing the Science Question in *Frankenstein*," Suparna Banerjee argues that *Frankenstein* does not condemn the science that Dr. Frankenstein uses because it seeks to reproduce women's reproductive power. Instead, Banerjee offers an alternative to the popular view of "Frankenstein's science as a negative manipulation of nature, an attempt, specifically, to usurp woman's creative power through scientific technology" (2010, 1). For Banerjee *Frankenstein* is instead "a subversion of the thematic itself of nature-versus-culture and . . . a critique of the Baconian concept of modern science—a concept that is symptomatic of this hierarchical opposition in cultural thinking . . . and the gender division created and sustained by this discursive and attitudinal schism" (1–2). Instead of the novel separating culture from nature, Banerjee suggests that it argues for blurring the boundaries between these two poles and seeks to redefine science outside such binaries.

Kim Hammond's "Monsters of Modernities: Frankenstein and Modern Environmentalism" also provides a reading of the novel "as a critical questioning of both anti-Enlightenment Romanticism and anti-Enlightenment science that provides a framework for evaluating contemporary ecobiocentric ideals . . . drawing our attention instead to important questions about what kind of socio-nature we want produced, by whom, for what purposes, and under what conditions" (2004, 181). For Hammond, too, the nature-versus-culture theme may lead to destructive consequences. Scholarship examining film adaptations of the novel takes a similar stance.[4]

In "'A Blot upon the Earth': Nature's 'Negative' and the Production of Monstrosity in *Frankenstein*" (2010), on the other hand, Helena Feder explores the environment within and outside the novel. Feder looks closely at "monstrosity and acculturation in the context of western culture's objectification of nonhuman nature, circling back to bodies of water and the extraordinary environmental conditions of the novel's production." And Julie Cruikshank's "Glaciers and Climate Change: Perspectives from Oral Tradition" highlights how "Shelley wrote his poem 'Mont Blanc' while visiting the Alps in 1816, the reputed 'year without a summer' (Harington, 1992) in which Mary Shelley also wrote *Frankenstein*, sending her protagonist into alpine glaciers during his tormented struggle to become human" (2001, 378).

Adaptations of the novel highlight a few of these environmental themes. Film adaptations since Thomas Edison's 1910 silent *Frankenstein* have critiqued humanity's manipulation of nature and the nature/culture binary undergirding Frankenstein's drive to create life. As with many science fiction novels and films, science and the scientist are under suspicion in these

Frankenstein films because they separate themselves from nature in their attempts to "play god." As in the novel, both the monster and its creator, Dr. Frankenstein, must be punished as "abominations." In the 1931 Universal adaptation, for example, a narrator introduces the play with a warning against manipulating nature: "We're about to unfold the story of Frankenstein, a man of science who sought to create a man after his own image without reckoning upon God." That warning takes shape when Frankenstein (Colin Clive) succeeds and highlights his own superiority to nature, exclaiming, "Look! It's moving. It's alive. It's alive . . . It's alive, it's moving, it's alive, it's alive, it's alive, it's alive, IT'S ALIVE!" And when his partner, Victor Moritz (John Boles), admonishes him, "in the name of God," Frankenstein declares, "Oh, in the name of God! Now I know what it feels like to be God!" Similar themes predominate in most adaptations of the novel, even in social social-statement horror such as *Blackenstein* (1972) and the hybrid vampire feature, *I, Frankenstein*.[5]

A few adaptations more blatantly integrate environmental themes, however, reinforcing arguments made by Feder and Cruikshank. Kenneth Branagh's *Mary Shelley's Frankenstein* (1994) highlights the glacial setting as a frame for the film. Unlike the novel the film portrays the Alpine glaciers as both setting and antagonist, disrupting Captain Robert Walton's (Aiden Quinn) voyage to the North Pole and thwarting Frankenstein's (Kenneth Branagh) attempts to destroy his creation (Robert De Niro). In Roger Corman's sci-fi horror *Frankenstein Unbound* (1990), that glacial setting explicitly illustrates humanity's destruction of its own environment. The opening scenes even highlight a tribute for the last remaining parts of the Brazilian rainforest. In 2031 scientist Dr. Joe Buchanan (John Hurt) creates a powerful weapon with catastrophic consequences. It not only will destroy whole cultures but also produces time slippages that knock Buchanan back to 1817 Switzerland, where he meets Dr. Frankenstein (Raul Julia) and his creature (Nick Brimble).[6]

As in *The Bride of Frankenstein* (1935), *Mary Shelley's Frankenstein*, and multiple other adaptations of the novel, the creature in *Frankenstein Unbound* pressures Dr. Frankenstein to build him a wife and companion because the human world has rejected him. When Frankenstein refuses, the creature grows increasingly violent, and neither Frankenstein nor Buchanan can destroy him. As a last attempt Buchanan uses his weapon once more and thrusts the creature, Frankenstein, and himself into the lifeless glacial wasteland that opened the film. Unlike *Mary Shelley's Frankenstein*, however, *Frankenstein Unbound* makes clear that humans are the cause of this wasteland. Centuries of war have destroyed both humanity and the natural world. Although the separation between humans and the natural world is critiqued in these films, however, they all amplify our difference from nonhuman nature rather than our connections to it.[7]

New Feminist Representations of Body Modification: *American Mary* and Nature's Drive for Survival

The body modification explored in *American Mary* builds on the drive to create life explored in various *Frankenstein* movies. But it also replicates behaviors found in the natural world. The modifications Mary performs most closely connect with the actions of a particular species of *Cyclosa* spider, *Cyclosa mulmeinensis*. According to a BBC News report on the work of biologists Ling Tseng and I-MinTso, the species "decorates its web with both the remains of dead insect prey and egg sacs. Intriguingly, the spiders made prey pellets and egg sacs that were the same size as its own body." The researchers found that "these decorations appeared to wasps to be the same color, and reflect light in the same way, as the spider's body." In the report Tseng and Min Tso explain, "Our results show that this vulnerable spider protects itself from predator attacks by constructing decoys that increase the conspicuousness of the web, and resemble its own appearance in size and color" (quoted in Walker 2009). These *Cyclosa* spiders build decoys that look so much like themselves that wasps strike the decoy rather than the spider. A "Smarter Every Day" video reveals how authentically this spider replicates its body, even including eight artificial legs on its decoy self.[8] This species of spider, then, acts like Frankenstein, building a spider replica to stand in for itself.

Whereas *Elysium* illustrates both the benefits and the negative consequences of merging nature with technology, Jen and Sylvia Soska's *American Mary* (2012) explores surgically modified bodies in an update of *Frankenstein* and its film adaptations. C. Jerry Cutner defines it as female-centered horror distinguished by its female directors. According to Cutner, "Thematically, *American Mary* draws from the fetishism and 'body horror' of David Cronenberg films like *Dead Ringers* and *Crash*. Though shot on a comparatively low budget, it has the style and gloss of Hollywood erotic thrillers like De Palma's *Dressed to Kill* or Verhoeven's *Basic Instinct*" (2013) *American Mary* tells the story of a medical student, Mary Mason (Katharine Isabelle), using her skills as a surgeon in three settings: in a hospital residency program, in a strip club where she looks for work when her restaurant job falls through, and in her own body modification practice. Because of its body modification focus, however, we see the film explicitly connecting with *Frankenstein*, its offshoots, and the natural world.[9]

In *American Mary* Mason revises the figure of Dr. Frankenstein as the unethical scientist unwilling to take responsibility for his "monstrous" creation. As a product of date rape perpetrated by her medical school professors, Dr. Grant (David Lovgren) and Dr. Walsh (Clay St. Thomas), Mary becomes both monster and "mad" scientist. Instead of creating new life forms by assembling discarded body parts, Mary transforms the bodies of her "patients" so they can, as Beatrice (Tristan Risk), a stripper and body modification advocate who looks like Betty Boop explains, "look the same on the outside as they do on the inside." These transformations become monstrous, however, only when they serve as revenge.[10]

American Mary's opening illustrates Mary's strengths as artist and surgeon, while also foreshadowing the body modification focus of the film. In an early scene, Mary practices sutures on a turkey carcass wearing only a black petticoat, apron, and rubber gloves but looks more like a torture artist than a doctor, despite the skill on display. These images of sealing deliberately made incisions are reinforced by a medical school lecture Mary attends the next day focused on reattaching amputated body parts. Grant explains, "An amputated arm . . . can be surgically reattached if the patient receives surgical attention within four hours. An amputated hand within eight, amputated fingers within twelve. So, four, eight, twelve." Mary has already demonstrated her ability to reattach amputated arms, hands, and fingers with her careful work on the turkey. The stage has been set for Mary's entrance into the body modification community and the film's connection to the Frankenstein genre.

Mary's experiences as a medical student also expose Grant as the oppressor who encourages her decision to adopt body modification surgery as a profession instead of traditional medicine. These experiences also serve as a critique of the nature-culture binary explored in *Frankenstein* and its adaptations. He verbally attacks her during his lectures and threatens her over the phone despite noting her potential as a surgeon. He attacks her in one scene, warning her not to bring her cell phone into his classroom; "It's fucking rude," he exclaims. When she excels as a resident under Walsh, he tells her, "You're going to be a great slasher," both denigrating his profession and making an explicit connection between surgery and the body-modification community. His words also amplify the work that Mary performs for nightclub owner Billy Barker (Antonio Cupo) when she sutures the slashes Barker's henchmen have cut into a victim who failed to pay a debt.

When Grant tyrannizes Mary even more, drugging and raping her para-lyzed body and capturing the violent act on video, Walsh's words gain even more force. Although it does prompt Mary to seek revenge, the rape scene primarily demonstrates Grant's role as monster. While encouraging Mary to drink a drugged cocktail, he tells her, "Don't fuck up" and claims, "Everything else is forgivable if the work is good." To hide his intentions, Grant continues to question Mary about her work, asking her, "How are those turkeys coming along?" and claiming, "It's an old pro's secret" before nonchalantly taking her glass as the drug begins to work. As she falls further into unconsciousness, Grant continues presenting his monstrous act as normal, telling her he hopes the party is "matching up well to the ones [she] usually attend[s]," adding, "We do things a little differently." The reason for her invitation to this party of surgeons becomes clear when Grant explains, "I noticed that you were doing better financially. Nice new clothes, brand-new stethoscope. I never thought I'd see you at one of these." When the drug leaves Mary feeling sick and immo-bile, Grant sees it as an invitation instead of a call for help, declaring, "Maybe you just need to lie down on your back for a moment.... Lie down on a nice bed here; you'll feel much better." Reinforcing her helpless state, the camera stays on Mary's terrified face during the rape scene. Seemingly unaware of the horror of his act, Grant compliments Mary as he thrusts her paralyzed body: "You are so pretty. So pretty," he tells her as her body moves helplessly.

Although mostly offscreen the rape connects Grant to both monsters and their creators. He is a monster, but he also serves as an exaggerated version of Dr. Frankenstein, who perhaps inadvertently changes Mary into a "monster" seeking revenge. To avenge Grant's horrific act, Mary becomes a different kind of "slasher." Because his brutal violation turns Mary against medical school, it also transforms her into an unconventional Frankenstein-like scientist who chooses to perform body modifications rather than remain in the world of a surgeon where "everything is forgiven if the work is good." As she tells Grant before slicing into him, "I quit med school today. That shouldn't come as a surprise to you. I'm changing specialties, Dr. Grant. Have you ever heard of body modification?"

Mary revises the Dr. Frankenstein role in at least two ways. First of all, she primarily modifies only those patients who choose willingly to transform themselves. She does not create a creature without his or her consent, as does Mary Shelley's Frankenstein. Instead, she begs for Beatrice's reassurance before modifying her friend Ruby (Paula Lindberg) from sex goddess to a sexually featureless doll. Mary tries only to address Beatrice's complaint: "I don't think it's really fair that God gets to decide what we look like on the outside."

Ruby's explanation of her changes clarifies this first revision of the Dr. Frankenstein role by illustrating the gendered world of body modification. Ruby tells Mary, "It'll probably surprise you, but I've never had any of these surgeries to become a sexual object." Instead she wants to remove any sexual appeal because "no one looks at dolls in a sexual manner . . . . A doll can be naked and never feel shy or sexualized or degraded. That's what I want. . . . Just take these off, and seal up this as much as possible. Take off the extra bits too." Unlike women undergoing plastic surgery, in the body-modification community, alterations to the female body may not meet traditional ideals of beauty. Instead, they may blur sexuality. As film critic Jon Towlson asserts, "The desires of the female body modification characters to radically alter their appearances are largely motivated by a profound sense of alienation from a society that promotes the sexual objectification of the female" (2014, 205).

Although her decision to modify Ruby is driven by her need for rent money, ultimately Mary opens her own body-modification clinic with the support of the strip joint owner, Billy Barker (Antonio Cupo), and his bodyguard, Lance (Twan Holliday). According to Towlson, "As the first film to focus on body modification culture, the Soskas wanted *American Mary* to provide a fair and honest representation and their portrayal of that subculture is largely sympathetic" (2014, 205). The film highlights how professionally Mary runs her practice in several scenes, reinforcing her evolution from medical student to business owner, as well as her transformation from helpless rape victim to autonomous woman. As Andy Webster (2013) explains, "We've seen medical gear—gurneys, rubber aprons, cutlery—in myriad horror movies.... But maybe not metaphors like the caged bird Mary keeps, in a nod to Jean-Pierre Melville, or her uncommon path to self-sufficiency." In one scene, for example, she refuses to treat a possible client because he lacks conviction. In a few quick but sympathetically presented scenes, we see actual modified bodies—a forked tongue, a horned forehead, and various bodily inserts. We also see the planning necessary to perform a complicated surgery for a pair of twins played by the Soska sisters. In order to stay connected even after their deaths, the sisters have an unusual request. They want Mary to take off their left arms and exchange them with one another. To highlight Mary's work, the twins offer to build Mary a website. Her work has become so popular in the body-mod community that she has gained a nickname Bloody Mary.

The strip joint connection broaches the second way in which Mary revises the Dr. Frankenstein role. Shelley's Frankenstein refuses to take responsibility for his creation and decides instead to destroy it because his choices have transformed the being into a monster. Although Mary had entered the club only to make money as a stripper, when club owner Billy discovers her work as a surgeon, he offers her an alternative that ties together the three settings of the film: saving the life of a victim who failed to pay a debt. When Mary sutures the tortured cheat, she also builds a reputation that prepares her for both vengeance and body modification. Billy and his bodyguard, Lance, capture Grant, so Mary can use her surgical skills to take Beatrice's words literally and change Grant's outside into something that looks more like his "inside." Mary's actions do not turn Grant into a monster. He is already a monster. His callous and cruel behavior toward her and other women illustrate his monstrous interior. But his exterior does not mirror this horrific interior. Mary takes revenge on Grant, transforming him into a monstrous limbless experiment. For Mary he looks on the outside like he does on the inside.

Mary explains the process as she works, reinforcing this revision of the Frankenstein role:

> You're always telling me that surgeons can't make any mistakes. So, in the spirit of practice, I've come up with a little list of the most popular procedures that we are going to try on you tonight. So we have tongue

splitting ... implants, sometimes referred to as 3D implants, teeth filing, genital modification, and voluntary amputation. So I think we should get started. We have at least fourteen hours of surgery ahead of us. I would like to get it all done in one session. So I'm just going to grab your little tongue right here. Isn't this fun? I'm still learning from you.

Mary transforms Grant into a powerless and inhuman limbless torso in an act of vengeance meant to protect herself and the other women on which he might prey. Yet within even the body modification subculture, such attempts prove unattainable. As Towlson asserts, she "begins to really lose all sense of who she once was when she is driven to murder the innocent security guard who discovers her torture chamber" (2014, 209). Perhaps because she has become the monster she attacked in Grant, her attempts to thwart the patriarchal surgeon community fail. Beatrice's last call to Mary demonstrate the extent of that failure: "I'm sorry, Mary," Beatrice whispers. "Ruby's husband. He wanted to know who you were, and where you lived. I didn't want to tell him. He forced me. He wanted to hurt me. I'm so sorry, Mary." His attack ends Mary's revenge narrative, perhaps punishing Mary's aberrant behavior but also emphasizing the film's alliance with earlier *Frankenstein* adaptations that condemn attempts to "play God."

What sets *American Mary* apart from other Frankenstein horror is its hero. Mary chooses a subculture with connections to the natural world rather than the science of surgeons, a choice she continues even during the film's conclusion when she sutures her own wounds. Like the *Cyclosa mulmeinensis*, Mary has constructed a monster not unlike herself. Brian D. Johnson (2013) notes that "*American Mary* is riddled with astute references, from its nod to Mary Harron's *American Psycho* to a shot of Isabelle in red surgical scrubs that echoes Cronenberg's *Dead Ringers*. But the Soskas are facelifting horror archetypes with their own brand of genre modification." As Sylvia Soska explains, "You see Freddie, you see Pinhead, you see Jason, but you rarely see a female character like that. ... You hear, 'Oh, women don't have that capacity for evil.' But I'm a woman. I know the crazy thoughts that go through my head sometimes" (quoted in Johnson 2013). Mary has become nearly as monstrous as the predator she seeks to destroy.

American Mary: Beatrice introduces Mary to her first client.

In the process she challenges the nature-culture binary not only through her professional choices but also because her behaviors recall those found in a particular species of *Cyclosa* spider, the *Mulmeinensis*. Entomologists Eunice J. Tan and Daiqin Li explains how the "C. mulmeinensis usually rests at the hub, in line with its web decorations" (2009, 1833). According to Tan and Li, "Often the egg sacs covered in prey remains vertically radiate from the hub upwards to the web frame in the webs of female spiders. Positioning itself at the hub, the spider appears to be part of the line of cryptic prey remains and egg sacs" (1833). Tan and Li see this behavior functioning "primarily to reduce the rate of detection by insects, at least at close proximity, thus increasing the rate of insect interception" (1838).

But like Mary's attempts to thwart patriarchy through various forms of body modification, the spider's "Frankenstein monsters" sometimes fail. As Tan and Li explain, "prey-remains and egg-sac decorations exhibit varying success as camouflage against predators, depending on the types of predators. These decorations seem to be effective as predator defences against bird predators but not against wasps" (2009, 1838). Body modifications in both human and nonhuman nature provide evolutionary advantages, sometimes heightening beauty and protecting prey, but they also sometimes fail. Bowerbirds do not always attract mates. Mud-covered sandhill cranes may still be hunted. Looper caterpillars are sometimes eaten despite their flower camouflage. And spider decoys may not always fool birds.

The Day of the Animals: A depleted ozone layer creates deadly animals.

Conclusion

Monstrous Nature and the New Cli-Fi Cinema

In a May 2014 interview, deep-green activist Dan Bloom—arguably the first to use the term cli-fi for climate fiction and film—asserts, "I believe that cli fi novels and movies can serve to wake up readers and viewers to the reality of the Climapocalypse that awaits humankind if we do nothing to stop it" (Vemuri 2014). Bloom's claims echo those of Rahman Badalov, who in 1997 declared, "Blazing oil gushers make marvelous cinematographic material.... Only cinema can capture the thick oil bursting forth like a fiery monster." But Badalov not only views these oil gushers as monstrous nature. He also notes the dual message of monstrous nature cinema: to both condemn environmental degradation and entertain with spectacle. According to Badalov, cinema does not just highlight the fiery monster of the gusher. For him "only cinema can [also] display such an awesome inferno in its terrifying beauty and majesty." Bloom's admission that "the impact of cli fi novels and films has been minor, very minor" may point to the same dual role of cli-fi and other monstrous cinema. For Badalov and Bloom, cinema has the potential to bring environmental issues such as climate change to the forefront. But the cinematic mechanism also has the potential to obscure that message with spectacular beauty.

Such is the conundrum we face when writing about monstrous nature film, a puzzle amplified in recent spectacular cli-fi films from *The Day after Tomorrow* (2004) to *Elysium* (2013), *The Colony* (2013), *Snowpiercer* (2013), *Noah* (2014), and *Into the Storm* (2014). Monstrous cinema and its cli-fi offshoots may present important environmental messages, but they also must entertain viewers with spectacular effects to attract the audiences needed for big profits. And these awesome cinematic presentations may actually obscure the ecological points on display. Despite the challenge the film experience presents, however, we see recent cli-fi films aligning well with the four eco-approaches we explore in *Film and Monstrous Nature*: anthropomorphism, human ecology, evolution, and gendered landscapes. Reading the spectacular images in each of these films through an ecocritical lens can make the workings of the spectacular events transparent.

Although most cli-fi films from *Soylent Green* (1973) forward connect well with a human ecology approach, some also emphasize evolutionary narratives (as does *The Thaw*), as well as gendered landscapes (as in *Frankenstein Unbound*) and anthropomorphism (as in *Damnation Alley*). One of our first excursions into ecocinema studies provides an early exploration of human ecology in relation to the 1896 Lumière Brothers' *Oil Wells of Baku: Close View*. In our *Film Quarterly* article, "The First Eco-Disaster Film?," we examined the view as both spectacle and eco-disaster (at least from a more contemporary perspective). The questions our reading broached apply well to the recent influx of "cli-fi" films of the in the second decade of this century and their forerunners in the 1970s.

As we then suggested, when Bertrand Tavernier asserts that *Oil Wells of Baku: Close View* "may be the first ecological film ever made" (1996), he is, to a certain extent, reading the footage of burning oil wells from an ecocritical perspective. The film invites such a reading, one that centers on environmental concerns, because of what appears to be the devastating effects of drilling for oil. This thirty-six-second "view," shot by Kamill Serf with a stationary camera, shows huge flames and black smoke streaming from burning oil wells in Baku, Azerbaijan, seemingly sure signs of environmental disaster. But disaster looks more like spectacle in this closely shot scene, and both Serf and the film's viewers serve as attentive spectators. Although the camera never moves during the film, the vibrant image it captures also captures its viewers.

The film appears to be strategically framed. The oil wells in the frame look like miniatures until the immensity of the oil derricks is emphasized by a human figure moving in front of the center well. This figure looks minuscule as it walks away from the center derrick and out of the frame of the shot. The two tall derricks in the view behind the tiny striding male figure show us that the view was shot from a distance. This extreme long shot accentuates the power of both the tall derricks and the rising flames and smoke, smoke that darkens into the distance from the right side of the frame. We see enormous flames shoot up and clouds of heavy black smoke plume from the fire, but more smoke comes from similar oil well fires off-screen. To the right of the center derrick, as far away as the horizon line, two blazes flame up from what look like vertical pipes. Gray and black smoke flows out of the fires in a plume that covers the sky. The enormity of these flaming plumes mesmerizes because their powerful blaze shocks us. But the raging flames also bring forth images of phoenixes rising from the flames and hearths stoked by Hestia, broaching the question, "Is this beautiful?"[1]

All this smoke and uncontrolled fire supports Tavernier's assertion that this is an eco-disaster film. Such a disaster, from a current point of view, begs for an ecological reading. More than just spectacle, these burning oil fields, these obfuscating clouds of smoke, this general conflagration of the natural world, signify humans' rape of the landscape for personal gain—oil at any price to the natural world. But the figure walking in front of the derricks suggests another reading altogether. He moves without the urgency an ecological reading might spur. In fact, he walks in front of the derricks and the burning oil fields with quite a normal gait, as if he's unconcerned about anything. But as the Lumières' brief film offers no explanation for its fires, nor does its title: *Oil Wells of Baku: Close View*, it leaves today's viewers wondering, is this a picture of business as usual or an account of eco-disaster?

What the Lumières' view "means" may be different now than it was in the late 1890s, but spectacular events continue to overpower environmental statements on film. So, what does the view tell us about what we would now call our "concerns about nature"? And what did the view tell its original viewers? When (if ever) does the destruction "wrought" by gushing oil wells—"monsters," according to A. V. W. Jackson ([1911] 2002, 40)—become seen as something other than a spectacle "surpassed only by the awful grandeur when fire adds terror to the scene" (40)? When, in other words, does a burning oil well gain the status of ecological disaster? When does it come to be perceived that the costs of such flames include not only money and human lives but also nature? This brief view can certainly be read as stating a message, but if we are to presume there is a message here, that message at first is subsumed by its context. That is, the spectacular event serves as the context of a possible environmental message—oil well fires and gushers not only waste resources; they also destroy the surrounding ecology. The 2014 massive gas flare burn-offs in North Dakota oil fields support this perspective. In North Dakota, as in Baku, money trumps the environment. Instead of building pipelines to capture the gas, they burn it off to produce the more lucrative oil. This view, like that in later films highlighting oil-driven eco-disasters, begs a question: How does disaster come to be turned into a spectacular image that leaves spectators struck more with awe than with concern? And how can that disaster be revealed?

These same questions apply to the "cli-fi" films popularized by Roland Emmerich's *The Day after Tomorrow*. Critiques of *The Day after Tomorrow* point to its exaggerated claims regarding global warming not as a way to highlight the film's environmental ideologies but to highlight one of its biggest weaknesses. The environmental message seems lost because it rests on such a poor interpretation of climatology. Instead, critics valorize the film's spectacular effects and faithful execution of the eco-disaster formula. A surface reading of the environmental politics on display in the film, then, deconstructs the film's environmental leanings.

But director Roland Emmerich's assertion that the film's climate-change exaggerations were intended as a way to add to its dramatic appeal points to another consequence of the "sublimely ridiculous" ecological disasters: large box office sales. All of the 258 reviews on the Internet Movie Database admit that the environmental catastrophes on display in the film are spectacularly powerful, drawing audiences who crave the entertainment value that a highly special effects–driven disaster movie provides. The special effects paid off: *The Day after Tomorrow* grossed $528 million worldwide and earned a stunning $85.8 million during its opening weekend. For us more appealing are ecological themes beyond the surface meaning, themes that help us answer questions such as, How is this cli-fi-disaster? How is this cli-fi-disaster film different from those that have come before it? And (as Dan Bloom suggests) can cli-fi movies serve to wake up readers and viewers to the reality of the Climapocalypse? Our readings of early and contemporary cli-fi films suggest they can, at least potentially, reveal the eco-horror behind the spectacle on display.

Monstrous Cli-Fi in the 1960s and 1970s

For us cli-fi films continue some of the same trends we note occurring in monstrous nature cinema, including drawing on anthropomorphism to both humanize and vilify nonhuman nature. Dan Bloom (2014) asserts, "In order to be a cli-fi short story or novel, the book will have a climate theme, of course. It can be set in the past, the present or the future, and it can be dystopian or utopian." The same definition applies to filmic cli-fi, which, like short stories and novels, explores climate change and global warming explicitly. Bloom also differentiates cli-fi from environmental literature and film, declaring, "But if the book is just about the environment, such as protecting rivers or stopping air pollution, then it wouldn't really be a cli-fi novel [or film]. There are other categories such as eco-fiction or calling a book an eco-thriller if it is about the environment."

Earlier cli-fi films that anthropomorphize monstrous nature explicitly fit Bloom's criteria.[2] Considered one of the earliest eco-horror films, *Frogs* (1972) confronts environmental destruction with a vengeful bevvy of psychic frogs. During an annual Jason Crockett (Ray Milland) birthday celebration on the Fourth of July, these frogs telepathically communicate with other animal species, enticing them to attack Crockett's family and guests one by one. The film highlights how almost every family member despises nature so much they spread harmful chemicals to eradicate all nonhuman animal life. The film suggests that the frogs recognize the source of these animal deaths—humans, especially the spoiled rich Crockett patriarch and his family. On the night of Jason Crockett's birthday, frogs, snakes, alligators, lizards, birds, and spiders begin to pay Crockett back, and in *Frogs* nature

wins. Like humans, frogs and other animals in the Florida swamp surrounding Crockett's mansion sense the source of their oppression and fight back.

Despite the deaths of family and houseguests, millionaire Crockett still
maintains his superiority to nonhuman nature, exclaiming, "I still believe man
is master of the world." Nature photographer and environmentalist Pickett
Smith (Sam Elliot) offers an alternative view, asking, "Does that mean he
can't live in harmony with the rest of it?" In *Frogs* anthropomorphizing these
swamp creatures provides an environmental message, but it also humanizes
nature and provides a means to punish the real monster—Jason Crockett
and the human oppressors he represents.

The Day of the Animals (1977) addresses the greenhouse effect more blatantly,
anthropomorphizing the animals that seek vengeance against humanity for
its mistreatment of nature. The film's opening title cards explicitly states its
focus on humanity's contribution to Earth's damaged ozone layer and suggests that *The Day of the Animals* serves as a warning regarding the possible
negative consequences of our environmental exploitation.

In June 1974, Drs. F. Sherwood Rowland and Mario Molina of the University
of California startled the scientific world with their finding that fluorocarbon
gases used in aerosol spray cans are seriously damaging the Earth's protective ozone layer. Thus, potentially dangerous amounts of ultraviolet rays
are reaching the surface of our planet, adversely affecting all living things.
This motion picture dramatizes what could happen in the near future if we
continue to do nothing to stop this damage to nature's protective shield for
life on this planet.

In *The Day of the Animals*, humans are constructed as villains when they
are dropped off for a hike in the mountains. In response to a chemical
imbalance caused by the depletion of the ozone layer, animals from con-
dors and vultures to bears, mountain lions, and wolves attack the hikers as
their known enemies. In *The Day of the Animals*, then, animals have become
more like humans, able to determine the cause for their possible demise—a
human-caused hole in the ozone layer.

The film illustrates humanity's culpability by constructing at least some of
the hikers as monstrous. Advertising executive Paul Jenson (Leslie Nielson)
embodies all the negative qualities that have led to the animal attacks. In
one scene he even exclaims, "If there's a God left up there to believe in. My

father who art in heaven you've a made a jackass out of me for years. Neville's God, that's the God I believe in! You see what you want you take. You take it! And I am going to do just that!" Hiker Sam (Walt Gorney), on the other hand, explains why nature is assaulting them when he declares, "God sent a plague down on us because we're just a bunch of no-good fellers." Ultimately the only defense against these animal executioners is military intervention, but the film makes a case for changing our destructive behaviors to preserve nature and ourselves.

Other early monstrous cli-fi films incorporate evolutionary narratives and tragic or comic heroes drawn from Darwinian theory. We have talked in some detail about the evolution of monstrous parasites in *The Thaw* (2009) unearthed by a climate change caused thaw in the Arctic. But other cli-fi films explore evolutionary narratives in more classical ways. *Soylent Green* (1973), for example, emphasizes what Joseph W. Meeker calls a tragic evolutionary narrative. In a world completely overrun with humans, food sources for the masses come in the form of "soylents," including the infamous soylent green: people. *Soylent Green* provides a picture of what would happen on Earth if Paul Ehrlich's predictions came true: "Population will inevitably and completely outstrip whatever small increases in food supplies we make," Ehrlich asserted in 1970 (Collier 1970, 189). But the film's protagonist Thorn (Charlton Heston) serves as a prophet revealing the most horrifying result: "Soylent Green is people." Constructing Thorn as a prophet also establishes him as a tragic eco-hero like that described by Meeker: "the supreme importance of the individual personality" (1997, 24). In his earlier essay, "The Comic Mode," Meeker also defines this tragic hero in relation to biology and evolution, asserting, "Pioneer species are the loners of the natural world, the tragic heroes who sacrifice themselves in satisfaction of mysterious inner commands which they alone can hear" (1996, 161).

Thorn more than fulfills Meeker's criteria for a tragic hero, gaining force as an eco-hero who both strives to save humanity and to remind it of its pristine past. Thorn is a pioneer, a tragic hero willing to speak up and resist homogenizing forces as an individual whose morality transcends all those around him. Even his name suggests that he is a prickly plant, one of the pioneering outsiders "whose life styles resemble behavior that men have admired most when they have seen it in other men. We celebrate the qualities in human pioneers that we despise in the pioneers of other plant and animal species" (Meeker 1996, 161)

First as a rogue detective in a police state and then (after his roommate's death) as the sole rational voice in the film, Thorn serves as an eco-hero, a human pioneer stamping out dehumanizing forces. Thorn proves the dreadful truth about Soylent Green for the intellectuals' Supreme Exchange, and he stands alone, morally superior to the corporate heads who control the food supply. For him the crime is against humanity, not nature, since his biggest fear is that the company will raise humans "like cattle." "It's people," he says. "Soylent Green is made out of people." Thorn proclaims his message after fighting off bullets and punches from corporate thugs, first to his police captain and then to the scores of others sleeping in what is left of a church.

A suffering, tragic eco-hero to the end, Thorn speaks the last words we hear, and he passes the task of taking evidence to "the Exchange," the intellectual "Books'" haven, to his captain. Here the prophet, Thorn, reveals himself as a pioneer, a tragic eco-hero with a message that becomes his dying words. The film's cultural backdrop and its hero's role are obvious, but both serve as a direct response to the 1970s environmental movement and its prophets of doom.

Early monstrous cli-fi can also be read through the lens of gender. Most monstrous cli-fi cinema masculinizes the bodies of both heroes and oppressors, adding climate change as a plot device problem that these heroes solve. As we discussed in *Film and Everyday Eco-Disasters*, *Our Man Flint* (1966), an action-adventure spoof of James Bond films of the 1960s, showcases an ecoterrorist plot by a group of scientists to force climate changes that will melt the Arctic and Antarctic glaciers and flood major coastal cities if global governments refuse to comply with their ultimatum to destroy all military forces and agree to become docile "programmed" but peaceful automatons. In this comic action adventure, world leaders rely on a computer program to choose their savior, Derek Flint (James Coburn), an ex-intelligence officer with 007 gadgets and numerous female conquests. Directed by Daniel Mann, the film masculinizes the genre by suggesting that only a male action hero can save humanity from global warming.

Cli-fi films from at least the 1970s forward primarily highlight human approaches to ecology. For example, *No Blade of Grass* (1970) provides a blatant and bleak picture of the costs of a toxic atmosphere to human and nonhuman life that brings to mind postapocalyptic films such as *Silent Running* (1972), *Soylent Green*, and *The Road Warrior* (1981). As we noted in *Film and Everyday Eco-Disasters*, in *No Blade of Grass* those effects include both atmospheric pollution and deadly climate change. Reinforcing Ellen Swallow Richards's definitions of human ecology, the film powerfully illustrates the human causes for the disaster humanity now faces: Because humans have polluted the Earth's air, water, and soil, a strange new virus has appeared that attacks only strains of grasses such as wheat and rice, and the world is descending into famine and chaos.

When the virus reaches London, architect and former military officer John Custance (Nigel Davenport), escapes the city with his wife, Ann (Jean Wallace); daughter, Mary (Lynne Frederick); and Mary's boyfriend, Roger (John Hamill). Polluted rivers and industrial smokestacks provide the terrible backdrop for a truth exposed by their son, David (Nigel Rathbone), who explains, "Earth gets warmer because of pollution," and he maps out the aftermath of melting glaciers and polar ice causing flooded coastlines and cities, "so we all drown," he exclaims. Together with those who join them along the way, however, they fight their way to John's brother's farm, where survival seems possible. Despite this hopeful road-film narrative, however, the film maintains its fierce critique of humanity's destruction of the natural world. *No Blade of Grass* showcases a family's attempts to survive in a postapocalyptic world. It illustrates the toxic environment created by humanity, but it purveys only a message of humanity's preservation, not a biotic community.

Monstrous Cli-Fi from the Early Twenty-First Century Forward

Monstrous cli-fi after *The Day after Tomorrow* continues the trend begun in the 1970s. Multiple films respond to the context in which anthropogenic climate change becomes horror. They also draw on some of the same trends in the horror genre found throughout the eco-horror genre. Some contemporary monstrous cli-fi films draw on anthropomorphic views of the monster. In a new wave of anthropomorphized monsters in cinema, *Godzilla* may draw on films such as *Frogs* (as well as the earlier Godzilla films it remakes).

Many critics argue that the recent *Godzilla* qualifies as cli-fi and continues a pattern of 2014 cli-fi films from *Noah* (2014) to *Into the Storm* (2014). In a *Time* magazine review, Lily Rothman (2014) claims "the misdeeds that rouse the beast [Godzilla] from slumber now aren't so much what humans do to one another but what they do to the earth—and how the planet might get revenge." According to Rothman "in *Godzilla*, nature doesn't just bite back, it stomps and smashes too." Co-star Aaron Taylor-Johnson (who plays Ford Brody in the film) concurs with Rothman's claim, suggesting that director "Gareth [Edwards] definitely wanted this element that we as mankind should feel conscious of what we're doing and almost guilty that we're polluting the planet. . . . Nature has a way of fighting back, represented by Godzilla" (quoted in Rothman). In *Godzilla* (2014) the monster fights MUTOs rather than humans, however, to restore nature's balance, a move that anthropo-morphizes Godzilla but may set the film apart from more blatant cli-fi. *Godzilla* (2014) definitely meets Bloom's criteria for environmental cinema, but whether the film fulfills Bloom's definition of cli-fi is unclear. Godzilla, however, is explicitly anthropomorphized in the film, benevolently fighting the MUTO to protect humans and the natural world.

The Day after Tomorrow highlights a different way to envision evolutionary narratives and the heroes that drive them. In cli-fi films from the 1970s and eco-comic disaster films from the 1980s forward (such as *Eight Legged Freaks* [2002] and *Warm Bodies* [2013]), disaster plots are driven by two different kinds of heroes: tragic pioneers and comic community builders. *The Day after Tomorrow*, on the other hand, relies on a different kind of hero, one that arguably combines both tragic and comic characteristics. Our reading of *The Day after Tomorrow* attempts to make the idea of the new ecological (eco-) hero more transparent rather than rearticulating the obvious ecologi-cal messages on display in the film. In *The Day after Tomorrow*, heroic roles are filled not by tragic pioneers or even bumbling comic heroes, but by a father seeking to save his own child from an environment that humanity has made toxic in multiple ways. In *The Day after Tomorrow* eco-hero and father Jack Hall (Dennis Quaid) attempts not only to save the world from global warming but also to save his son, Sam (Jake Gyllenhaal), from a flooded and frozen New York City.

This new breed of eco-hero fails to fit in categories of tragic or comic heroes as defined by either Aristotle or Joseph W. Meeker. Meeker expands Aristotle's categories to include the natural world in his ecocritical approach to classic literature. Meeker's tragic heroes in the natural world are the ecological pioneers, "the loners of the natural world, the tragic heroes who sacrifice themselves in satisfaction of mysterious inner commands which they alone can hear" (1996, 161). His comic heroes build community. Meeker argues that once ecosystems mature, heroic, solitary pioneers become not only unnecessary but also subordinate to the group. In a mature or climax ecosystem, "it is the community itself that really matters, and it is likely to be an extremely durable community so long as balance is maintained among its many elements" (Meeker 1996, 163). Comic heroes emerge from these climax ecosystems.

Jack Hall serves the community while maintaining a solitary quest, however. This new eco-hero combines the best qualities of the tragic and comic heroes to build a better world community while also saving children who are closest to them. As an intellectually driven hero seeking to save the world from the consequences of climate change he endured at the North Pole, Jack looks like Al Gore in *An Inconvenient Truth* when he explains global warming to a world delegation but like Thorn when he saves himself from a glacial collapse. In spite of these two daring acts—one physical and the other intellectual—Jack's many weaknesses are also on display in the film. When he returns from his latest Arctic trip, his houseplants have nearly died, his son has failed calculus, and his ex-wife has lost faith in his ability even to pick up his son in time to get him to the airport for a scholastic bowl tournament.

These everyday events, however, are juxtaposed with images of worldwide eco-disaster. Professor Terry Rapson (Ian Holm), an oceanographer, discusses the possibility of a new ice age, and reports of its oncoming effects soon arrive from all over the world. Pieces of ice fall from the sky in Tokyo, destroying cars and killing any people they strike. Snowstorms drift into New Delhi. Storms hit Sam's flight on its way to New York. And when Sam and his friend Laura (Emmy Rossum) reach the city, they watch from their taxi as flocks of birds migrate away from the city, seemingly disturbed by climate change. When Jack enters Rapson's data into his climate model, the results are devastating. According to their conclusions the Earth will be in a full-scale ice age in six to eight weeks. More disastrous events point to this upcoming ice age: frozen helicopter pilots in Scotland and massive flooding in New York City with tidal waves catapulting down its broad avenues. Sam and the rest of his scholastic bowl friends make their way into the New York Public Library, and the father-son narrative takes center stage. Sam finds a waterlogged pay phone in the library, calls his father, and hears his father's promise: "Wait it out and burn what you can. I will come for you. I will come for you." The rest of the film revolves around Jack's quest to save his son and his son's and ex-wife's evolution into new eco-heroes like Jack.

The family melodrama becomes the main focus until the film's end, even though it is occasionally broken with more global concerns, like the death of the president and the fate of American refugees in Mexico. The heroism of Jack's ex-wife Lucy (Sela Ward) is highlighted when an ambulance arrives to save her and a young patient, Peter, whom she has refused to leave alone. And when Sam gathers penicillin and food from an iced-in Russian ship, he too demonstrates his potential as an eco-hero. Jack serves as the most daring eco-hero when he saves his son and the remaining New York survivors from the library. As Jack explains, "I made my son a promise. I'm going to keep it."

This eco-drama ends with father and son reunited (and possibly husband and wife). The cli-fi disaster closely resembles most disaster films other than the way in which the image of the hero is constructed. In *The Day after Tomorrow*, the hero is a true eco-hero, attempting to save the world from environmental disaster, but his most heroic act is localized and less than self-sacrificial. Jack makes his heroic journey not to save the world—as we might expect an eco-hero and a climatologist to do—but to save his son. And both Lucy and Sam act heroically for similar reasons: to save the individuals they love, not the world, the nation, or even the community.

Gender also plays a role in contemporary monstrous cli-fi films. In *The Colony* (2013), directed by Jeff Renroe, masculinity takes center stage for the few human survivors forced underground by a sudden ice age caused by global warming. Colony 7, one of these outposts, receives a distress signal from another outpost, Colony 5. Masculine bodies rule in this post-climate apocalypse world where its heroes and villains are all male. The leader of Colony 7, Briggs (Laurence Fishburne), organizes an expedition with his assistant Sam (Kevin Zegers) and young recruit Graydon (Atticus Dean Mitchell) to investigate, leaving one of the few women, biologist Kai (Charlotte Sullivan), in charge. But Briggs's former military partner Mason (Bill Paxton) quickly seizes control. After a two-day walk, Briggs, Sam, and Graydon reach Colony 5 and discover the reason for the signal: a savage group of male cannibals has slaughtered all but one of the colonists. In *The Colony* men (Briggs and Sam) must save humanity from other savage men (Mason and the cannibals). The cli-fi message comes through mainly in the frozen landscape and a message showing that another colony has successfully manipulated the weather to reveal the sun and the fertile soil beneath the ice. Kai's role connects to this message, since as a biologist she has gathered and preserved the seeds they will need to survive. Although focused on another repercussion of climate change, ferocious tornadoes, *Into the Storm* (2014) explores a similar gender dynamic between storm chaser Pete (Matt Walsh) and meteorologist Allison (Sarah Wayne Callies).

One of the few cli-fi films directed by a woman, Jennifer Phang's *Half-Life* (2008), focuses less on monstrous nature than family drama. But by connecting eco-disasters caused by climate change with the destruction of the family unit, the film provides a way to personalize these issues, adding relevance to destruction caused by anthropogenic climate change. The film centers on the coming-of-age stories of a precocious boy Timothy (Alexander Agate) and his jaded sister, Saura (Julia Nickson). Timothy's drawings and Saura's imaginative powers provide them with an escape from a confining home life. Together they save their self-destructive mother (Sanoe Lake) from her charmingly manipulative boyfriend (Leonardo Nam) and finally reinvent their world in a spectacular conclusion.

Half-Life draws on multiple genres to fulfill this challenging conclusion, integrating animation and supernatural elements with generic expectations of the typical family melodrama. This story, however, literally parallels the troubling consequences of climate change surrounding them, amplifying global cataclysms from species extinction to tsunamis by associating them with their personal traumas in the home. In many scenes a television in the background shows these scenes of destruction, clearly associating coastal flooding with global warming as the tension in the household "warms up." In *Half-Life* the destruction of the natural world is in direct relationship with the destruction of the family. The only escape is the creation of a new world that hybridizes approaches, a point illustrated by the ethnically ambiguous family members and their friends.

Some contemporary monstrous cli-fi films also embrace human approaches to ecology. Although they also highlight a masculine action hero, both *The Road* (2009) and *The Book of Eli* stress recovery from Anthropocene apocalypses. Directed by Darren Aronofsky, *Noah* (2014) continues the human focus found in films such as *No Blade of Grass*. In this rewriting of the biblical Genesis story, Noah (Russell Crowe) gains the trust of God and his "Watchers" by contesting the environmental disasters caused by Tubal-cain (Ray Winstone), a descendent of Cain. According to the film's opening, Cain and his offspring "build a great industrial civilization" that has "devoured the world." Instead of exploiting the earth's resources, Noah teaches his family to live sustainably, protecting nature as a steward rather than a figurative rapist. As a descendent of Seth, he "defend[s] and protect[s] what is left of creation," according to the opening narration.

But Noah also serves as a super-masculine action hero protecting his family and the Earth at any cost. In this reboot of the biblical story, Noah decisively revises God's plan to rebuild all life, including humans, by eliminating wives and children from the ark. In this version Noah believes that because "everything that was beautiful, everything that was good we shattered, mankind must end." After the flood ends, Noah tells his family that when his adopted infertile daughter, Ila (Emma Watson), and the last of his sons, Japheth (Leo McHugh Carroll), die, so will humanity. In Noah's mind humans will only repeat their mistakes and destroy creation if given the chance.

Instead, Noah's grandfather Methuselah (Anthony Hopkins) has miraculously restored Ila's fertility. When she gives birth to twins girls, Noah cannot kill his granddaughters, so human ecology prevails. In *Noah* as in the Bible, however, it is a higher power that intervenes to cleanse the world and provide the space for a new beginning after the great flood. As the narrator explains, Noah and his family must "be fruitful and multiply and replenish the Earth." Most of humanity is destroyed, but the remaining extended family serves as a curious genesis for the rise of human populations around the world.

The more blatantly eco-horror cli-fi film *Snowpiercer* (2013) emphasizes both its climate-change catalyst and its human focus through its steampunk sensibility. The film's opening shows us the consequences of climate change and the negative repercussions of treating the warming atmosphere with an experimental chemical CW7 to cool the Earth. Instead of combating climate change, the experiment has frozen the planet and killed all life, according to the opening narration. Only a few humans have survived on a massive climate-controlled train and are relegated into carriages by class. Unsurprisingly, the third-class masses like Tanya (Octavia Butler) and her children envy the first-class passengers in the comfort of the opulent front. As Salon.com's Andrew O'Hehir (2014) explains, "In the filthy, overcrowded rear cars where Curtis (Chris Evans), Edgar (Jamie Bell) and the cryptic, prophetic elder statesman called Gilliam (John Hurt) are confined, anger is building toward another uprising." Set seventeen years after the freeze, *Snowpiercer* shows us the results of such exploitation: a rebellion led by young revolutionary Curtis (Chris Evans) with sometimes devious goals.

The bulk of *Snowpiercer* examines this rebellion while also revealing the intricacies of the train as biosphere with every new carriage Curtis and his crew penetrate. The ultimate goal is disrupting the hierarchy by seizing the means of production: the engine that runs the train and its climate. In one car they free a drug-addicted security specialist Namgoong Minsoo (Kang-ho Song) and his daughter, Yona (Ah-sung Ko). When Curtis offers him a month of the hallucinogen Kronole for every carriage door he opens, Minsoo agrees to join them. With Minsoo's help the rebels fight their way through a car where a sole worker cooks their insect protein blocks, a vegetable-and-flower-garden carriage, an aquarium car where seafood is raised for the upper classes, and even an elite elementary school. The rebel group dwindles with each battle, but according to A. O. Scott (2009), the sometimes slapstick violence "produc[es] a volatile blend of humor and horror that pays tribute to the source material while coloring its themes with the director's distinctively perverse and humane sensibility."

Ultimately Curtis reaches the engine at the front of the train, but the rebellion ends not in capturing control but in initiating a new beginning like that depicted in *Noah*. As O'Hehir (2014) declares, "This may be the most ambitious and capacious dystopian critique since "The Matrix" 15 years ago, and it's one that seeks to offer a hopeful and even transcendent vision." The last scenes of *Snowpiercer* support this claim when Yona and Timmy climb outside the train and live to see a polar bear on a hill. In *Noah*, according to Noah's vision, "water cleanses." In *Snowpiercer* that cleansing water is frozen.

The Power of Monstrous Cli-Fi

With a Metacritic score of 84 that points to universal acclaim, *Snowpiercer* seems to suggest that monstrous cli-fi film has the potential to move audiences to both awareness of and action to address climate change. Whether cli-fi movies can wake up viewers to the dangerous repercussions of climate change seems to depend on audience size and demographic composition. Preliminary results suggest that cli-fi can potentially alert audiences to these dangers. These results, however, are as yet limited in scope. For example, a study by Anthony Leiserowitz, a risk-perception analyst and the director of the Climate Change Center at Yale, concludes that *The Day after Tomorrow* "had a significant impact on the climate change risk perceptions, conceptual models, behavioral intentions, and even voting intentions of moviegoers" in the United States (2004, 34), based on results from a global audience research survey published in a 2004 *Environment* journal article.

But these results were constrained by the numbers who attended the film (10 percent of adults in the United States) and by the level of national exposure. According to Leiserowitz, "Surveys conducted immediately before *The Day after Tomorrow* was released and three weekends afterward found no shift in broad public attitudes or in behaviors" (2004, 35). And an international study published in a later *Environment* issue found that when U.S. viewers were asked, "Why did you watch this movie?" "only 17 percent said they went because they were 'interested in global warming.' By contrast, 83 percent of moviegoers went because they liked the trailer' (29 percent), 'like disaster movies' (21 percent), 'like to see all big films' (21 percent), or 'another reason' (12 percent)" (2005, 44). Leiserowitz concludes, "We have only scratched the surface . . . in the effort to understand the role of popular representations of risk (such as movies, books, television, fiction, and nonfiction) or of cross-national differences in public risk perception and behavior" (2005, 44).

Although there are few studies of the effects that cli-fi and other eco-horror films have on viewers' awareness of environmental issues, the environmental

Snowpiercer: Yona and the boy discover life outside the train.

movement has definitely made its mark in classic and contemporary horror cinema. Despite their emphasis on monstrous nature, the horror films we explore here also demonstrate the true monster in the Anthropocene age: humanity itself. Anti–nuclear energy films from *Them!* to the recent *Godzilla* highlight a nonhuman monster, perhaps, but in each not only do humans create these radioactive creatures. They also anthropomorphize them, emphasizing their similarity to ourselves. Evolutionary narratives in zombie and parasite films also point to humanity as the cause for their demise, but they also include humans in the evolutionary narratives they explore. Horror films examining human ecology and the gendered body even more explicitly integrate humans into the natural world.

All the films explored here suggest the horrors on display are human made. As Paul Wells explains, they examine the repercussions of humanity's desire to challenge natural selection and "'artificially' impose itself upon the conditions of material existence, while nature slowly but surely, organically and often invisibly, changes the world" (2000, 5). Whether addressing cockroaches or climate change, these films also seem to suggest that monstrous horrors can be solved not through mad-scientist experiments but through a return to an interdependent biotic community with or without humanity.

FILMOGRAPHY

Alien. Dir. Ridley Scott. Perf. Sigourney Weaver, Tom Skerritt, John Hurt. Twentieth-Century Fox, 1979. DVD.

Alien 3. Dir. David Fincher. Perf. Sigourney Weaver, Charles S. Dutton, Charles Dance. Twentieth-Century Fox, 1992. DVD.

Alien: Resurrection. Dir. Jean-Pierre Jeunet. Perf. Sigourney Weaver, Winona Ryder, Dominique Pinon. Twentieth-Century Fox, 1997. DVD.

Aliens. Dir. James Cameron. Perf. Sigourney Weaver, Michael Biehn, Carrie Henn. Twentieth-Century Fox, 1986. DVD.

Alive. Dir. Frank Marshall. Perf. Ethan Hawke, Vincent Spano. Paramount Pictures, 1993. DVD.

American Mary. Dir. Jen Soska, Sylvia Soska. Perf. Katherine Isabelle, Antonio Cup. IndustryWorks Pictures, 2012. DVD.

American Psycho. Dir. Mary Harron. Perf. Christian Bale, Chloe Sevigny, Reese Witherspoon, Willem Dafoe. Lions Gate Films, 2000. DVD.

American Zombie. Dir. Grace Lee. Perf. Austin Basis, Jane Edith Wilson, Al Vicente. Lee Lee Films, 2008. DVD.

Arachnophobia. Dir. Frank Marshall. Perf. Jeff Daniels, Harley Jane Kozak. John Goodman. Buena Vista Pictures, 1990. DVD.

Audition. Dir. Takashi Miike. Perf. Ryo Ishibashi, Eihi Shiina, Tetsu Sawaki. Basara Pictures, 1999. DVD.

Bambi. Dir. James Algar et al. Walt Disney Productions, 1942. DVD.

The Bay. Dir. Barry Levinson. Perf. Will Rogers, Kristen Connolly, Kether Donohue. Automatik Entertainment, 2012. DVD.

Beetle Queen Conquers Tokyo. Dir. Jessica Oreck. Myriapod Productions, 2009. DVD.

The Beetle's Deception. Dir. Loyshki. 1913.

Biozombie. Dir. Wilson Yip. Perf. Matt Chow, Siu Man Sing. Brilliant Idea Group, 1998. DVD.

Blacula. Dir. William Crain. Perf. William Marshall, Vonetta McGee. American International Pictures, 1972. DVD.

Blade. Dir. Stephen Norrington. Perf. Wesley Snipes, Kris Kristofferson. Amen Ra Films, 1998. DVD.

Blade II. Dir. Guillermo del Toro. Perf. Wesley Snipes, Kris Kristofferson, Ron Perlman. New Line Cinema, 2002. DVD.

Blade: Trinity. Dir. David S. Goyer. Perf. Wesley Snipes, Kris Kristofferson. New Line Cinema, 2004. DVD.

The Blair Witch Project. Dir. Daniel Myrick, Eduardo Sánchez. Perf. Heather Donahue, Michael C. Williams, Joshua Leonard. Haxan Films, 1999. DVD.

The Blood Beast Terror. Dir. Vernon Sewell. Perf. Peter Cushing. Tigon British Film Productions, 1968. DVD.

Blood Diner. Dir. Jackie Kong. Perf. Rick Burks, Carl Crew, Roger Dauer. PMS Filmworks Films, 1987. DVD.

Blood Feast. Dir. Herschell Gordon Lewis. Perf. William Kerwin, Mal Arnold, Connie Mason. Friedman-Lewis Productions, 1963. DVD.

Body Snatchers. Dir. Abel Ferrara. Perf. Gabrielle Anwar, Meg Tilly, Terry Kinney. Dorset Productions, 1993. DVD.

The Book of Eli. Dir. Albert Hughes, Allen Hughes. Perf. Denzel Washington, Mila Kunis, Ray Stevenson. Alcon Entertainment, 2010. DVD.

Boxing Helena. Dir. Jennifer Chambers Lynch. Perf. Julian Sands, Sherilyn Fenn, Bill Paxton. Mainline Pictures, 1993. DVD.

The Brain Eaters. Dir. Bruno VeSota. Perf. Ed Nelson, Alan Jay Factor, Cornelius Keefe. American International Pictures, 1958. DVD.

Bram Stoker's Dracula. Dir. Francis Ford Coppola. Perf. Gary Oldman, Winona Ryder, Anthony Hopkins. American Zoetrope, 1992. DVD.

The Bride of Frankenstein. Dir. James Whale. Perf. Boris Karloff, Elsa Lanchester, Colin Clive. Universal Pictures, 1935. DVD.

Buffy, the Vampire Slayer. Creator Josh Whedon. Perf. Sarah Michelle Gellar, Nicholas Brendon. Mutant Enemy, 1997–2003. DVD.

Bug. Dir. Jeannot Szwarc. Perf. Bradford Dillman, Joanna Miles. William Castle Productions, 1975. DVD.

The Cameraman's Revenge. Dir. Wladyslaw Starewicz. Milestone Films, 1912. DVD.

The China Syndrome. Dir. James Bridges. Perf. Jane Fonda, Jack Lemmon, Michael Douglas. Columbia Pictures, 1979. DVD.

Citizen Toxie: The Toxic Avenger IV. Dir. Lloyd Kaufman. Perf. David Mattey, Clyde Lewis, Heidi Sjursen. Troma Studios, 2000. DVD.

City of Lost Children. Dir. Marc Caro, Jean-Pierre Jeunet. Perf. Ron Perlman, Daniel Emilfork, Judith Vittet. Club d'Investissement Média, 1995. DVD.

Class of Nuke 'Em High. Dir. Richard Haines, Lloyd Kaufman. Perf. Janelle Brady, Gilbert Brenton, Robert Prichard. Troma Studios, 1986. DVD.

Class of Nuke 'Em High Part 2: Sub-Humanoid Meltdown. Dir. Richard Haines, Lloyd Kaufman. Perf. Brick Bronsky, Lisa Gaye, Leesa Rowland. Troma Studios, 1991. DVD.

Class of Nuke 'Em High Part 3: The Good, the Bad, and the Subhumanoid. Dir. Eric Louzil. Perf. Brick Bronsky, Lisa Star, John Tallman. Troma Studios, 1994. DVD.

Cloverfield. Dir. Matt Reeves. Perf. Mike Vogel, Jessica Lucas, Lizzy Caplan. Paramount Pictures, 2008. DVD.

Colin. Dir. Marc Price. Perf. Alastair Kirton, Daisy Aitkens. Nowhere Fast Productions, 2008. DVD.

The Colony. Dir. Jeff Renfroe. Perf. Kevin Zegers, Laurence Fishburne, Bill Paxton. Alcina Pictures, 2013. DVD.

Crocodile Hunter: Collision Course. Dir. John Stainton. Perf. Steve Irwin, Terri Irwin, Magda Szubanski. MGM, 2002. DVD.

Cronos. Dir. Guillermo del Toro. Perf. Federico Luppi, Ron Perlman, Tamara Shanath. Instituto Mexicano de Cinematografía (IMCINE), 1997. DVD.

Damnation Alley. Dir. Jack Smight. Perf. Jan-Michael Vincent, George Peppard. Twentieth-Century Fox, 1977. DVD.

Dark Shadows. Dir. Tim Burton. Perf. Johnny Depp, Michelle Pfeifer. Warner Bros. Pictures, 2012. DVD.

Dawn of the Dead. Dir. George A. Romero. Perf. David Emge, Ken Foree, Gaylen Ross. Laurel Group, 1978. DVD.

The Day after Tomorrow. Dir. Roland Emmerich. Perf. Dennis Quaid, Jake Gyllenhaal, Emmy Rossum, Sela Ward. Twentieth-Century Fox, 2004. DVD.

Daybreakers. Dir. Michael Spierig, Peter Spierig. Perf. Ethan Hawke, Willem Dafoe, Sam Neill. Lions Gate Films, 2009. DVD.

The Day of the Animals. Dir. William Girdler. Perf. Christopher George, Leslie Nielsen, Lynda Day George. Film Ventures International, 1977. DVD.

The Day of the Triffids. Dir. Steve Sekely. Perf. Howard Keel, Kieron Moore. United Artists, 1963. DVD.

Dead Alive. Dir. Peter Jackson. Perf. Timothy Balme, Diana Penalver. WingNut Films, 1992. DVD.

Deadheads. Dir. Brett Pierce, Drew T. Pierce. Perf. Michael McKiddy, Ross Kidder, Markus Taylor. FroBro Films, 2011. DVD.

The Deadly Mantis. Dir. Nathan Juran. Perf. Craig Stevens, William Hopper, Alix Talton. Universal International Pictures, 1957. DVD.

Death Becomes Her. Dir. Robert Zemeckis. Perf. Meryl Streep, Bruce Willis, Goldie Hawn. Universal Pictures, 1992. DVD.

The Devil Comes on Horseback. Dir. Ricki Stern, Anne Sundberg. Perf. Nicholas Kristof, Brian Steidle. Break Thru Films, 2007. DVD.

The Devil's Backbone. Dir. Guillermo del Toro. Perf. Marisa Paredes, Eduardo Noriega, Federico Luppi. El Deseo, 2001. DVD.

Diary of the Dead. Dir. George A. Romero. Perf. Michelle Morgan, Joshua Close, Shawn Roberts. Artfire Films, 2007. DVD.

District 9. Dir. Neil Blomkamp. Perf. Sharito Copley, David James, Jason Cope. Tristar Pictures, 2009. DVD.

Dracula. Dir. Tod Browning. Perf. Bela Lugosi, Helen Chandler. Universal Pictures, 1931. DVD.

Dracula: Dead and Loving It. Dir. Mel Brooks. Perf. Leslie Nielsen. Gaumant, 1995. DVD.

Dracula Has Risen from the Grave. Dir. Freddie Francis. Perf. Christopher Lee. Hammer Film Productions, 1968. DVD.

Dreamcatcher. Dir. Lawrence Kasdan. Perf. Morgan Freeman, Thomas Jane, Jason Lee. Castle Rock Entertainment, 2003. DVD.

Dredd. Dir. Pete Travis. Perf. Karl Urban, Olivia Thirlby, Lena Headey. DNA Films, 2012. DVD.

Eight Legged Freaks. Dir. Ellory Elkayem. Perf. David Arquette, Kari Wuhrer, Scott Terra, Scarlett Johansson, Doug E. Doug. Warner Brothers, 2002. DVD.

Elysium. Dir. Neill Blomkamp. Perf. Matt Damon, Jodie Foster, Sharlto Copley. TriStar Pictures, 2013. DVD.

ExistenZ. Dir. David Cronenberg. Perf. Jude Law, Jennifer Jason Leigh, Ian Holm. Alliance Atlantis Communications, 1999. DVD.

Eyes without a Face. Dir. Georges Franju. Perf. Pierre Brasseur, Alida Valli, Juliette Mayniel. Champs-Élysées Productions, 1960. DVD.

The Faculty. Dir. Robert Rodriguez. Perf. Jordana Brewster, Clea DuVall, Laura Harris. Dimension Films, 1998. DVD.

Fido. Dir. Andrew Currie. Perf. Billy Connolly, Mary Black, Kesun Loder. Lions Gate Films, 2006. DVD.

Flesh and Blood. Dir. Larry Silverman. GRB Entertainment, 2007. DVD.

The Fly. Dir. David Cronenberg. Perf. Jeff Goldblum, Geena Davis, John Getz. SLM Production Group, 1986. DVD.

Frankenstein. Dir. J. Searle Dawley. Edison Manufacturing Company, 1910. YouTube.

Frankenstein. Dir. James Whale. Perf. Colin Clive, Mae Clarke, Boris Karloff. Universal Pictures, 1931. DVD.

Frankenstein Unbound. Dir. Roger Corman. Perf. John Hurt, Raul Julia, Nick Brimble. Mount Company, 1990. DVD.

The Freshman. Dir. Andrew Bergman. Perf. Marlon Brando, Matthew Broderick, Bruno Kirby. TriStar Pictures, 1990. DVD.

Frogs. Dir. George McCowan. Perf. Ray Milland, Sam Elliott, Joan Van Ark. American International Pictures, 1972. DVD

Ganja and Hess. Dir. Bill Gunn. Perf. Duane Jones, Marlene Clark, Bill Gunn. Kelly/Jordan Enterprises, 1973. DVD.

Germany Year Zero. Dir. Roberto Rossellini. Perf. Edmund Moeschke. Produzione Salvo D'Angelo, 1948. DVD.

Godzilla. Dir. Gareth Edwards. Perf. Aaron Taylor-Johnson, Elizabeth Olsen, Bryan Cranston. Warner Brothers, 2014. DVD.

Half-Life. Dir. Jennifer Phang. Perf. Sanoe Lake, Julia Nickson, Leonardo Nam. Fade to Blue Films, 2008. DVD.

The Hellstrom Chronicle. Dir. Walon Green, Ed Spiegel. Perf. Lawrence Pressman. Wolper Pictures, 1971. DVD.

The Hills Have Eyes. Dir. Wes Craven. Perf. John Steadman, Janus Blythe, Suze Lanier-Bramlett. Blood Relations, 1977. DVD.

Horror of Dracula. Dir. Terence Fisher. Perf. Peter Cushing, Christopher Lee. Hammer Film Productions, 1958. DVD.

How a Mosquito Operates. Dir. Winsor McCay. Vitagraph Company of America, 1912. YouTube.

The Hurricane. Dir. John Ford. Perf. Dorothy Lamour, John Hall, Mary Astor. United Artists, 1937. DVD.

I, Frankenstein. Dir. Stuart Beattie. Perf. Aaron Eckhart, Bill Nighy, Miranda Otto. Hopscotch Features, 2014.

I Am Legend. Dir. Francis Lawrence. Perf. Will Smith, Alice Braga. Warner Bros, 2007. DVD.

Into the Storm. Dir. Stephen Quale. Perf. Richard Armitage, Sarah Wayne Callies, Matt Walsh. Broken Road Productions, 2014. Film.

Invasion of the Body Snatchers. Dir. Don Siegel. Perf. Kevin McCarthy, Dana Wynter, Larry Gates. Allied Artists Pictures, 1956. DVD.

Invasion of the Body Snatchers. Dir. Philip Kaufman. Perf. Donald Sutherland, Brooke Adams, Jeff Goldblum. Solofilm, 1978. DVD.

Jennifer's Body. Dir. Karyn Kusama. Perf. Megan Fox, Amanda Seyfried, Johnny Simmons. Fox Atomic Films, 2009. DVD.

Land of the Dead. Dir. George A. Romero. Perf. Simon Baker, John Leguizamo, Dennis Hopper. Universal Pictures, 2005. DVD.

The Last Man on Earth. Dir. Ubaldo Ragona. Perf. Vincent Price, Franca Bettoia. Produzioni La Regina, 1964. DVD.

The Lone Ranger. Dir. Gore Verbinski. Perf. Johnny Depp, Armie Hammer, William Fichtner. Walt Disney Pictures, 2013. Film.

The Machine Girl. Dir. Noboru Iguchi. Perf. Minase Yashiro, Asami, Kentarô Shimazu. Fever Dreams, 2008. DVD.

Mad Max 2: The Road Warrior. Dir. George Miller. Perf. Mel Gibson, Bruce Spence, Michael Preston. Kennedy Miller Entertainment 1981. DVD.

Mary Shelley's Frankenstein. Dir. Kenneth Branagh. Perf. Robert De Niro, Kenneth Branagh, Helena Bonham Carter. Tristar Pictures, 1994. DVD.

May. Dir. Lucky McKee. Perf. Angela Bettis, Jeremy Sisto, Anna Faris. 2 Loop Films, 2002. DVD.

Men at Work. Dir. Emilio Estevez. Perf. Charlie Sheen, Emilio Estevez. Epic Productions, 1990. DVD.

Men in Black. Dir. Barry Sonnenfeld. Perf. Tommy Lee Jones, Will Smith, Linda Fiorentino. Columbia Pictures Corporation, 1997. DVD.

Microcosmos. Dir. Claude Nuridsany, Marie Pérennou. Galatée Films, 1996. DVD.

Milagro Beanfield War. Dir. Robert Redford. Perf. Rubén Blades, Richard Bradford, Sonia Braga. Universal Pictures, 1988. DVD.

Milk of Sorrow. Dir. Claudia Llosa. Perf. Magaly Solier, Susi Sánchez, Efraín Solís. Institut Català de les Indústries Culturals (ICIC), 2009. DVD.

Mimic. Dir. Guillermo del Toro. Perf. Mira Sorvino, Jeremy Northam. Dimension Films, 1997. DVD.

Modify. Dir. Jason Gary, Greg Jacobson. Committed Films, 2005. DVD.

Monsters inside Me. Perf. Dan Riskin, Kevin Kazacos, Daniel Caplivsky. Animal Planet, 2009–. Television.

Motel Hell. Dir. Kevin Connor. Perf. Rory Calhoun, Paul Linke, Nancy Parsons. Camp Hill, 1980. DVD.

Mr. Bug Goes to Town. Dir. Dave Fleischer. Max Fleischer Studios, 1941. DVD.

Naked Gun 2½: The Smell of Fear. Dir. David Zucker. Perf. Leslie Nielsen, Priscilla Presley, George Kennedy, O. J. Simpson, Robert Goulet. Paramount Pictures, 1991. DVD.

The Naked Jungle. Dir. Byron Haskin. Perf. Charlton Heston, Eleanor Parker, Abraham Sofaer. Paramount Pictures, 1954. DVD.

Nature's Half Acre. Dir. James Algar. Walt Disney Productions, 1951. YouTube.

Near Dark. Dir. Kathryn Bigelow. Perf. Adrian Pasdar, Jenny Wright, Lance Henriksen. F/M, 1987. DVD.

The Nest. Dir. Terrence H. Winkless. Perf. Robert Lansing. Concorde Pictures, 1988. DVD.

Night of the Creeps. Dir. Fred Dekker. Perf. Jason Lively, Tom Atkins, Steve Marshall. TriStar Pictures, 1986. DVD.

Night of the Living Dead. Dir. George A. Romero. Perf. Duane Jones, Judith O'Dea. Image Ten, 1968. DVD.

Noah. Dir. Darren Aronofsky. Perf. Russell Crowe, Jennifer Connelly, Anthony Hopkins. Paramount Pictures, 2014. DVD.

No Blade of Grass. Dir. Cornel Wilde. Perf. Nigel Davenport, Jean Wallace, John Hamill. Theodora Productions, 1970. DVD.

Nosferatu. Dir. F. W. Murnau. Perf. Max Schreck, Greta Schröder, Ruth Landshoff. Jofa-Atelier Berlin-Johannisthal, 1922. DVD.

Nova: Kings of Camouflage. Dir. Gisela Kaufmann. Perf. Jean Geary Boal, Roger Hanlon, Lance Lewman. Kaufman Productions, 2007. Television.

Oil Wells of Baku: Close View. Dir. Lumière brothers. Kino, (1896) 1996. DVD.

The Outlaw Josey Wales. Dir. Clint Eastwood. Perf. Clint Eastwood, Sandra Locke. Warner Brothers, 1976. DVD

The Pack. Dir. Franck Richard. Perf. Yolande Moreau, Émilie Dequenne, Benjamin Biolay. La Fabrique 2, 2010. DVD.

Paisan. Dir. Roberto Rossellini. Organizzazione Film Internazionali (OFI), 1946. DVD.

Pale Rider. Dir. Clint Eastwood. Perf. Clint Eastwood, Carrie Snodgrass, Michael Moriarty. Warner Brothers, 1985. DVD.

Paranormal Activity. Dir. Oren Peli. Perf. Katie Featherston, Micah Sloat, Mark Fredrichs. Solana Films, 2007. DVD.

Phase IV. Dir. Saul Bass. Perf. Michael Murphy, Nigel Davenport. Paramount Pictures, 1974. DVD.

The Plague of the Zombies. Dir. John Gilling. Perf. Andre Morell, Diane Clare, Brook Williams. Hammer Film Productions, 1966. DVD.

Poisoned Waters. Dir. Rick Young. Perf. Martin Baker, Will Baker, Ken Balcomb. Frontline, 2009. DVD.

Prometheus. Dir. Ridley Scott. Perf. Noomi Rapace, Logan Marshall-Green, Michael Fassbender. Twentieth-Century Fox Films, 2012. DVD.

The Puppet Master. Dir. David Schmoeller. Perf. Paul Le Mat, William Hickey, Irene Miracle. Empire Pictures, 1989. DVD.

The Puppet Masters. Dir. Stuart Orme. Perf. Donald Sutherland, Eric Thal, Julie Warner. Hollywood Pictures, 1994. DVD.

Rabid. Dir. David Cronenberg. Perf. Marilyn Chambers, Frank Moore, Joe Silver. CFDC, 1976. DVD.

Ravenous. Dir. Antonia Bird. Perf. Guy Pearce, Robert Carlyle, David Arquette. ETIC Films, 1999. DVD.

Red-Blooded American Girl. Dir. David Blyth. Perf. Andrew Stevens, Heather Thomas, Christopher Plummer. Prism Entertainment, 1990. DVD.

The Return of the Vampire. Dir. Lew Landers. Perf. Bela Lugosi, Frieda Inescort, Nina Foch. Columbia Pictures, 1944. DVD.

Return to Nuke 'Em High Volume 1. Dir. Lloyd Kaufman. Perf. Asta Paredes, Catherine Corcoran, Vito Trigo. Troma Studios, 2013. DVD.

The Revenant. Dir. D. Kerry Prior. Perf. David Anders, Chris Wylde, Louise Griffiths. Putrefactory, 2012. DVD.

A River Runs through It. Dir. Robert Redford. Perf. Craig Sheffer, Brad Pitt, Tom Skerritt. Allied Filmmakers, 1992. DVD.

The Road. Dir. John Hillcoat. Perf. Viggo Mortensen, Charlize Theron, Kodi Smit-McPhee. Dimension Films, 2009. DVD.

RoboCop. Dir. Paul Verhoeven. Perf. Peter Weller, Nancy Allen, Dan O'Herlihy. Orion Pictures, 1987. DVD.

RoboCop. Dir. José Padilha. Perf. Joel Kinnaman, Gary Oldman, Michael Keaton. MGM, 2014. Film.

Robo Geisha. Dir. Noboru Iguchi. Perf. Asami, Naoto Takenaka, Yoshihiro Nishimura, Kadokawa Eiga K.K., 2009. DVD.

Rome Open City. Dir. Roberto Rossellini. Perf. Anna Magnani. Excelsa Film, 1945. DVD.

The Ruins. Dir. Carter Smith. Perf. Shawn Ashmore, Jena Malone, Jonathan Tucker. DreamWorks SKG, 2008. DVD.

Scream Blacula Scream. Dir. Bob Kelljan. Perf. William Marshall, Don Mitchell, Pam Grier. American International Pictures, 1973. DVD.

Secrets of Life. Dir. James Algar. Walt Disney Productions, 1956. DVD.

Shaun of the Dead. Dir. Edgar Wright. Perf. Simon Pegg, Kate Ashfield, Nick Frost. Universal Pictures, 2004. DVD.

Shivers. Dir. David Cronenberg. Perf. Paul Hampton, Joe Silver, Lynn Lowry. Canadian Film Development Corporation (CFDC), 1975. DVD.

Silent Running. Dir. Douglas Trumbull. Perf. Bruce Dern. Universal Pictures, 1972. DVD.

Silkwood. Dir. Mike Nichols. Perf. Meryl Streep, Kurt Russell, Cher. Twentieth-Century Fox, 1983. DVD.

Skeeter. Dir. Clark Brandon. Perf. Tracy Griffith, Jim Youngs, Charles Napier. New Line Cinema, 1993. DVD.

The Skin I Live In. Dir. Pedro Almodóvar. Perf. Antonio Banderas, Elena Anaya, Jan Cornet. Blue Haze Entertainment, 2011.DVD.

Slither. Dir. James Gunn. Perf. Nathan Fillion, Elizabeth Banks, Michael Rooker. Gold Circle Films, 2006. DVD.

Snowpiercer. Dir. Joon-Ho Bong. Perf. Chris Evans, Jamie Bell, Tilda Swinton. Moho Film, 2013. DVD.

Something for the Birds. Dir. Robert Wise. Perf. Patricia Neal, Victor Mature. Twentieth-Century Fox, 1952. DVD.

Soylent Green. Dir. Richard Fleischer. Perf. Charlton Heston, Edward G. Robinson, Leigh Taylor-Young. MGM Pictures, 1973. DVD.

Splinter. Dir. Toby Wilkins. Perf. Shea Whigham, Jill Wagner, Paulo Costanzo. Indion Entertainment Group, 2008. DVD.

Stake Land. Dir. Jim Mickle. Perf. Connor Paolo, Nick Damici, Kelly McGillis. Glass Eye Pix, 2010. DVD.

Starship Troopers. Dir. Paul Verhoeven. Perf. Caspar Van Dien, Dina Meryer. TriStar Pictures, 1997. DVD.

Star Trek 2: The Wrath of Khan. Dir. Nicholas Meyer. Perf. William Shatner, Leonard Nimoy, DeForest Kelley. Paramount Pictures, 1982. DVD.

The Strength and Agility of Insects. Dir. Percy Smith. 1911. YouTube.

Strigoi. Dir. Faye Jackson. Perf. Catalin Paraschiv, Rudy Rosenfeld, Constantin Barbulescu. St. Moritz Productions, 2009. DVD.

Survival of the Dead. Dir. George A. Romero. Perf. Alan Van Sprang, Kenneth Welsh, Kathleen Munroe. Blank of the Dead Productions, 2009. DVD.

Tabu: A Story of the South Seas. Dir. F. W. Murnau. Murnau/Flaherty Productions, 1931. DVD.

Tetsuo: The Iron Man. Dir. Shin'ya Tsukamoto. Perf. Kei Fujiwara, Tomorowo Taguchi, Nobu Kanaoka. Japan Home Video, 1989. DVD.

The Texas Chainsaw Massacre. Dir. Tobe Hooper. Perf. Marilyn Burns, Allen Danziger, Paul A. Partain. Vortex Films, 1974. DVD.

The Thaw. Dir. Mark A. Lewis. Perf. Val Kilmer, Alexandra Staseson, Brad Dryborough. Anagram Pictures, 2009. DVD.

Them! Dir. Gordon Douglas. Perf. James Whitmore, Edmund Gwenn, Joan Weldon. Warner Bros. Pictures, 1954. DVD.

The Thing. Dir. John Carpenter. Perf. Kurt Russell, Wilford Brimley, Keith David. Universal Pictures, 1982. DVD.

The Thing. Dir. Matthijs van Heijningen Jr. Perf. Mary Elizabeth Winstead, Joel Edgerton, Ulrich Thomsen. Morgan Creek Productions, 2011. DVD.

The Thing from Another World. Dir. Christian Nyby, Howard Hawks. Perf. Kenneth Tobey, Margaret Sheridan, James Arness. Winchester Pictures, 1951. DVD.

Thirst. Dir. Chan-wook Park. Perf. Kang-ho Song, Ok-bin Kim, Hae-suk Kim. CJ Entertainment, 2009. DVD.

The Time Machine. Dir. George Pal. Perf. Rod Taylor, Alan Young, Yvette Mimieux. MGM Pictures, 1960. DVD.

The Tingler. Dir. William Castle. Perf. Vincent Price, Judith Evelyn, Darryl Hickman. Columbia Pictures, 1959. DVD.

To Be or Not to Be. Dir. Alan Johnson. Perf. Mel Brooks, Anne Bancroft, Christopher Lloyd. Twentieth-Century Fox, 1983. DVD.

Tokyo Gore Police. Dir. Yoshihiro Nishimura. Perf. Eihi Shiina, Itsuji Itao, Yukihide Benny. Fever Dreams, 2008. DVD.

The Toxic Avenger. Dir. Michael Herz, Lloyd Kaufman. Perf. Andree Maranda, Mitch Cohen, Jennifer Babtist. Troma Studios, 1984. DVD.

The Toxic Avenger Part II. Dir. Michael Herz, Lloyd Kaufman. Perf. Ron Fazio, John Altamura, Phoebe Legere. Troma Studios, 1989. DVD.

The Toxic Avenger Part III: The Last Temptation of Toxie. Dir. Michael Herz, Lloyd Kaufman. Perf. Ron Fazio, Phoebe Legere, John Altamura. Troma Studios, 1989. DVD.

Trouble Every Day. Dir. Claire Denis. Perf. Vincent Gallo, Tricia Vessey, Beatrice Dalle. Arte Pictures, 2001. DVD.

True Blood. Creator: Alan Ball. Perf. Anna Paquin, Stephen Moyer, Sam Trammell. HBO, 2008–. TV.

Tucker and Dale vs. Evil. Dir. Eli Craig. Perf. Tyler Labine, Alan Tudyk, Katrina Bowden. Reliance Big Picture, 2010. DVD.

Twelve Monkeys. Dir. Terry Gilliam. Perf. Bruce Willis, Madeleine Stowe, Brad Pitt. Universal Pictures, 1995. DVD.

28 Days Later. Dir. Danny Boyle. Perf. Cilian Murphy, Alex Palmer, Naomie Harris. DNA Films, 2002. DVD.

28 Weeks Later. Dir. Juan Carlos Fresnadillo. Perf. Robert Carlyle, Rose Byrne, Jeremy Renner. Fox Atomic, 2007. DVD.

Twilight. Dir. Catherine Hardwicke. Perf. Kristen Stewart, Robert Pattinson, Billy Burke. Summit Entertainment, 2008. Film.

Underworld. Dir. Len Wiseman. Perf. Kate Beckinsale, Scott Speedman, Shane Brolly. Lakeshore Entertainment, 2003. DVD.

Upstream Color. Dir. Shane Carruth. Perf. Amy Seimetz, Frank Mosley, Shane Carruth. Erbp, 2013. DVD.

Vamps. Dir. Amy Heckerling. Perf. Alicia Silverstone, Krysten Ritter, Larry Wilmore. Lucky Monkey Pictures, 2012. DVD.

Van Helsing. Dir. Stephen Sommers. Perf. Hugh Jackman, Kate Beckinsale, Richard Roxburgh. Universal Pictures, 2004. DVD.

WALL-E. Dir. Andrew Stanton. Perf. Ben Burtt, Elissa Knight. Pixar Films, 2008. DVD.

War Witch. Dir. Kim Nguyen. Perf. Rachel Mwanza, Alain Lino Mic Eli Bastien, Serge Kanyinda. Item 7, 2012. DVD.

Warm Bodies. Dir. Jonathan Levine. Perf. Nicholas Hoult, Teresa Palmer. Summit Entertainment, 2013. DVD.

White Zombie. Dir. Victor Halperin. Perf. Bela Lugosi, Madge Bellamy. Edward Halperin Productions, 1932. DVD.

World War Z. Dir. Marc Forster. Perf. Brad Pitt, Mireille Enos, Daniella Kertesz. Paramount Pictures, 2013. DVD.

Zombieland. Dir. Ruben Fleischer. Perf. Jesse Eisenberg, Emma Stone, Woody Harrelson. Columbia Pictures, 2009. DVD.

NOTES

2. "AS BEAUTIFUL AS A BUTTERFLY"?

1. Mixed versions of the cockroach myth appear in films such as *Naked Lunch* (1991) and *Joe's Apartment* (1993) as well.

2. Stacy Alaimo notes that "the film counter-poses Dr. Tyler's reproductive capacities with her ability to scientifically create creatures.... By associating Dr. Tyler with her monstrous progeny, the film can discipline her scientific pretensions without invoking woman as the uneasy, unstable, border zone between man and beast" (2001, 288).

4. THROUGH AN ECO-LENS OF CHILDHOOD

1. *A Foreign Affair* (1948) and *The Search* (1948), two Hollywood films of the period, also document the devastated postwar city of Berlin, but from the perspective of the Allies.

5. ZOMBIE EVOLUTION

1. See, for example, *White Zombie* (dir. Victor Halperin, 1933), *The King of the Zombies* (dir. Jean Yarbrough, 1941), *I Walked with a Zombie* (dir. Jacques Tourneur, 1943), *Plague of the Zombies* (dir. John Gilling, 1966), and later stragglers such as *Sugar Hill* (dir. Paul Maslansky, 1974), *The Serpent and the Rainbow* (dir. Wes Craven, 1988), *Pet Sematary* (dir. Mary Lambert, 1989), *Bubba Ho-Tep* (dir. Don Coscarelli, 2002), *Exit Humanity* (dir. John Geddes, 2011), and *Paranorman* (dir. Chris Butler and Sam Fell, 2012).

2. See, for example, *Return of the Living Dead* (dir. Dan O'Bannon, 1985), *Zombie High* (dir. Ron Link, 1987), *Biozombie* (dir. Wilson Yip, 1998), *Severed: Forest of the Dead* (dir. Carl Bessai, 2005), *The Revenant* (dir. D. Kerry Prior, 2009), *Dead Snow* (dir. Tommy Wirkola, 2009), *Chernobyl Diaries* (dir. Bradley Parker, 2012), *Night of the Living Dead—Reanimation* (dir. Jeff Broadstreet, 2012), and *Doomsday Book—A Brave New World* (dir. Pil-Sug Yim, 2012).

3. Other zombie films highlighting a virus as the agent for the change include *Dawn of the Dead* (dir. George A. Romero, 1978), *Day of the Dead* (dir. George A. Romero, 1985), *Cemetery Man* (dir. Michele Soavi, 1994), *Shaun of the Dead* (dir. Edgar Wright, 2004), *Dawn of the Dead* (dir. Zack Snyder, 2004), *Fido* (dir. Andrew Currie, 2006), *The Zombie Diaries* (dir. Michael Bartlett, 2006), *Diary of the Dead* (dir. George Romero, 2007), *[REC]* (dir. Jaume Balaguero, 2007), *American Zombie* (dir. Grace Lee, 2007), *The Dead Outside* (dir. Kerry Anne Mullaney, 2008), *Pontypool* (dir. Bruce McDonald, 2008)—a language virus!, *Xombies: Dead on Arrival* (dir. James Farr, 2008), *Zombies of Mass Destruction* (dir. Kevin Hamadani, 2009), *The Horde* (dir. Yannick Dahan, 2009), *Mutants* (dir. David Morlet, 2009), the very funny *Zombieland* (dir. Ruben Fleischer, 2009), *Rambock* (dir. Marvin Kren, 2010), *Devil's Playground* (dir. Mark McQueen, 2010), *Juan of the Dead* (dir. Alejandro Brugues, 2011), and *Dead Season* (dir. Adam Deyoe, 2012).

8. GENDERING THE CANNIBAL

1. In her *Rural Gothic in American Popular Culture* (2013) chapter, "Going Windigo: Civilisation and Savagery," Bernice M. Murphy further explains this history.
2. In a May 2012 *Smithsonian Magazine* article, Maria Dolan suggests a contemporary form of medicinal cannibalism might be the black market in body parts for transplants.
3. See the following examples: Darling 1998 and Conklin 1997.
4. Regarding genre, see also Met 2003. Regarding style, see also Morrey 2004; and Murphy 2012.

9. *AMERICAN MARY* AND BODY MODIFICATION

1. Other documentaries include *Flesh and Blood*, dir. Larry Silverman (GRB Entertainment, 2007), DVD; *Moana*, dir. Robert Flaherty (Famous Players-Lasky Corporation, 1926), DVD; *Tabu: A Story of the South Seas*, dir. F. W. Murnau (Murnau/Flaherty Productions, 1931), DVD; and *Pumping Iron*, dir. George Butler and Robert Fiore (White Mountain Films, 1977), DVD.
2. The assassin bug also uses decoys for protection, cloaking itself in the exoskeleton of its prey.
3. These Japanese horror films draw on the revenge narrative found in *Audition* (1999), directed by Takashi Miike, but they add the critique of mechanization found in male-driven films such as Shin'ya Tsukamoto's *Tetsuo: The Iron Man* (1989) with a feminist take on body modification.
4. See, for example, Gould 1994; J. A. W. Heffernan 1997; Laplace-Sinatra 1998; Shor 2003; and A. M. Adams 2009.

5. IMDB lists at least seventy movies explicitly noting Frankenstein's monster. Offshoots are even more numerous, and include films as diverse as female-centered horror films *Eyes without a Face* (1960), *Death Becomes Her* (1992), *Boxing Helena* (1993), *May* (2002), and *The Skin I Live In* (2011); masculine action horror-sci-fi films such as *Robocop* (1987 and 2013) and *Dredd* (2012); European sci-fi horror such as *City of Lost Children* (1995); and David Cronenberg body horror films such as *The Fly* (1986) and *ExistenZ* (1999).

6. Earlier film adaptations address nuclear power and atomic warfare. See, for example, *Frankenstein 1970* (1958) and *Frankenstein Conquers the World* (1965). *Blackenstein* (1972) inserts an anti–Vietnam War message.

7. Other responses to and loose and close adaptations of the novel highlight this Arctic setting. See, for example, *Frankenstein: The True Story* (1973), *Subject 2* (2006), and *The Frankenstein Theory* (2013).

8. "First Video of New Spider Species," *Smarter Every Day 78*, Web, http://youtu.be/RrWnz7vySac, *YouTube*. See also the *National Geographic* website at http://news watch.nationalgeographic.com/2013/01/23/spider-decoy/#.u3aqdbDkE_A.email.

9. Ian Woolstencroft describes *American Mary* as "a *Frankenstein* for the 21st Century which makes it surprisingly apt that Universal has picked up the distribution rights for the film" (2012, available at https://letterboxd.com/dr_movie/film/american-mary/).

10. This approach to rape-revenge body modification horror differs from *Frankenhooker* (1990), a "campy throwback movie" (1992, 235) according to Carol J. Clover.

CONCLUSION

1. This image is nearly replicated in Thomas Hart Benton's painting *Boomtown* (1928), which captures a scene of nonchalance toward oil well fires in a Borger, Texas. Benton also discusses the dilemma we face when environmental destruction is masked by spectacular beauty in *An Artist in America*. According to Benton,

> Out on the open plain beyond the town a great thick column of black smoke rose as in a volcanic eruption from the earth to the middle of the sky. There was a carbon mill out there that burnt thousands of cubic feet of gas every minute, a great, wasteful, extravagant burning of resources for momentary profit. All the mighty anarchic carelessness of our country was revealed in Borger. But it was revealed with a breadth, with an expansive grandeur, that was as effective emotionally as are the tremendous spatial reaches of the plains country where the town was set. (1983, 201–2)

2. Bernice Murphy offers an overview of these 1970s animal attack movies in her *The Rural Gothic in American Popular Culture* chapter "Why Wouldn't the Wilderness Fight Us? American Eco-Horror and the Apocalypse."

WORKS CITED

Adams, Ann Marie. 2009. "What's in a Frame? The Authorizing Presence in James Whale's *Bride of Frankenstein. Journal of Popular Culture* 42, no. 3 (June): 403–18. Print.

Adams, Josh. 2009. "Bodies of Change: A Comparative Analysis of Media Representations of Body Modification Practices." *Sociological Perspectives* 52, no. 1 (Spring): 103–29. Print.

Alaimo, Stacy. 2001. "Discomforting Creatures: Monstrous Natures in Recent Films." In *Beyond Nature Writing: Expanding the Boundaries of Eco-Criticism*, edited by Karla Armbruster, 279–96. Richmond: University Press of Virginia. Print.

Amorok, Tina. 2007. "The Eco-Trauma and Eco-Recovery of Being." *Shift: At the Frontiers of Consciousness* 15 (June–August 2007): 28–31, 37. Print.

Anonymous. 2005. *A Woman in Berlin*. New York: Metropolitan Books. Print.

Apte, Mahadev. 1985. *Humor and Laughter: An Anthropological Approach*. Ithaca NY: Cornell University Press.

Armstrong, Derek. 2002. "*Eight Legged Freaks* Review." *All Movie Guide*. Web. 1 June 2007.

Arens, W. 1979. *The Man-Eating Myth: Anthropology and Anthropophagy*. New York: Oxford University Press. Print.

Asibong, Andrew. 2011. "Claire Denis's Flickering Spaces of Hospitality." *L'Esprit Createur* 51, no. 1 (Spring): 154–67. Print.

Avramescu, Catalin. 2003. *An Intellectual History of Cannibalism*. Princeton NJ: Princeton University Press. Print.

Badalov, Rahman. 1997. "Oil Revolution, and Cinema." *Azerbaijan International* 5, no. 3 (Autumn). Web. 2 Dec. 2005.

Banerjee, Superna. 2010. "Home Is Where Mamma Is: Reframing the Science Question in *Frankenstein.*" *Women's Studies: An Interdisciplinary Journal* 40, no. 1:1–22. Print.

Barker, Francis, et al., eds. 1998. *Cannibalism and the Colonial World*. Cambridge: Cambridge University Press. Print.

Basso, Ellen B. 1995. *The Last Cannibal: A South American Oral History*. Austin: University of Texas Press. Print.

Beaver, Dan. 2002. "Flesh or Fantasy: Cannibalism and the Meanings of Violence." *Ethnohistory* 49, no. 3 (Summer): 671–85. Print.

Becker, Matt. 2006. "A Point of Little Hope: Hippie Horror Films and the Politics of Ambivalence." *Velvet Light Trap* 57 (Spring): 42–59. Print.

Beevor, Antony. 2002. *The Fall of Berlin, 1945*. New York: Penguin Books. Print.

Bekoff, Marc. 2006. *Animal Passions and Beastly Virtues: Reflections on Redecorating Nature*. Philadelphia: Temple University Press. Print.

———. 2007. *The Emotional Lives of Animals*. Novato CA: New World Library. Print.

Bekoff, Marc, and Jessica Pierce. 2009. *Wild Justice: The Moral Lives of Animals*. Chicago: University of Chicago Press. Print.

Bell, William J., Louis M. Roth, and Christine A. Nalepa. 2007. *Cockroaches: Ecology, Behavior, and Natural History*. Baltimore: Johns Hopkins University Press. Print.

Benton, Thomas Hart. 1983. *An Artist in America*. 4th rev. ed. Columbia: University of Missouri Press.

Berry, Thomas. (1988) 2006. *The Dream of the Earth*. San Francisco: Sierra Club Books. Print.

Beville, Maria. 2013. *The Unnamable Monster in Literature and Film*. New York: Routledge. Print.

Biggs, Shelby Brooke. 2011. "Ethnobiology Enthusiast Filmmaker versus MOTHRA!" *Independent Lens Blog*, 17 May. Web. 25 May 2012.

Bishop, Kyle. 2006. "Raising the Dead." *Journal of Popular Film and Television* 33, no. 4:196–205. Print.

———. 2010. "The Idle Proletariat: *Dawn of the Dead*, Consumer Ideology, and the Loss of Productive Labor." *Journal of Popular Culture* 43, no. 2: 234–48. Print.

Bloom, Dan. 2014. "Interview: Dan Bloom on the New Cli-Fi Genre and Where It Is Headed." *Hollywood Goes "Cli-Fi"* (1 June). Web. 1 Nov. 2014.

Bondanella, Peter. 2004. "The Making of *Roma citta aperta*: The Legacy of Fascism and the Birth of Neorealism. In Gottlieb 2004, 43–66. Print.

Boucher, Phillip P. 1992. *Cannibal Encounters: Europeans and Island Caribs, 1492–1763*. Baltimore: Johns Hopkins University Press. Print.

Bower, Bruce. 2013. "Cannibalism in Colonial America Comes to Life." *Science News* 183, no. 11 (June): 5. Print.

Bradley, Linda. 1995. *Film, Horror, and the Body Fantastic*. Westport CT: Greenwood. Print.

Brinks, Ellen. 2004. "'Nobody's Children': Gothic Representation and Traumatic History in *The Devil's Backbone*." *JAC: A Journal of Composition Theory* 24, no. 2:291–312. Print.

Brooks, Daniel R., and Eric P. Hoberg. 2007. "How Will Global Climate Change Affect Parasite-Host Assemblages?" *Trends in Parasitology* 23, no.12:571–74. Print.

Brottman, Mikita. 2005. *Offensive Films*. Nashville: Vanderbilt University Press. Print.

Brown, Eric C., ed. 2006a. *Insect Poetics*. Minneapolis: University of Minnesota Press. Print.

———. 2006b. "Introduction." In Brown 2006a, ix–xxiii. Print.

Brown, Jennifer. 2013. *Cannibalism in Literature and Film*. New York: Palgrave Macmillan. Print.

Brush, Pippa. 1998. "Metaphors of Inscription: Discipline, Plasticity and the Rhetoric of Choice." *Feminist Review* 58 (Spring): 22–43. Print.

Bundtzen, Linda K. 1987. "Monstrous Mothers: Medusa, Grendel, and Now *Alien*." *Film Quarterly* 40, no. 3 (Spring): 11–17. Print.

Cahill, Ann J. 2003. "Feminist Pleasure and Feminine Beautification." *Hypatia* 18, no. 4:42–64. Print.

Cameron, Allan. 2012. "Zombie Media: Transmission, Reproduction, and the Digital Dead." *Society for Cinema and Media Studies Journal* 52, no. 1 (Fall): 66–89. Print.

Canby, Vincent. 1971. "'Hellstrom Chronicle' Opens: Nature Provides Topic of Documentary." *New York Times*, 29 June. Web. 29 May 2012.

———. 1986. "*Class of Nuke 'Em High* Review." *New York Times*, 12 Dec. Web. 3 Dec. 2014.

Carroll, Noel. 1990. *The Philosophy of Horror or Paradoxes of the Heart*. New York: Routledge University Press. Print.

Chau, N., L. Benamghar, Q. T. Pham, D. Teculescu, E. Rebstock, and J. M. Muret. 1993. "Mortality of Iron Miners in Lorraine (France): Relations between Lung Function and Respiratory Symptoms and Subsequent Mortality." *British Journal of Industrial Medicine* 50, no. 11 (Nov.): 1017–31. Print.

Cherry, Brigid. 2013. *True Blood: Investigating Vampires and Southern Gothic*. New York: I. B. Taurus. Print.

Clarke, Robert. 1973. *Ellen Swallow: The Woman Who Founded Ecology*. New York: Follett. Print.

Clasen, Mathias. 2010. "Vampire Apocalypse: A Biocultural Critique of Richard Matheson's *I Am Legend*." *Philosophy and Literature* 34, no. 2 (Oct.): 313–28. Print.

Cleese, John. 1994. "Synopsis of Humour and Psychoanalysis Conference." London: Freud Museum. 5 Nov. Web. 3 Dec. 2005.

Click, Melissa. 2010. *Bitten by Twilight: Youth Culture, Media and the Vampire Franchise*. New York: Peter Lang. Print.

Clover, Carol J. 1992. *Men, Women and Chainsaws: Gender in the American Horror Film*. Princeton NJ: Princeton University Press. Print.

Cohen, Jeffery J., ed. 1996. *Monster Theory: Reading Culture*. Minneapolis: University of Minnesota Press. Print.

———. 2014. "Grey." In *Prismatic Ecology: Ecotheory beyond Green*, edited by Jeffrey Jerome Cohen, 270–89. Minneapolis: University of Minnesota Press. Print.

Cohen, Rich. "Sugar Love: A Not So Sweet Story." 2013. *National Geographic*, August, 78–97. Print.

Collier, Peter. 1970. "Ecological Destruction Is a Condition of American Life: An Interview with Ecologist Paul Ehrlich." *Mademoiselle* (April), 189, 293.

Comaroff, Jean, and John Comaroff. 2002. "Alien-Nation: Zombies, Immigrants, and Millennial Capitalism." *South Atlantic Quarterly* 101, no. 4 (Fall): 779–805. Print.

Combes, Claude. 2005. *The Art of Being a Parasite*. Chicago: University of Chicago Press. Print.

Conklin, Beth A. 1997. "Consuming Images: Representations of Cannibalism on the Amazonian Frontier." *Anthropological Quarterly* 70, no. 2 (Apr.): 68–78. Print.

Conrich, Ian, Editor. 2010. *Horror Zone*. New York: I. B. Taurus. Print.

Copeland, Marion W. 2003. *Cockroach*. London: Reaktion Books. Print.

———. 2006. "Voices of the Least Loved: Cockroaches in the Contemporary American Novel." In Brown 2006a, 153–78. Print.

Creed, Barbara. 1993. *The Monstrous-Feminine: Film, Feminism, Psychoanalysis*. London: Routledge. Print.

Creed, Barbara, and Jeannette Hoorn, eds. 2001. *Body Trade: Captivity Cannibalism and Colonialism in the Pacific*. New York: Routledge. Print.

Crowther, Bosley. 1946. "The Screen: How Italy Resisted." *New York Times*, 26 Feb. Web. 4 July 2012.

Cruikshank, Julie. 2001. "Glaciers and Climate Change: Perspectives from Oral Tradition." *ARCTIC* 54, no. 4 (Dec.): 377–93. Print.

Cubitt, Sean. 2005. *EcoMedia*. Amsterdam: Rodopi. Print.

———. 2013. "Everybody Knows This Is Nowhere: Data Visualization and Ecocriticism." In Rust, Monani, and Cubitt 2013, 279–96.

Cutner, Jerry C. 2013. "*American Mary* and Female-Centered Horror." *Bright Lights Film Journal*, 12 Oct. Web. 3 Aug. 2014.

Dargis, Manohla. 2005. "Not Just Roaming, Zombies Rise Up: *Land of the Dead* Review." *New York Times*, 24 June. Web. 20 May 2013.

Darling, Andrew J. 1998. "Mass Inhumation and the Execution of Witches in the American Southwest." *American Anthropologist*, n.s., 100, no. 3 (Sept.): 732–52. Print.

Darwin, Charles. (1859) 2001. *On the Origin of the Species*. State College: Penn State Electronic Classics Series. Web. 22 May 2013.

Daston, Loraine, and Gregg Mitman, eds. 2005. *Thinking with Animals: New Perspectives on Anthropomorphism*. New York: Columbia University Press. Print.

Del Toro, Guillermo. 1993. "*Cronos* Production Notes." Criterion Collection. Print.

DiMarco, Danette. 2011. "Going Wendigo: The Emergence of the Iconic Monster in Margaret Atwood's *Oryx and Crake* and Antonia Bird's *Ravenous*." *College Literature* 38, no. 4 (Fall): 134–55. Print.

Dolan, Maria. 2012. "The Gruesome History of Eating Corpses as Medicine." *Smithsonian Magazine*, 7 May. Web. 1 July 2013.

Dowler, Andrew. 2009. "Toronto After Dark Fest." *Now* 28, no. 50 (12–19 Aug.). Web. 2 Feb. 2013.

Drew, C. Harvel, et al. 2013. "Climate Warming and Disease Risks for Terrestrial and Marine Biota." *Science Magazine.com*, 19 Jan. Web. 3 Oct. 2013.

Dufour, Eve. 2012. "Lesbian Desires in the Vampire Subgenre: *True Blood* as a Platform for a Lesbian Discourse." *Prandium: The Journal of Historical Studies* 1, no. 1 (Mar.). Web. 1 June 2013.

Dunn, Robert B., and Matthew C. Fitzpatrick. 2012. "Every Species Is an Insect (or Nearly So): On Insects, Climate Change, Extinction, and the Biological Unknown." In *Saving a Million Species: Extinction Risk from Climate Change*, edited by Lee Hannah and Thomas Lovejoy, 217–38. Washington DC: Island Press. Print.

Dutch, Steve. 2010. "Military Impacts on the Environment." 2 June. University of Wisconsin–Green Bay. http://www.uwgb.edu/dutchs. Web. 4 July 2012.

Ebert, Roger. 1971. "The Hellstrom Chronicle." *Chicago Sun Times*, 1 Jan. Web. 1 June 2012.

———. 1994. "*Cronos* Review." *Chicago Sun Times*, 6 May. Web. 5 Aug. 2012.

———. 2009. "*Jennifer's Body* Review." *Chicago Sun Times*, 16 Sept. Web. 2 July 2013.

Edmonds, Alexander. 2007. "'The Poor Have the Right to Be Beautiful': Cosmetic Surgery in Neoliberal Brazil." *Journal of the Royal Anthropological Institute* 13, no. 2 (June): 363–81. Print.

Eldridge, David. 2008. "The Generic American Psycho." *Journal of American Studies* 42, no. 1:19–33. Print.

Ellis, Bret Easton. 1991. *American Psycho*. New York: Vintage. Print.

Erickson, Glenn. 2011. "*Hellstrom Chronicle* Review." 31 Dec. Web. 2 June 2012.

Ertung, Celan. 2011. "Bodies That [Don't] Matter: Feminist Cyberpunk and Transgressions of Bodily Boundaries." *Edebiyat Fakültesi Dergisi / Journal of Faculty of Letters* 28, no. 2 (Dec.): 77–93. Print.

Etcoff, Nancy. 2010. "Born to Adorn: Why We Desire, Display, and Design." *Premsela.org*, 26 May. Web. 5 July 2014.

Fay, Jennifer. 2008. "Dead Subjectivity: White Zombie, Black Baghdad." *CR: The New Centennial Review* 8, no. 1 (Spring): 81–101. Print.

Feder, Helena. 2010. "'A Blot upon the Earth': Nature's 'Negative' and the Production of Monstrosity in *Frankenstein*." *Journal of Ecocriticism (JOE)* 2, no. 1 (Jan.). Web. 2 July 2014.

Forbes, Jack D. 1992. *Columbus and Other Cannibals: The Wetiko Disease of Exploitation, Imperialism, and Terrorism*. New York: Seven Stories Press. Print.

Freud, Sigmund. 1963. *Jokes and Their Relation to the Unconscious*. New York: W. W. Norton. Print.

Gangestad, Steven W., and Glenn J. Scheyd. 2005. "The Evolution of Human Physical Attraction." *Annual Review of Anthropology* 34: 523–48. Print.

Garland-Thomas, Rosemarie. 2012. "Feminist Disability Studies." *Signs* 30, no. 2 (Winter): 1557–87. Print.

Gervais, Matthew, and Wilson, David Sloan. 2005. "The Evolution and Functions of Laughter and Humor: A Synthetic Approach." *Quarterly Review of Biology* 80, no. 4 (Dec.): 395–430. Print.

Gibron, Bill. 2004. "La Cu-Ca-Racha!" *PopMatters*, 5 Oct. Web. 10 Aug. 2012.

Gottlieb, Sidney, ed. 2004. *Roberto Rossellini's Rome Open City*. New York: Cambridge University Press. Print.

Gould, Stephen Jay. 1994. "The Monster's Human Nature." *Natural History* 103, no. 7 (July): 14–20. Print.

Grisanti, Mary Lee. 2010. "Roberto Rossellini's War Trilogy." *Films in Review*, 17 Apr. Web. 2 July 2012.

Guarner, José Luis. 1970. *Roberto Rossellini*. New York: Praeger. Print.

Gupta, Sujata. 2014. "The Silencing of the Deaf." *Matter*, 9 Apr. Web. 2 Aug. 2014.

Hale Mike. 2010. "Beetle Queen Conquers Tokyo." *New York Times*, 11 May. Web. 1 June 2012.

Hallenbeck, Bruce G. 2009. *Comedy-Horror Films: A Chronological History, 1914–2008*. Jefferson NC: McFarland, 2009. Print.

Hammond, Kim. 2004. "Monsters of Modernities: Frankenstein and Modern Environmentalism." *Cultural Geographies* 11, no. 2 (Apr.): 181–98. Print.

Hand, Richard J., and Jay McRoy. 2007. *Monstrous Adaptations: Generic and Thematic Mutations in Horror Film*. Manchester: Manchester University Press. Print.

Hanke, Ken. 2004. "*Blood Diner* Review." *Mountain Xpress*, 29 Jan. Web. 30 June 2013.

Haraway, Donna. 1991. "The Cyborg Manifesto: Science, Technology, and Socialist Feminism in the Late Twentieth Century." In *Simians, Cyborgs, and Women: The Reinvention of Nature*, 149–81. New York: Routledge. Print.

Harvey, Dennis. 2010. "*Strigoi* Review." *Variety*, 18 July. Web. 3 Feb. 2013.

Heffernan, James A. W. 1997. "Looking at the Monster: 'Frankenstein' and Film." *Critical Inquiry* 24, no. 1 (Autumn): 133–58.

Heffernan, Kevin. "Inner-City Exhibition and the Genre Film: Distributing *Night of the Living Dead*." *Cinema Journal* 41, no. 3 (Spring 2002): 59–77. Print.

Hendrix, Grady. 2010. "From Nuclear Nightmare to Networked Nirvana." *World Literature Today*, 1 May 2010. *The Free Library*. Web. 3 Dec. 2014.

Hess, David E. 2013. PA *Environment Daily*. 29 Apr. Web. 5 Oct. 2013.

Hoberman, J. 2001. "Ghost Worlds." *Village Voice*, 20. Web. 3 Aug. 2014.

Hogle, Linda F. 2005. "Enhancement Technologies and the Body." *Annual Review of Anthropology* 34: 695–716. Print.

Holden, Stephen. 1986. "*Toxic Avenger* Review." *New York Times*, 4 Apr. Web. 3 Dec. 2014.

———. 2000. "*American Psycho*: Murderer! Fiend! Cad! (but Well-Dressed)." *New York Times*, 14 Apr. Web. 3 July 2013.

Hollingsworth, Christopher. 2006. "The Force of the Entomological Other: Insects as Instruments of Intolerant Thought and Oppressive Action." In Brown 2006a, 262-80. Print.

Horowitz, Alexandra C., and Bekoff, Marc. 2007. "Naturalizing Anthropomorphism: Behavioral Prompts to Our Humanizing of Animals." *Anthrozoos* 20, no. 1: 23–35. Print.

Howe, Desson. 1994. "*Cronos* Review." *Washington Post*, 20 May. Web. 6 Aug. 2012.

Humphries, Reynold. 2006. *The Hollywood Horror Film, 1931–1941: Madness in a Social Landscape*. Lanham MD: Scarecrow Press. Print.

Jackson, Abraham V. W. (1911) 2002. *From Constantinople to the Home of Omar Khayyam*. Piscataway NJ: Gorgias Press. Print.

Jagernauth, Kevin. 2013. "'Warm Bodies' Exhumes a Zombie Romance without Much of a Pulse." *Playlist*, 29 Jan. Web. 20 May 2013.

James, Caryn. 1987. "*Blood Diner* Review." 4 Sept. Web. 2 July 2013.

Johnson, Brian D. 2013. "Two Nightmares on the Cult Circuit: *American Mary* Has Made Jen and Sylvia Soska Global Sensations. *MacLean's*, 11 Jan. Web. 5 July 2014.

Jowett, Lorna. 2005. *Sex and the Slayer: A Gender Studies Primer for the Buffy Fan*. Middletown CT: Wesleyan University Press. Print.

Joyce, Rosemary A. 2005. "Archaeology of the Body." *Annual Review of Anthropology* 34 (Oct.): 139–58. Print.

Kaminsky, Stuart M. 1985. "Comedy and Social Change." In *American Film Genres*, 2nd ed., 135–70. Chicago: Nelson-Hall. Print.

Kavanagh, James H. 1980. "'Son of a Bitch': Feminism, Humanism, and Science in *Alien*." *October* 13: 90–100. Print.

Keane, Stephen. 2001. *Disaster Movies: The Cinema of Catastrophe*. London: Wallflower. Print.

Kellert, Stephen R. 1993. "The Biological Basis for Human Values of Nature." In *The Biophilia Hypothesis*, edited by Stephen R. Kellert and Edward O. Wilson, 57–58. Washington DC: Island Press. Print.

Kelley, Laura, and Endler, John. 2012. "Bowerbird Builds a House of Illusions to Improve His Chances of Mating." *Guardian*, 19 Jan. Web. 3 July 2014.

Kermode, Mark. 2013. "*The Devil's Backbone*: The Past Is Never Dead . . ." Criterion Collection. 30 July. Web. 1 Aug. 2014.

King, Geoff. 2002. *Film Comedy*. New York: Wallflower Press. Print.

Kirksey, S. Eben. 2014. "Interspecies Love in an Age of Excess: Being and Becoming with a Common Ant, *Ectatomma ruidum* (Roger)." In *The Politics of Species: Reshaping Our Relationships with Other Animals*, edited by Anette Lanjouw and Raymond Corbey. Cambridge: Cambridge University Press. Essay available at http://agrarianstudies.macmillan.yale.edu/sites/default/files/files/colloqpapers/07kirksey.pdf. Web. 2 Aug. 2012.

Kohn, Eric. 2013. "Shane Carruth Explains Why 'Upstream Color' Isn't So Difficult to Understand and Talks about His Next Project." *IndieWire*, 3 Apr. Web. 2 Oct. 2014.

Kolodny, Annette. 1975. *The Lay of the Land*. Chapel Hill: University of North Carolina Press. Print.

———. 1984. *The Land before Her: Fantasy and Experience of the American Frontiers, 1630–1860*. Chapel Hill: University of North Carolina Press. Print.

Landy, Marcia. 2004. "Diverting Clichés: Femininity, Masculinity, Melodrama, and Neo-realism in *Open City*. In Gottlieb 2004, 85–105. Print.

Laplace-Sinatra, Michael. 1998. "Science, Gender and Otherness in Shelley's *Frankenstein* and Kenneth Branagh's Film Adaptation." *European Romantic Review* 9, no. 2 (Spring): 253–70.

Lazaro-Reboll, Antonio. 2007. "The Transnational Reception of *El Espinazo del Diablo* (Guillermo del Toro 2001)." *Hispanic Research Journal* 8, no. 1 (Feb.): 39–51. Print.

Leiserowitz, Anthony. 2004. "Before and after *The Day after Tomorrow*: A U.S. Study of Climate Change Risk Perception." *Environment* 46, no. 9:22–37. Print.

———. 2005. "The International Impact of *The Day after Tomorrow*." *Environment* 47, no. 3:41–44. Print.

Leavenworth, Maria Lindgren. 2012. "'What Are You?' Fear, Desire, and Disgust in the Southern Vampire Mysteries and *True Blood*. *Nordic Journal of English Studies* 11, no. 3:36–54. Print.

Leopold, Aldo. 1949. *A Sand County Almanac, and Sketches Here and There*. London: Oxford University Press. Print.

Levinson, Barry. 2012. "The Bay After: An Interview with Barry Levinson." *Mother Jones*, 27 Nov. Web. 6 Oct. 2013.

Lindenbaum, Shirley. 2004. "Thinking about Cannibalism." *Annual Review of Anthropology* 33, no. 1 (Oct.): 475–98. Print.

Lumenick, Lou. 2014. *"Return to Nuke 'Em High* Review." *New York Post*, 10 Jan. 3 Dec. 2014.

Mannion, A. M. 2003. "The Environmental Impact of War and Terrorism." *Geographical Paper* no. 169 (June). Web. 3 July 2012.

Marks, Laura U. 2000. *The Skin of the Film: Intercultural Cinema, Embodiment, and the Senses*. Durham NC: Duke University Press. Print.

Maslin, Janet. 1997. "Six-Foot Cockroach, Waiting for the Train." *New York Times*, 22 Aug Web. 3 Aug. 2012.

Matheson, Richard. 1954. *I Am Legend*. New York: Tor Books. Print.

Matthews, Melvin E., Jr. 2009. *Fear Itself: Horror on Screen and in Reality during the Depression and World War II*. Jefferson NC: McFarland. Print.

McAlister, Elizabeth. 2012. "Slaves, Cannibals, and Infected Hyper-Whites: The Race and Religion of Zombies." *Anthropological Quarterly* 85, no. 2 (Spring): 457–86. Print.

McAllister, Matt. 2011. *"Strigoi* DVD Review." *Sci-Fi Bulletin*. Web. 4 Feb. 2013

Meeker, Joseph W. 1996. "The Comic Mode." In *The Eco-criticism Reader: Landmarks in Literary Ecology*, edited by Cheryll Glotfelty and Harold Fromm, 155–69. Athens: University of Georgia Press. Print.

———. 1997. *The Comedy of Survival: Literary Ecology and the Play Ethic*. Tucson: University of Arizona Press. Print.

Melton, J. Gordon. 1999. *The Vampire Book*. 2nd ed. Detroit: Invisible Ink Press. Print.

Merchant, Carolyn. 2013. *Reinventing Eden: The Fate of Nature in Western Culture*. 2nd ed. New York: Routledge. Print.

Mertins, James W. 1986. "Arthropods on the Screen." *Bulletin of the Entomological Society* 32, no. 2: 85–90. Print.

Met, Phillippe. 2003. "Looking for Trouble: The Dialectics of Lack and Excess, Claire Denis' *Trouble Every Day* (2001)." *Kinoeye: New Perspectives on European Film* 3, no. 7 (9 June). Web. 3 July 2013.

Mintzer, Jordan. 2010. "*The Pack* Review." *Variety*, 20 May. Web. 4 Feb. 2013.

Mitchell, Kaye. 2006. "Bodies That Matter: Science Fiction, Technoculture, and the Gendered Body." *Science Fiction Studies* 33, no. 1 (Mar.): 109–28. Print.

Mitman, Gregg. 2005. "Pachyderm Personalities: The Media of Science, Politics, and Conservation." In Daston and Mitman 2005, 175–95. Print.

Mokoena, Tshepo. 2011. "Beetle Queen Conquers Tokyo: One Six-Legged Step at a Time." *Don't Panic Magazine*, 29 June. Web. 3 June 2012.

Morrey, Douglas. 2004. "Textures of Terror: Claire Denis's *Trouble Every Day*." *Belphegor: Littérature populaire et culture médiatique* 3, no. 2 (Apr.). Web. 1 July 2013.

Morris, Clint. 2005. "*Blood Diner* Review." *Film Threat*, 11 Mar. Web. 1 July 2013.

Morriss-Kay, Gillian M. 2010. "The Evolution of Human Artistic Creativity." *Journal of Anatomy* 216, no. 2 (Feb.): 158–76. Print.

Murphy, Bernice M. 2013. *The Rural Gothic in American Popular Culture: Backwoods Horror and Terror in the Wilderness*. New York: Palgrave Macmillan. Print.

Murphy, Ian. 2012. "Feeling and Form in the Films of Claire Denis." *Jump Cut: A Review of Contemporary Media* 54 (Fall). Web. 30 June 2013.

Murray, Noel. 2009. "*The Thaw* Review." *A.V. Club*, 14 Oct. Web. 20 Oct. 2013.

———. 2010. "Beetle Queen Conquers Tokyo." *A.V. Club*, 13 May. Web. 3 June 2012.

Narine, Anil. 2015. *Eco-Trauma Cinema*. New York: Routledge. Print.

Newbury, Michael. 2012. "Fast Zombie, Slow Zombie: Food Writing, Horror Movies, and Agribusiness Apocalypse." *American Literary History* 24, no. 1 (Spring): 87–114. Print.

New Jersey Office of Science. 2012. *Solid Waste and Recycling*. New Jersey Environmental Trends Report. Oct. Web. 3 Mar. 2014.

New York Times. 2012. "Mapping Hurricane Sandy's Deadly Toll," 17 Nov. Web. 12 Sept. 2013.

Nhanenge, Jytte. 2011. *Ecofeminism: Towards Integrating the Concerns of Women, Poor People, and Nature into Development*. New York: University Press of America. Print.

Nunes, Zita. 2008. *Cannibal Democracy: Race and Representation in the Literature of the Americas.* Minneapolis: University of Minnesota Press. Print.

O'Brien, Brad. "Fulcanelli as a Vampiric Frankenstein and Jesus as His Vampiric Monster: The Frankenstein and Dracula Myths in Guillermo del Toros' *Cronos*." In Hand and McRoy, 172–180. Print.

Ochoa, George. 2011. *Deformed and Destructive Beings: The Purpose of Horror Films.* Jefferson NC: McFarland. Print.

O'Hehir, Andrew. 2014. "*Snowpiercer*: Movie of the Year, at Least So Far." *Salon.com.* 26 June. Web. 3 Dec. 2014.

Oppermann, Serpil. 2013. "Feminist Ecocriticism: The New Ecofeminist Settlement." *Feminismo* 22 (Dec.): 65–88. Print.

Packham, Chris. 2013. "Warm Bodies: Bloodless Romance and Bloodless Carnage." *Village Voice*, 30 Jan. Web. 20 May 2013.

Palamar, C. R. 2008. "The Justice of Ecological Restoration: Environmental History, Health, Ecology, and Justice in the United States." *Human Ecology Review* 15, no. 1:82–94. Print.

Parke, Maggie, and Natalie Wilson, eds. 2011. *Theorizing "Twilight": Critical Essays on What's at Stake in a Post-Vampire World.* Jefferson NC: McFarland. Print.

Parmesan, Camille. 2006. "Ecological and Evolutionary Responses to Recent Climate Change." *Annual Review of Ecology, Evolution, and Systematics.* 37:637–69. Print.

Persson, Per, Laaksolahti, Jarmo, and Lonnquist, Peter. 2000. "Anthropomorphism—A Multi-Layered Phenomenon." *American Association for Artificial Intelligence.* Web. 31 May 2012.

Pinkerton, Nick. 2009. "*Jennifer's Body* East Men, Forces Awkward Teen Dialogue." *Village Voice*, 15 Sept. Web. 1 July 2013.

Pitts, Victoria. 2000. "Visibly Queer: Body Technologies and Sexual Politics." *Sociological Quarterly* 41, no. 3 (Summer): 443–63. Print.

Ponder, Justin. 2012. "Dawn of the Different: The Mulatto Zombie in Zack Snyder's *Dawn of the Dead*." *Journal of Popular Culture* 45, no. 3 (2012): 551–71. Print.

Poulin, Robert. 2007. *Evolutionary Ecology of Parasites.* 2nd ed. Princeton NJ: Princeton University Press. Print.

Pulliam, June. 2009. "Our Zombies, Ourselves: Exiting the Foucauldian Universe in George A. Romero's *Land of the Dead*." *Journal of the Fantastic in the Arts* 20, no. 1:42–56. Print.

Rainer, Peter. 2010. "Beetle Queen Conquers Tokyo: Movie Review." *Christian Science Monitor*, 30 May. Web. 20 May 2012.

Rayfuse, Rosemary. 2014. *War and the Environment: New Approaches to Protecting the Environment in Relation to Armed Conflict.* Leiden: Brill. Print.

Richards, Ellen Swallow. 1907. *Sanitation in Daily Life.* Boston: Whitcomb and Barrows. Print.

———. 1908. *The Cost of Cleanness.* New York: John Wiley and Sons. Print.

Richards, Ellen Swallow, and Alpheus G. Woodman. 1909. *Air, Water, and Food*. New York: Scientific Press. Print.

Risen, Clay. 2010. "The Environmental Consequences of War: Why Militaries Almost Never Clean Up the Messes They Leave Behind." *Washington Monthly*, Jan./Feb. Web. 2 July 2012.

Roberts, Sue Lloyd. 2009. "The Lost Children of Franco-Era Spain. *BBC*, 27 Aug. Web. 3 Aug. 2014.

Robinson, David. 2006. "The Unattainable Narrative: Identity, Consumerism, and the Slasher Film in Mary Harron's *American Psycho*." *Cineaction* 68 (Winter): 26–35. Print.

Roeper, Richard. 2013. "*Warm Bodies* Review." *Chicago Sun Times*, 30 Jan. Web. 21 May 2013.

Ross, Marina Devila, M. J. Owren, and E. Zimmermann. 2009. "Reconstructing the Evolution of Laughter in Great Apes and Humans." *Current Biology* 19, no. 13 (14 July): 1106–11. Print.

Rothman, Lily. 2014. "*Godzilla, Into the Storm* and More Summer Cli-Fi Thrillers." *Time*, 8 May. Web. 1 Dec. 2014.

Rudolf, Volker H. W., and Janis Antonovic. 2007. "Disease Transmission by Cannibalism: Rare Event or Common Occurrence?" *Proceedings of the Royal Society of Biological Sciences*, 7 May:1205–10. Print.

Rust, Amy. 2011. "Hitting the Vérité Jackpot: The Ecstatic Profits of Freeze-Framed Violence." *Cinema Journal* 50, no. 4 (Summer): 48–72. Print.

Rust, Stephen. 2014. "Comfortably Numb: Material Ecocriticism and the Postmodern Horror Film." *ISLE: Interdisciplinary Studies in Literature and the Environment* 21, no. 3 (Summer): 550–61. Print.

Rust, Stephen, and Carter Soles. 2014. "Editor's Choice: Ecohorror Special Cluster; "Living in Fear, Living in Dread, Pretty Soon We'll All Be Dead." *ISLE: Interdisciplinary Studies in Literature and the Environment* 21, no. 3 (Summer): 509–12. Print.

Rust, Stephen, Salma Monani, and Sean Cubitt, eds. 2013. *Ecocinema Theory and Practice*. New York: Routledge. Print.

Sahlins, Marshall. 2003. "Artificially Maintained Controversies: Global Warming and Fijian Cannibalism." *Anthropology Today* 19, no. 3 (June): 3–5. Print.

Salopek, Paul. 2015. "Fleeing Terror, Finding Refuge." *National Geographic*, Mar. Web. Apr. 2015.

Savlov, Marc. 2009. "Vamping on an Old Folk Myth." *Austin Chronicle*, 23 Oct. Web. 3 Feb. 2013.

Schildkrout, Enid. 2001. "Body Art as Visual Language." *AnthroNotes* (Winter). Web. 30 June 2014.

Schwartz, Dennis. 2006. "*Germany Year Zero* DVD Review." *Ozus' World Movie Reviews*, 22 Feb. Web. 3 Mar. 2013.

Scott, A. O. 2009. *"Jennifer's Body* Review: Hell Is Other People, Especially the Popular Girl." *New York Times*, 17 Sept. Web. 2 July 2013.

Shor, Esther. *"Frankenstein* and Film." In *The Cambridge Companion to Frankenstein*, 63–83. Cambridge: Cambridge University Press, 2003. Print.

Siegal, Sarita. 2006. "Reflections on Anthropomorphism in *The Disenchanted Forest.* In Daston and Mitman 2006, 196–222. Print.

Soles, Carter. 2014. "'And No Birds Sing': Discourses of Environmental Apocalypse in *The Birds* and *Night of the Living Dead." Interdisciplinary Studies in Literature and the Environment* 21, no. 3 (Summer): 526–37. Print.

———. 2013. "Sympathy for the Devil: The Cannibalistic Hillbilly in the 1970s Rural Slasher Film." In Rust, Monani, and Cubitt 2013, 233–50. Print.

Solomons, Jason. 2011. "Beetle Queen Conquers Tokyo—Review." *Observer*, 2 July. Web. 2 June 2012.

Stevens, Dana. 2009. *"Jennifer's Body* Review." *Slate.com*, 17 Sept. Web. 2 July 2013.

Stoker, Bram. (1897) 2000. *Dracula*. New York: Dover. Print.

Sutherland, Meghan. 2007. "Rigor/Mortis: The Industrial Life of Style in American Zombie Cinema." *Framework: The Journal of Cinema and Media* 48, no. 1 (Spring): 64–78. Print.

Tan, Eunice J., and Li, Daiqin. 2009. "Detritus Decorations of an Orb-Weaving Spider, Cyclosa Mulmeinensis." *Journal of Experimental Biology* 212, no. 2 (24 Mar.): 1832–39. Print.

Tavernier, Bertrand. 1996. "Commentary." *Lumière Brothers: First Films.* "Oil Wells of Baku: Close View." Kino DVD. Print.

Thiele, Leslie Paul. 1999. "Evolutionary Narratives and Ecological Ethics." *Political Theory* 27, no. 1 (Feb.): 6–38. Print.

———. 2006. *The Heart of Judgment: Practical Wisdom, Neuroscience, and Narrative.* Cambridge: Cambridge University Press. Print.

———. 2011. *Indra's Net and the Midas Touch: Living Sustainably in a Connected World.* Cambridge MA: MIT Press. Print.

Thiessen, Ilka. 2001. "The Social Construction of Gender: Female Cannibalism in Papua New Guinea." *Anthropos* 96, no. 1 (2001): 141–56. Print.

Towlson, Jon. 2014. *Subversive Horror Cinema: Countercultural Messages of Films from Frankenstein to the Present.* Jefferson NC: McFarland. Print.

Travis-Henikoff, Carole. 2008. *Dinner with a Cannibal: The Complete Story of Mankind's Oldest Taboo.* Santa Monica CA: Santa Monica Press. Print.

Treiber, Miklos. 1979. "Composites as Host Plants and Crypts for *Synchlora Aerata* (Geometridae)." *Journal of the Lepidopterists' Society* 33, no. 4:239–44. Print.

Trenberth, Kevin. 2012. "Hurricane Sandy Mixes Super-Storm Conditions with Climate Change." *The Conversation*, 29 Oct. http://theconversation.com/hurricane-sandy-mixes-super-storm-conditions-with-climate-change-10388. Web. 10 Sept. 2013.

Tsutsui, William M. 2004. "Landscapes in a Dark Valley: Toward an Environmental History of Wartime Japan." In Tucker and Russell 2004, 195–216. Print.

———. 2007. "Looking Straight at *Them!*: Understanding the Big Bug Movies of the 1950s." *Environmental History* 12 (Apr.): 1, 237–53. Print.

Tucker, Richard P., and Edmund Russell, eds. 2004. *Natural Enemy, Natural Ally.* Corvallis: Oregon State University Press. Print.

Turner, Frederick Jackson. 1893. "The Significance of the Frontier in American History." *Report of the American Historical Association*, 199–227. Print.

"Vandalism Hampers Sanitation Efforts in Jordan's Za'atari Camp." 2013. *IRIN: Humanitarian News and Analysis*, 19 July. Web. 13 Sept. 2013.

Vemuri, Vicas. 2014. "Climate Change with Cli Fi Coiner." *Guardian Liberty Voice*, 27 May. Web. 3 Dec. 2014.

Wade, Nicholas. 2013. "Girl's Bones Bear Signs of Cannibalism by Starving Virginia Colonists." *New York Times*, 1 May. Web. 1 July 2013.

Walker, Matt. 2009. "Spider Builds Life-Size Decoys." *BBC Earth News*, 6 July. Web. 10 July 2014.

Weber, Brenda R. 2013. "Masculinity, American Modernity, and Body Modification: A Feminist Reading of *American Eunuchs*." *Signs: Journal of Women in Culture and Society* 38, no. 3 (Jan.): 671–94. Print.

Webster, Andy. 2013. "Warning: Woman Wields a Scalpel; 'American Mary,' by Jen and Sylvia Soska." *New York Times*, 30 May. Web. 5 Aug. 2014.

Weiner, Robert G., and John Cline, eds. 2010. *Cinema Inferno: Celluloid Explosions from the Cultural Margins.* Lanham MD: Scarecrow Press. Print.

Wells, Paul. 2000. *The Horror Genre: From Beelzebub to Blair Witch.* New York: Wallflower Press. Print.

Wexler, Rebecca. 2008. "Onward, Christian Penguins: Wildlife Film and the Image of Scientific Authority. *Stud. Hist. Phil. Biol. & Biomed. Sci.* 39:273–79. Print.

Wilson, Edward O. 2007. "Foreword." In Bell, Roth, and Nalepa 2007, ix–x. Print.

Wissinger, Scott A., H. H. Whiteman, M. Denoël, M. L. Mumford, and C. B. Aubee. "Consumptive and Nonconsumptive Effects of Cannibalism in Fluctuating Age-structured Populations." *Ecology* 91, no. 2 (Feb.): 549–59. Print.

Wood, Robin. 2008. "'Fresh Meat': *Diary of the Dead*." *Film Comment*, Jan.–Feb., 28–31. Print.

Yacowar, Maurice. 1977. "The Bug in the Rug: Notes on the Disaster Genre." In *The Genre Film*, edited by B. K. Grant, 277–95. Baltimore: Scarecrow Press. Print.

Yarbro, Chelsea Quinn. 1983. *Saint Germain Chronicles.* New York: Pocket. Print.

Zacharek, Stephanie. 2013. "*Warm Bodies* Makes You Care about the Undead." *Film.com*, 31 Jan. Web. 20 May 2013.

Zelazny, Roger. (1969) 2004. *Damnation Alley.* New York: Mass Market. Print.

INDEX

Page numbers in italic indicate illustrations.